PRAISE FOR
THE WITCHING HERBS

Harold Roth is an extraordinary man—wise, generous, and deeply entwined in the mysteries of the green world from first-hand experience growing, using, and loving plants. His work adds to our deeper understanding of our plant allies, fleshing out folklore and putting our traditions into deeper context. I've learned so much from him and know that with The Witching Herbs, *you will too.*

> —CHRISTOPHER PENCZAK, award-winning author and
> co-founder of the Temple of Witchcraft

Harold Roth is a master of the witchcraft plants. His knowledge encompasses their magical, spiritual, and therapeutic aspects, their blessings and their banes. In The Witching Herbs, *his long-awaited first book, Roth has crafted a brilliant guide to the witches' garden, teaching us how to grow and nurture its most prized plants, how best to access their gifts, navigate their dangers, and communicate with their plant spirit familiars. The* Witching Herbs *is a must for every witch's library.*

> —JUDIKA ILLES, author of *Encyclopedia of Witchcraft,*
> *Encyclopedia of 5000 Spells, The Big Book of Practical Spells,*
> and other books devoted to the magical arts.

I grew up with books detailing hundreds of herbs and their magical uses. I would then go to the botanica or the occult store and buy bags of the herbs for my spells. Harold Roth's book, The Witching Herbs, *is for anyone ready to put down the plastic bags of dried herbs and go deep into the mystery and power of the whole plant. Rather than going wide with hundreds of herbs, he delves deep into 13 witching herbs and in so doing gives us not only a master's comprehension of these, but the tools to understand any other plant magic. This book is the best thing to happen to wortcunning this century.*

> —JASON MILLER, author of *Financial Sorcery* and *The Sorcerer's*
> *Secrets,* and creator of The Strategic Sorcery Course.

Harold Roth's The Witching Herbs *offers an original perspective on the magical dimension of plants, rooted not in the repetition of occult texts but in the soil itself, as accessed by hands, head, and heart.*

—DANIEL A. SCHULKE, author of *The Green Mysteries* and *Veneficium: Magic, Witchcraft and the Poison Path*

At last! A guide to a subject very dear to my heart, and Harold Roth is just the man for the job. Added bonus: several of the most important plants from the correspondences of the Fifteen Behenian Stars. A must-have for goetic gardeners everywhere!

—JAKE STRATTON-KENT, editor of *Conjure Codex, author of The True Grimoire (Encyclopaedia Goetica Book 1),* and other books of power

A book that will take you far beyond the basics of magickal herbalism. Much more than a "this for that" compendium, it will teach you to open your eyes, ears, feelings, touch, and sense of taste to any herb you may encounter, so that you may divine its magical use.

—ELLEN EVERT HOPMAN, author of *Secret Medicines from Your Garden: Plants for Healing, Spirituality, and Magic, A Druid's Herbal of Sacred Tree Medicine,* and other books devoted to herbalism and Celtic plant lore.

In The Witching Herbs, *Harold Roth has approached the plant as book and narrative; seeing the plant itself as the author of its own mystery; a mystery only grasped in fullness by the direct interaction with the plant, where it is nurtured from seed to adulthood and in the process turns into a teaching spirit. Roth roots his work in the doctrine of signatures, mediated by the patient dedication to the plant itself, and, in this, he has manifested a work softly born by the whispers of the 13 plants themselves, flanked with folklore, myths, and the frustrating and rewarding poetry of practice. It is a book easy to recommend, a delight to read, a book that deserves a place not only on the bookshelf, but as a companion in the garden of witching herbs.*

—NICHOLAJ DE MATTOS FRISVOLD, author of *Craft of the Untamed, Palo Mayombe: The Garden of Blood and Bones, and Exu and the Quimbanda of Night and Fire.*

Harold Roth's website alchemy-works.com *has been a constant companion and guide for me over the years. What made me come back were not only the well-researched tables of planetary correspondences, but also the many interesting and neatly structured info articles spiced up with Harold's personal insights on the spiritual nature of magical herbs and incense ingredients and what could be done with them. When I research the magical properties of a plant or resin, Harold Roth is an author I rely on, as he provides substantiated and well informed advice, founded on decades of practical experience in Kabbalah, Hermeticism, alchemy, European witchcraft, Native American medicine, Afro-American folk-magical traditions, and, of course, gardening. What is truly unique about Harold is that his approach is literally rooted in the same ground that the plants grow on, as well as his ability to bring us closer to them, not only in word but also through beautifully done illustrations. And as if this would not be enough, we are given plenty of recipes to try by ourselves. To say that Harold's first book,* The Witching Herbs, *is highly anticipated is an understatement. Whether you are interested in the magical uses of herbs such as mandrake, poppy or clary sage, their medicinal properties, or simply the joy of gardening and growing your own green familiars, this book is a must-have.*

—WIEBKE ROST, herbalist and proprietor of Teufelskunst

THE
WITCHING
HERBS

THE
WITCHING
HERBS

13 Essential Plants and Herbs for Your Magical Garden

HAROLD ROTH

WEISER BOOKS

This edition first published in 2017 by Weiser Books, an imprint of
Red Wheel/Weiser, LLC
With offices at:
65 Parker Street, Suite 7
Newburyport, MA 01950
www.redwheelweiser.com

ISBN: 978-1-57863-599-3

Library of Congress Cataloging-in-Publication Data available upon request

Cover design by Jim Warner
Cover illustration: Mandragora officinarum, 1836 (hand-coloured engraving),
    Bessa, Pancrace (1772-1835) / Private Collection / The Stapleton Collection /
    Bridgeman Images
Interior illustrations by the author
Interior by Maureen Forys, Happenstance Type-O-Rama
Typeset in Adobe Garamond Pro and Koch Antiqua

Printed in Canada
MAR
10 9 8 7 6 5 4 3 2 1

With thanks to the spirits

CONTENTS

INTRODUCTION

When I began gardening in the 1980s, I learned the difference between what was written about a plant—the lore—and how that plant would act in my own garden—the practice. Zucchinis might overrun other people's gardens; I was lucky if I got three or four. Mandrakes might drop dead at the slightest bit of unhappiness in other gardens; in mine, they were tough and robust. It wasn't that the lore of plants was useless, but rather that it sometimes clashed with my own experience in the garden. Lore and practice didn't seem to match up.

When I became interested in herbal magic, I thought: What better way to work with an herb magically than by actually growing it in the garden and harvesting it for magical use myself? I had already grown lots of flowers and veggies, so I began growing the witching herbs, especially members of the nightshade family so beloved by the ancestors of witches. By doing this, I not only got to know these herbs more deeply, but I also learned how they grow and act for me in my practice, in my situation. But the gulf between lore and practice turned up again.

What I'd read or heard about the magical properties of herbs was often different from what I learned by growing them. Since I sometimes could not make lore and practice fit together very well, I thought I must be doing something wrong. I heard about people working with plant spirits or gushing about devas, but I did not perceive any such things in my own garden. Daturas, belladonna, and henbane grew fat and happy in my plots, but I didn't see any witchy Tinkerbells or hear the voices of any wise plant guides.

When I went out into my garden, what I felt was its life. It brought me joy. Yet I kept feeling that I was missing the magical knowledge part. I didn't realize then that I had already started to learn directly about the spirits of these plants simply by growing them attentively. I observed them in the different stages of their lives—from birth to death, alone and among their comrades, in the isolation of a pot and in the community of the garden.

Since I kept running into the problem of my practical knowledge of plants growing in my garden being quite different from what the lore had to teach about them, I decided to take an idea I'd learned from alchemy and apply it to the witching herbs: As above, so below; as below, so above. I figured that if I wanted to know the magical and spiritual properties of a plant and approach the plant spirit itself, I should look at how those properties and that spirit (the "above") were manifested in the material world (the "below")—how the plant's spirit was crystallized in its physical existence.

When you have a living plant in front of you, you are more apt to allow the natural world to whisper to you what its magic is. You have to be ready to listen, yes. But this kind of learning doesn't require any special "blood" or secret wisdom, only patience and the ability to wonder. In this way, I learned exactly how I could best use the witching herbs in my magic, and I came to experience plant spirits firsthand. This technique, which I used to acquire the knowledge of a plant's magical capabilities and gain an acquaintance with its spirit, is what I want to share with you in this book.

There is so much information embedded in a living plant that is not accessible to us when dealing with a dried herb. With a living plant, we experience not only how it grows but also its living scent. We can see how it behaves toward other plants and toward animals. And if we are open to it, we can pick up its "vibe." We can observe and draw conclusions about how the magical properties of an annual, a plant that goes from seed to seed in one year, differ from those of a perennial, which can live for years by withdrawing into the Underworld for a season, as if dying and being reborn. We can go on to test those ideas in actual magical practice with plant material we have grown and gathered ourselves.

When you look at a plant in your own garden, you can consider how the number of petals on a flower may relate to the plant's planetary rulership. Such a small detail, such a tiny bit of "below," can tell you not only how the plant may best fit into a magical practice but also what you can expect from its ruling spirit. You can look at the shape of the leaves, the color and number of petals on the flower, and the type of "skin" on the plant (fuzzy, leathery, satiny, or prickly). When you combine that observation with what lore you do have about the plant, ideas about its magical capabilities can rise to the surface of your mind.

From what I have seen, few books actually encourage you to look closely at a plant to learn about its magical and spiritual properties. That is what I encourage you to do in this book. I've divided the chapters on each of the witching herbs into three sections: Lore, Practice, and In the Garden.

- *Lore* details how the plant has been used or conceived of in the past and is based on research in folklore. It includes information about planetary growth patterns, planetary rulership, the meaning of the shape of the plant's flowers and/or leaves, its scent, taste, and "habit," and where it's from—all the information that gives you a sense of the identity of the plant spirit.

- *Practice* outlines magical uses and projects to get you started working with the plant material that you yourself have grown and gathered, from how to make dream tinctures to compounding incense, washes, smokes, poppet stuffings, inks, and teas.

- *In the Garden* gives detailed information on how to grow the plant from germination to harvest.

I hope this will help you bring your firsthand observations of the living plants, your knowledge of their place in lore and magical practice, and the manifestation of their plant spirits together in an intuitive way. This is true depth of knowledge that is forged from your own personal experience, melding lore gathered from reading and tradition with your own garden work and magical practice.

THE
WITCHING
HERBS

13 Essential Plants and Herbs
for Your Magical Garden

CHAPTER ONE

LINKING THE MAGICAL AND THE MATERIAL

The closest we've come to successfully linking the magical and material worlds in the past is through the Doctrine of Signatures. The Doctrine of Signatures is an ancient way of looking at plants that goes back at least as far as Plato, although in its simplest form, in Western botanical medicine, it was most developed by Jacob Boehme in the 1600s and by William Cole in *The Art of Simpling* (1656). It provided a direct link between the material and the magical, and magic workers of the past were familiar with it, as it was a prevalent idea in medieval society.

THE DOCTRINE OF SIGNATURES

The primitive version of the Doctrine of Signatures most frequently bandied about is that a specific plant part signifies its medicinal use by its resemblance to the body part it treats—the classic example being lungwort, which has spots on its leaves that resemble the holes of the bronchial tubes in the lungs.

The true Doctrine of Signatures is not as mechanical as that, however. The alchemist Paracelsus (1493–1541) extended the doctrine from plants to people, other animals, celestial objects like the moon, and features of the landscape like rivers. He wrote that any natural object with lines, veins, wrinkles, or colors can be interpreted as having meaning and can tell us something about its nature. He considered that the Archeus, the lowest aspect of the astral plane that pervades all things, created signs in everything and argued that the art of recognizing signatures (which he extended to divinatory methods like palmistry, geomancy, hydromancy, pyromancy, and so on) in nature is a part of astronomy. Perhaps that was true for medieval astronomers, who were more mages than scientists, but the art of reading signatures has been and continues to be the stock in trade for many magic workers today.

Paracelsus warned that these signs could appear in a confusing mix, which he likened to a council meeting where everyone wants to have their way and the resolutions adopted end up being foolish. As an example, a plant may have thorns (Mars) but also lush, sweetly scented flowers (Venus). It may be a perennial, which tends to indicate that it works in the long term (Saturn). It may like to grow in sun (solar), but with cool, wet feet (lunar). It may have small, hard fruits (Jupiter) and a dill-like smell (Mercury). A wise person knows how to sift through all these competing signs to choose which part of the plant is most apt for the situation at hand. So we must be careful when we make use of signatures to determine which of them is most appropriate, most "true" for our purpose.

This is precisely the point that those who mock the Doctrine of Signatures miss—anything can contain within itself multiple signatures. It is the skill of the interpreter that determines whether the plant part indicated is usable in a particular situation or not. Our power here lies in the ability to go through all the signatures of any plant and find the one that is the most fitting for the work involved. That ability to sift and sort through a variety of information about a plant is part of the magic practitioner's job.

Planetary Rulership and Tables of Correspondence

Today, practitioners of magic have come to rely, perhaps a bit too much, on tables of correspondence when dealing with plants. It is true that the characteristics of planetary rulership that are always a part of tables of correspondence tend to cross cultural boundaries in a way few other indicators do. People of all cultures all over the world and in every era have been able to see the planets. Many cultures have assigned values to them, and often these values are surprisingly similar. This, to my mind, points out an underlying verification of planetary characteristics.

Do these characteristics or this energy have anything to do with the planets themselves? I honestly don't think that matters. It's something we can chat about while sitting on the porch on a summer night, but otherwise . . . ? What matters in my experience is that these characteristics identify particular types of energy streams that we can grasp and make use of in magical operations.

Tables can be very helpful when you are starting out in magic, because they give you a sense of a general tendency—for instance, why a particular plant is associated with Mars and is therefore good for protection. But you have to be able to think for yourself and not be dependent on planetary tables of correspondence. You should be able to look at any plant—whether or not it is included in a table or even established in magical lore—and determine by examining its appearance and behavior which planet rules it. From there, you can hypothesize about which parts of the plant are good for which magical task, knowing that each part and method of preparation will yield different results.

Knowledge that has been handed down, whether by tradition or in books, is only a foundation. The superstructure of knowledge is built on this foundation by folks working individually and directly with the natural world, concluding and practicing based on that knowledge, and building more on their own conclusions in turn. In other words, the book of magic is written by each individual and is a combination of lore and that person's own experience.

I think that, when we look at some common practices in magic, we see evidence of this type of building of a personal magical system in items like a magical journal, or Book of Shadows, or whatever we want to call it. These have become somewhat corrupted in our society, as some people simply copy spells from others. On a deeper level, however, I think these records represent a personal body of magic built upon a blend of received lore and lived experience in the garden and with the spirits. What I want this book to do for you is to show you how you can build on what you already know about the witching herbs from your reading or from tradition by getting you out there in the garden and observing and working to contact plant spirits. By doing this, you create your own personal magic that works best for you in the here and now. That is real magical power, in my opinion.

Where to begin, then?

BEYOND THE DOCTRINE OF SIGNATURES

The Doctrine of Signatures can be extremely helpful, but I believe that we can take it much further in order to get closer to understanding the spirit of a plant. We can look at the details and patterns of the plant in order to arrive at a deep understanding of the plant spirit. This approach assumes that everything about a plant means something—and probably more than one thing. Everything about a plant—the shape and color and smell of its flowers, how the leaves grasp the stalk, how it goes about reproducing itself and spreading its children, where it likes to grow, how it behaves with other plants, how it responds to animals—has meaning for the magic of that plant and is a signifier of the plant spirit's identity. These attributes are signatures of the plant's spirit and its magical abilities.

This kind of interpretation goes back to the interpretation of sacred texts in ancient times. Just as ancient scholars looked at a holy text on the level of individual words in order to tease out information about the divine spirit that inspired the text, so we can "read" a plant to discover a path to its magic and spirit. What is especially attractive to me about this method is that not only can we use it to find what may be hidden about a plant but also that our method for doing so is based solidly in the material world. It is not all personal gnosis—which can be insightful but can also be a bunch of ignorant baloney or wishful thinking. We can see the link between the material and the spiritual or magical in a rudimentary form in the Doctrine of Signatures. For instance, we decide that if a plant has thorns, it's a Mars plant, because thorns are tiny weapons and Mars is a warrior (or an angry red planet). But does that say something about the spirit of the plant? Let's look closer.

Starting with Lore

Lore doesn't have to come from a grimoire or a high priestess. It can come from any part of our culture, any practice with a plant. One of the first things I look at when I want to learn about the magic of an herb is how it has been used medicinally. Information about the medicinal actions of herbs tends to be widely available and to involve little axe-grinding, in contrast to any written or even spoken material you may gather about an herb's magical uses. One of my favorite texts to consult for herbal medicine is *Bartram's Encyclopedia of Herbal Medicine.* This British book is founded on a practice of herbal medicine that is a bit more rigorous than what we find here in the United States and includes many traditional herbs that are not part of American herbal medicine anymore.

For instance, if herbal medicine tells you that an herb is a stimulant, you have justification for identifying it provisionally as a Mercury herb and can look at other aspects of the herb (leaf shape, scent, growth pattern) to bolster that identification. Having established for yourself that an herb is ruled by Mercury, you can then go on to examine whether it may be helpful in rituals for the acquisition of particular magical skills or charms to improve communication between two people.

By doing this, you never need have recourse to a table of correspondence or feel concerned that an herb in your environment that attracts you—perhaps something native to your area—is not listed in any table you can find or has not been addressed in any magical context. You can begin to know that herb starting with information about its medicinal use.

I often go further and examine an herb's chemical properties. A good source for that is a website called Dr. Duke's Phytochemical and Ethnobotanical Database *(ars-grin.gov/duke/plants.html)*, which lists the various chemical components of a large number of herbs. Examining these components can reveal unsuspected aspects and potentialities of an herb—although often, the most potent chemicals are volatiles (things we can smell), and we can notice them right away when handling the herb.

English lavender, for example, is typically considered a Mercury herb, but the list of chemical components on the Dr. Duke website gives camphor as a component of its flowers. Camphor is typically connected to the Moon, since it's cooling and white and its scent is cold. If you click on camphor in that list, you find all the properties of camphor—for instance, that it's a stimulant of the central nervous system and can cause convulsions, making interesting connections between the Mercury aspect of this plant and Mercury's rulership of the mind. You also find a list of plants with the highest levels of camphor—which, surprisingly, includes sage. This implies that sage has some Moon qualities that you should watch out for. It also hints that perhaps English lavender and sage may be good partners in magical work, because they have significant volatile chemicals in common.

This is not the kind of relationship that would be revealed simply by examining the usual botanical plant families or looking at only the plant structure, flower color, growth habit, or even tables of correspondence, which may put sage under Jupiter or Earth. Lots of magical secrets are hidden in plain sight in the chemical makeup of plants. So already we can see that, even at the very base of the material level—chemistry—we can deduce what an herb's magical capabilities may be.

Just from examining the medicinal and chemical properties of a plant, we can begin to get a picture of its general magical aspects. But if we look at the plant itself—its pattern of growth, the shape of its flowers, the number of its petals, what kind of fruit it produces (succulent, poisonous, dry, no fruit at all), its scent or taste, its cycle of growth, and where and how it grows—we can get a good sense of not only how we may use the plant magically but also of who the plant spirit is.

The more different perspectives you have on a plant, the more you come to know it in depth and in truth, and thereby approach its spirit. Once you do have a handle on it, you can make incense, washes, smokes, inks, dyes and other colorants, poppet stuffing, oil infusions, and even mannekins for use in various rituals, taking the plant's planetary influences as rough guides and your experiences on the ground to refine your knowledge of its magical capabilities. You can use the information available on the material manifestation of the plant's spirit to make magic with that plant and approach its spirit.

How Lore and Practice Can Conflict

Now that we've covered the intellectual approaches to knowing an herb, let's look at the sensual. Most of the herbs that are part of Western witchcraft have been ingested in one form or another, whether as a medicinal herb, a culinary herb or spice, a smoke, or an incense. All of these are valid ways of further coming to know an herb magically. Sometimes ingestion is the primary way that an herb is used in ritual—mugwort, for example, which is a tried-and-true aid to increase dreaming and, by extension, a help in Sabbatic work. It's an herb of little toxicity and, in our day, little medicinal or culinary use. Another good example is tobacco. The ingestion of this herb's smoke is probably the single most widely used magical or spiritual tool in the Western world. It has definite psychoactive effects that are especially powerful when it is not habitually ingested. But there's a "but" about ingestion.

You have to be sure that an herb you intend to ingest for magical purposes does not have dangerous effects on the physical level. One example I encountered a little while ago was someone wanting to make a tea for fertility from the root of American mandrake (*Podophyllum peltatum*). Clearly, they were basing this on the lore surrounding Old World or European mandrake (*Mandragora officinarum*), which, in the Hebrew Bible and also in latter days, was used for fertility—especially the fruits. In fact, you can still buy a liqueur made from the fruits of mandrake that is supposed to encourage lust, which does tend to lead to fertility. Today, it's very common to substitute American mandrake in spellwork for European mandrake, which is so difficult to obtain and very expensive when you do find it (although I will teach you in this book how to grow your own).

The problem is that, although American mandrake is often used as a magical substitute for Old World or European mandrake, it actually has almost nothing in common with that plant and, in my opinion, does not work as a substitute on any level at all. Just look at the physical effects. Whereas Old World mandrake contains tropane alkaloids, which are known to produce frightening hallucinations, American mandrake contains the ferocious phyllotoxin, which causes vomiting and diarrhea that can be so violent that a person may have to be taken to the emergency room and can even die from dehydration.

What made people conflate American mandrake and Old World mandrake? Well, they share some physical aspects. They both grow in woodlands. They both have fragrant white flowers. They both have round, golden fruits with apple-like flesh that, when fully ripe, are pleasant to eat and not poisonous. If you just look at one similarity between these two plants, you might be tricked like the poor individual who was advised to drink a tea made from American mandrake root for fertility. But if you look at even the most superficial aspects of its growth, you find big differences that tip you off right away that you cannot substitute these herbs for each other magically or in any other way.

≋ Perfume of Love ≋

In fact, the fruit of the Old World mandrake is known to have the scent of fresh human sweat, and I believe that is the reason it came to be used in love magic.

Just for starters, the root of American mandrake is cord-like and grows horizontally in a line stretching out from the above-ground part of the plant. By contrast, the root of Old World mandrake is like that of a radish, growing directly down from the crown of the visible plant, and is famous for its resemblance to a human body. European mandrake grows from the same crown every year, penetrating deeper into the earth; American mandrake always produces new crowns as it moves across the forest floor, spreading outward in a very Uranian way (remember that Uranus rules purgatives in medicine). Thus, one plant sits still; the other travels. They are drastically different in the way they grow, which tells you they are drastically different in their medicinal uses—and implies that they are significantly different in their magical uses as well. So maybe using American mandrake as a substitute for European mandrake in spellwork is not such a good idea, regardless of who told you it was.

But let's say you are aware of any possible toxic effects of a plant and have taken them into account. Then you might, for instance, make tinctures using brandy for the fruits, rum for the leaves, potato vodka for the roots, regular vodka (usually made from grain) for the seeds, and so forth. You can then ingest the tincture in small amounts and note the effects. This will guide you further in identifying the magical properties and how the act of ingestion may itself be incorporated into ritual or give practitioners additional powers for magic.

That said, I do like what the respected author Paul Huson had to say about ingesting herbs in his book, *Mastering Witchcraft*: "The bludgeoning effect of drugs is the last resort of the ineffectual spell-binder. Witchcraft is effected by magical art, not chemical means." I think this is especially true for those herbs that contain tropane alkaloids (like mandrake, henbane, belladonna, datura)—which just so happen to be some of the same herbs that are traditionally associated with witchcraft. I also do not believe that the ingestion of truculent herbs like datura is advisable, especially when there are other less dangerous ways to get to know the plant spirit right there in front of us. I think that to use herbs in this mechanical way is to treat them like a bunch of dead molecules rather than like living beings with powerful, eternal spirits who may want to mess with us just for the hell of it.

PLANT SPIRITS

So far, we've been relating to herbs as herbs—as if they were, basically, tools not much different from a hammer or a pen. Hammers and pens can be well made or faulty, beautiful or ugly. They require skill from the user, as well as a certain amount of intrinsic capabilities as tools, but they are not capable of independent thought or of deliberately hindering or helping our work. When you work with an herb, rather than with its plant spirit, the herb is a tool. When you work with a plant spirit, the herb is a sacred text that you can read to learn about the spirit. And that spirit has its own will and its own desires that may not match what you want to achieve.

When you are silent, you have more of a chance of hearing what someone else has to tell you, and I think that this is especially true in the garden. In some ways, ordinary gardeners are closer to magic than most people, because of the opportunity gardening gives them to listen to other spirits and to relate to lives that are fundamentally different from their own. We can anthropomorphize animals to the point where it becomes difficult to perceive their "themness," but that doesn't usually happen with plants, because they are physically so different from us. To understand a life so alien from your own requires a real opening of the soul. I believe that anyone is capable of doing this, but it does take patience, work, and will.

If you are not cultivating a plant, or at least working with it in the wild, it is very difficult to come to know the spirit of that plant. If you want to work with henbane, but the only henbane you possess is in powdered form, you may have difficulty contacting the plant spirit, because powdered henbane seems always to be adulterated with flour, which can get in your way. This is not to say that magic work can't utilize herbs that you have bought rather than grown or harvested. Far from it. I sell herbs myself and often buy herbs that I cannot grow myself, as they derive from tropical trees. However, it is more difficult to contact a plant spirit using store-bought herbs.

When you grow an herb yourself, especially if it is one you grow on a regular basis, it is almost certain that, sooner or later, the spirit of that plant will contact you if you make yourself open to it. For one thing, when you grow the plant yourself, especially from seed, you are able to see it at various stages in its life, under many different weather conditions, in various seasons (sun phases), and through all the moon phases. I also see this activity—growing a plant—as being devotional to the plant spirit.

Yes, there are plants that grow without any human assistance, but many that are associated with magic actually seem to prefer to grow around people. They appear to get something from that proximity besides the benefits of cultivation. In fact, my sense is that they receive something spiritual or nonmaterial as well—something we lack the words to define at this time in our development.

I also view cultivating a plant as being akin to the Kabbalistic concept of *tzimtzum*, the Lurianic concept of how the Divine contracted to make room for the universe as an independent existence. Tending a plant can be a very caring and selfless activity. Moreover, many of the plants used in magic have aromatic foliage that, when brushed against, releases its signature scent. This may not always be a pleasant smell, but it is always an identifying characteristic.

Scent is among the primary ways that plants communicate with animals. This is certainly true with moths and butterflies, but even fruits begin to release a fragrant odor when they are ripe and ready for animals to eat them. If a plant can send out requests through scent for certain parts of it to be visited or even consumed, then it most likely can and will communicate other things about itself. However, we must be open to this communication and recognize that communication does not always have to occur in the form of words or even images.

Scent can be narrative, can tell a story. It can be a way for us to communicate with the plant spirit itself. Since scent is one of the least understood senses—and in our society, perhaps the least necessary and thus most mysterious—it is often accorded magical or spiritual properties. The *Zohar,* for instance, considers scent as the one food for the soul that is available on this plane and that can feed angels and other spirits as well as gods—which goes a long way toward explaining the importance of incense in magic.

It is certainly true that scent can affect the mind on the physical plane by being psychoactive. Examples include the perfume of brugmansias—which, if slept under, provides the sleeper with terrifying visions—or the uplifting scent of frankincense, or jasmine's ability to raise the seizure threshold. So one important means of communication between plants and people has to be scent—not only when plants send their scent to us but also when we, in turn, use that scent to evoke the plant spirit through magic oils or scented candles.

In my experience, being around and tending a growing plant every day—basically in a posture of helping and attentively listening—is a way to let the plant spirit know that you want to make contact and that you are ready to learn. Years ago, a rabbi told me that one way to indicate to the Divine that you want to make contact is to study holy books; by doing so, you indicate that you are open to contact with the sacred. I see tending plants in the same way. A plant is a sacred text—the description and plan, the story of the plant's spirit—and when you tend that plant and cultivate and groom it, you indicate to its spirit that you are open and ready and receptive to its contact. I see this posture as completely different from consuming plant parts.

Often, plants offer a particular part to animals for consumption—fruits, for instance—as an element in a bargain wherein they distribute their seeds. Even when we eat the leaves of a plant, I have sensed that these plants know that their siblings and their children will have more opportunities to propagate than if they were growing alone in the woods somewhere and no one ate their leaves. And, as with animals, propagation seems to be one of a plant's primary aims in life. So when we tend plants to help them grow or propagate, we let their spirits know that we are well disposed toward them and that, while we may kill masses of them during the harvest process, we intend to further their progeny more than would have been possible for them on their own.

We provide an important service to the community of that plant; the god of that plant, its spirit, must take heed of that service. I am certain that plant spirits notice our attentions to their avatars. If anything is equal to prayer in the relationship between people and plant spirits, it is our tending and helping to propagate their material manifestations as plants. I think it is also a good example of how prayer, in order to work, must be in the form of action.

It's also true that the plants we cultivate tend to be far less ferocious in their effects than those that grow in the wild. I have seen a lot of advice that claims that plants intended for use in magic should be harvested from the wild, rather than grown in the garden, because wild plants are considered to be more powerful. But plants grown in the optimal conditions of a garden tend to be far more relaxed and friendly. They don't produce the high amounts of alkaloids that wild plants do, because they don't have as much need for them, as they are not being gnawed on by every passing critter. A garden-raised baneful will likely have fewer alkaloids, because it is not as afraid of being eaten. A plant that is less afraid is a happier plant and one that may be more open to interaction with us, because it is not constantly in fear for its life or worrying that its babies will be destroyed.

My advice to people wanting to contact plant spirits: Choose a plant toward which you feel *simpatico* or one whose shape you just like (often the same thing) and grow it. Grow it in your yard or in a pot, on your windowsill or in your home—anywhere that provides the conditions for cultivation. Tend it and wait with an open heart.

We cannot demand that a plant spirit show itself. But my experience has been that, eventually, the spirit will reveal itself, and in a most unmistakable way—through dreams or visions, for instance. It is a mighty impressive and awe-inspiring experience, one that lets us know that our allies are extraordinarily powerful and also fundamentally different from us.

TRUE LEAVES AND TRUE MAGIC

The first pair of leaves for pretty much all plants except grasses is identical—a generic leaf shape. The second set of leaves, called the "true" leaves, will have the characteristic shape in miniature of their immediate family (their species). To me, these two sets of leaves have something to teach us. The first, generic, set shows how all plants are fundamentally the same; the second set shows how they are all different. Sameness and difference easily coexist in the plant world, just as they do for us. All of us are the same at the base, but we are all different at the same time.

This also implies that all magic is fundamentally the same and draws upon the same pool of energy. It is only externally that various rituals and works are different, aimed at different environments and situations and times. I think this shows that we are justified in tailoring magical works to particular events and need not copy the rituals from another time or place in order to be "authentic." We can create our own magic that suits the situation and our level of knowledge and power, knowing that we are drawing upon the same energy used by our ancestors or our neighbors on the next continent.

One of the most wonderful things about herb magic is that there can never be any doubt about whether a magical practitioner is capable of growing a plant. If an herb is sympathetic or a plant spirit willing to work with you, it lets you know in no uncertain terms. Plants will not grow for you if they don't want you; but if they do want you, then they will grow prolifically—even those that have a reputation for dropping dead at the slightest insult. Unlike other practices, in which the operator may always be in doubt regarding whether the work is "real," herb magic always gives strong indications of its potency and its reality. You can go around boasting about your magical accomplishments and no one can say a word against it. But if you cannot grow a marigold, then you cannot make any claims about doing green magic. This book shows you how to get on that path. But first, let's take a look at the practical aspects of working in your witch's garden.

CHAPTER TWO

CULTIVATING YOUR WITCH'S GARDEN

The best way to get to know a plant spirit is to help its material form go from seed to mature growth and harvest. By tending a plant, you not only come to know its quirks and habits, you also honor its spirit. And there are very few spirits that do not appreciate some honor being shown. Growing plants also helps build your confidence and sharpens your openness to other beings. You have to really look at a plant to notice whether bugs are eating it or disease is spreading its net. Growing your own plants not only shows you the influence of our actions on the material world but also demonstrates how much of the powers of that world are beyond our control.

When choosing plants for your witch's garden, try to identify plant spirits that are amenable to you. We all have a plant family or two that especially attracts us and that grows well for us. It's your job to approach a plant spirit by first finding those plants that do well for you in your place and time. Instead of growing all sorts of unrelated plants, discover by trial and error which plants want to grow for you.

Although the witching herbs have been grown in gardens for hundreds of years, most of them are still fairly wild and don't have "named varieties" that feature particular flower colors, size, or spread. Most important, remember that wild plants don't germinate all at once in the way that domesticated plants are likely to do. Instead, they feature staggered germination (which may occur over weeks, months, or even years) to take advantage of changes in growing conditions. Wild plants don't gamble with the same kind of confidence as domesticated plants, which seem to have become dependent on human judgment regarding the best time for them to germinate.

Wild plants hedge their bets. They are not regimented and so provide a huge amount of genetic variety in contrast to domesticated plants. This generally allows for at least some of any planting to survive in a variety of growing conditions.

STARTING YOUR SEEDS

Some folks have gotten the idea from old images of farm workers broadcasting grain seed that we can just throw seeds on the ground and expect them to grow. This is just a waste of seed. Most seeds, especially the more persnickety perennials, just die from too much or too little warmth, or too much or too little moisture, or too much or too little light. They also fall prey to birds and other critters. A few may beat the odds and grow either in the year of planting or—because they are wild—after a couple of years of waiting. They then have to compete with thousands of weed seeds and, worse, grass. Gardening requires a lot of planning and a certain amount of fiddlyness to succeed. That just goes with the territory. Nothing worth doing is easy.

Stratification

Some seeds are very wary about coming out of their shells and hesitate to germinate. Gardeners have to engineer conditions that will convince these embryos that it's a good time for them to be born. One of the ways you can do this is called "stratification." This technique tries to duplicate the period of cold moisture that seeds might experience outside.

The Baggie Method

My favorite method of stratification is called "the baggie method" by many gardeners. This requires a paper towel, some liquid kelp, and cheap, thin baggies that fold over instead of zipping—the thin plastic allows oxygen to flow through. Mix up the kelp solution according to the directions on the container, but be sure to use filtered water, not water right from the tap, because chlorine inhibits seed germination. Liquid kelp contains a chemical similar to gibberellic acid that will help the seeds germinate more dependably. Take a paper towel, dunk it in the kelp solution, and wring it out. Open it out and sprinkle some seeds into it. Typically, I never use more than half the seeds in a packet. That way, if things go wrong, I can start over. Now fold the paper towel into fourths, pressing it between your hands to ensure that the seeds are surrounded by dampness. Put the folded paper towel into the baggie and fold the top closed. Label the baggie with the seed name and the date that you started it.

What you do next depends on what kind of seed you have. You can remove annuals from the sun, for those that like room temperatures. Seeds that enjoy some warmth, such as the more exotic datura, like being on a heating pad set to low. For seeds that need cold to germinate—and this means many perennials—lots of folks have success putting the baggie in the fridge. But for these seeds, I have had the best luck with the outdoor treatment I describe below.

If the seed germination time is two weeks, start checking the seeds to see if they are germinating at the end of that time. Just take out the paper towel and carefully open it to see if any seeds have sprouted. If they haven't, fold it back up and put it back in the baggie. If the paper towel feels somewhat dry when you take it out, sprinkle some liquid kelp solution on it. Alternatively, sometimes I just quickly dunk it in some filtered water. Press the paper towel gently between your hands so it is not soaking wet and put it back in the baggie.

If you do see germination, gently tear off bits of the paper towel to isolate the area where the germinated seeds are, then gently press that whole piece of paper towel, seeds up, onto some wet planting soil. Try to have good contact between the paper towel and the soil so that the moisture does not evaporate and so that the roots grow directly from the paper towel into the soil. The paper towel will disintegrate on top of the planting soil as the seedlings grow and their roots reach into the soil.

The roots of seeds are very delicate and don't like to be touched. I usually put the pot in which I am planting germinated seeds inside a loose plastic bag like those that you get at the grocery store with your purchases. This confines some moisture around the pot without making it too humid. Don't close the top. Place the pot in indirect light, not direct sun. The seedlings are still too fragile to be exposed to the environment without some filtering.

Cold Stratification

Some especially difficult seeds that come from environments with cold winters need a bit more help than just a baggie. In the wild, this happens naturally in a process called "cold stratification," as the seeds fall from their parents, lie on the ground over the winter, and are often covered by leaves or half buried by frost heave and animals. If seeds requiring cold stratification do not receive it, they generally won't sprout. Eventually, they wither and die inside their shells.

You'd think that just leaving seeds outside on the ground would be enough to get them to sprout, but so many opposing forces exist outdoors—it gets too cold, too dry, too wet, and so on. Cold stratification is how we can partner with spirits to provide a winter awakening for the seeds that need it. There are five methods of cold stratification: cold-water soaking, refrigeration, fall planting, outdoor treatment, and snow planting.

Whichever method you decide to try, just remember that helping seeds germinate is not a science but an art. Witches know how important patience is to magical work, and helping a seed to germinate definitely has magical aspects. Even the most experienced magical workers fail sometimes, and so do the most experienced gardeners. That's why I always use only half the pack of seeds—that way, I have some left for another try if I fail.

Cold-Water Soaking

I usually use this method on belladonna, henbane, mandrake, and various monkshoods. It works best with seeds that are not too small. A small jar—a vitamin bottle or a baby food jar—is ideal for this technique. Put a label on it with the seed name and the date you start the soaking. (Sometimes I also put the date I'm supposed to stop the soaking.)

Put the seeds in the jar and fill it with cold filtered water. Cap the jar and put it in the fridge. Change the water for fresh cold filtered water each day. The point of this process is to imitate how, in the wild, snowmelt gradually washes away chemicals inside the seed's permeable coating that tend to inhibit germination. I sometimes empty the jar of seeds and water over a fine strainer. Alternatively, you can just pour it through your fingers and catch the seeds (but don't do this with aconites). If you don't change the water each day, the seeds will get moldy and die.

After two weeks of soaking, strain the seeds out and plant them. With the kind of biggish seeds that work well with the soaking method, I usually plant them in Jiffy pellets (see p. 25) and set them under fluorescent lights indoors. I don't use any sort of humidity dome or other covering.

Refrigeration

In Europe, where winters tend to be a bit milder than in North America, folks tend to plant seeds in pots outside in the fall for germination in the spring. Where I live, however, winters can suddenly get so bad that even seeds that tolerate cold well can be killed. Because of this, many Americans use refrigeration instead of planting outside in the fall.

Most people today use the baggie method described above and put the baggies in the fridge (or for aconites, in the freezer). But in the past, people mixed their seeds with substrates like sphagnum moss, peat moss, clean sand, or vermiculite. Simply soak the seeds in room-temperature filtered water overnight, then mix them with a couple of tablespoons of a sterile soil of your choice that has been moistened with liquid kelp solution. You want it moist, but not sopping wet. Put this into a plastic baggie, fold it closed, and put it in the fridge.

Most people leave the seeds refrigerated for three months, the usual length of the coldest part of the year. But you can experiment with starting cold stratification right after the Winter Solstice. This takes advantage of the growth energy of the Earth that starts as soon as the days begin to lengthen. You can make the planting a part of your observance of Yule or as a personal assertion that, despite the dark of winter, the Earth is alive and readying itself for spring. Try this at Summer Solstice if you're in the Southern Hemisphere.

After a month or so, open the baggie and see if any of the seeds are germinating in the soil. Some won't germinate in the darkness of the fridge, even though they need its cold. Others, however, will begin to sprout. When the three months are up, sprinkle the moist soil and seeds on wet planting soil and gently firm them in with your hand whether the seeds have visibly germinated or not.

The problem with using this more old-fashioned method is that the soil makes it much more difficult to see if mold or fungus is becoming a problem. That's why I use a paper towel instead. With that, if the seeds get brown halos around them on the towel or smell a little off—or worse, if they feel soft—then they are rotting and should be thrown out. This can happen if the seeds were DOA; but, more often, it's due to poor storage before putting them in the baggie to germinate. Stored seeds do best with cool, dry, and dark environments.

Another use for the refrigerator in germinating seeds is actually to plant the seeds in Jiffy pellets and put the pellets in some kind of small covered container—like the covered tins for baking little bread loaves. I used to do this with mandrake seeds before I began using the soaking method. This works well for seeds that don't need a whole pseudo-winter, but just a couple of weeks of cold before they germinate. Poppy seeds do well with this method when you are starting them during a time when the outside temperatures do not favor germination for them. Again, most seeds won't germinate inside the fridge, but will do so soon after you take them out.

Fall Planting

Fall planting is very traditional in Europe, but in North America this can be a very hit or miss method. Seeds planted in the fall are usually placed in a small pot that is covered and left in a protected area that does not get direct sun. That's important, because in winter, the south side of a house in a protected location—like right next to the wall—can get warm enough to kill seeds that expect cool temperatures. Likewise, don't put the seeds on the north side of the house (with the exception of aconites, which have a special love for the most Saturnian cold). A cold frame is really overkill for something like this and can get far too warm inside. Fall planting takes advantage of temperature fluctuation, snowmelt, and increasing day length, but it's also a bit riskier because of cold snaps.

The best time to start seeds in the fall is when temperature falls below 45°F (8°C). If you have snowy winters, cover the pot with a bit of screen held on with string or a strong rubber band. This will keep mice out and allow the snow to pile up on the screen and insulate the seeds from drastic temperature changes that can kill them. It will also allow the snow to melt through the screen and wash away germination inhibitors on the seeds.

Good placement for pots is on the east side of your house. You can use terra cotta pots as long as they don't fill with water and freeze, as they will then crack. I always used terra cotta pots in the past; however, lately I can only find thin slipware clay pots that can't withstand any freezing and thawing in the soil. So I switched to plastic pots. But be careful handling these—especially the big ones when it's very cold—because they become brittle and fragile. And don't forget to label each pot with the seed name. You can use stick-on labels on the outside of the pot, but a yogurt container cut up into little stakes and labeled with a marker or grease pencil works very well and seems to retain the writing longer than a printed label.

If, despite the best of intentions, you don't get your seeds put into pots outside until it's below 30°F (0°C), you can put them—pots and all—into the fridge for a week or so before putting them outside. This gets them used to the cold.

Too much water at any time of year can kill seeds, but this is especially true in winter. Make sure your outside pots are not under the drip line of the house or in standing water when you get a good rain or lots of snowmelt. Water has to be able to flow through the pot.

By late winter, your seeds should start to germinate. Surprisingly, the cold will not generally hurt them, especially if you have them close to the house or protected from wind and frost—for instance, if they are kept beneath bushes. Once the weather warms, check the soil to see if it's dry and needs water.

The Outdoor Treatment

The most successful method I have found for germinating seeds that require cold stratification is the outdoor treatment described in Norm Deno's *Seed Germination Theory and Practice* (1993). This book is well known in gardening circles for advocating the use of gibberellic acid to pretreat seeds, but Deno also tested a germination method he heard about at a bridge club. This starts with the baggie method that I described earlier, but rather than putting the baggies in the fridge, you put them outside in a protected location—a shed, a roofed patio, an unheated garage. The problem with refrigeration is that the temperature remains steady, and many seeds prefer the temperature to dip at night. The outdoor treatment is especially handy if you want to start a lot of seeds. In the past, I have cold stratified seeds of 150 different plants using the baggie method and a very small cardboard box in my garage. I had a 95 percent germination rate using this method and have never gone back to using the fridge. Yes, the paper towels do freeze solid, but this does not hurt the seeds at all. Just check for germination in the spring, just as you would at the end of a stint in the refrigerator.

Snow Planting

This method is very magical and works for seeds that like a bit of a cold boost, but don't need an actual stratification period—poppies of various types, heartsease, sweet alyssum, and various hardy annuals, biennials, and short-lived perennials. It calls for a good number of seeds.

After a heavy snow, go outside and broadcast the seeds onto the snow in an area where you want them to come up in the spring. I tried this with ten grams of California poppy seeds one year and was rewarded with a nice stand of poppies in the front of my house the following spring. It's very life-affirming to do this in the dead of winter.

Jiffy-7 Pellets and Kelp

For years, I've been using Jiffy-7 pellets and liquid kelp solution to help germinate seeds and grow plants. Jiffy-7 pellets are compressed peat wrapped in a kind of netting; they expand as they absorb water. You can get them at many garden centers in the spring or you can order them online all year round. Harris Seeds is a good source. If you buy a lot of Jiffy-7 pellets, actual flats designed for containing them can be very helpful. Otherwise, you can use any sort of pan.

Most big-box home-supply centers and gardening companies stock liquid kelp, which is a concentrate of kelp seaweed that's certified for organic growers. A popular brand is Maxicrop Liquid Seaweed. If a nearby store doesn't carry it, check for it online. A small bottle will last you for years, as typically liquid kelp is mixed with water in proportions of approximately one half teaspoon per gallon.

Use warm water, so that the peat pellets expand more readily. The kelp solution is great for soaking the peat pellets.

When the pellets are fully soaked with liquid kelp, pour out whatever has not been absorbed. You can save the liquid to water the pellets later, or use it as a fertilizer on other plants. The top of each pellet has an indentation or sometimes even a hole. Don't let your seeds go down into that hole; they should stay in contact with the soil. I usually use my finger to move away the top edge of the netting so there is plenty of planting room at the top of the pellet. My general rule for planting depth is to cover the seeds with peat about as thick as a dime. I just press the seeds into the soil with my fingertips, move a little peat over them, and gently tamp them down. For tiny seeds, just tamp them down and don't cover them with soil.

Directions for starting the seeds of all the plants in this book are contained within their respective chapters. These will tell you whether they should be covered or not. Keeping your fingertips dry while putting the seeds on the top of the planting soil really helps. Then you can go over all the pellets, tamp them in, and cover them with the barest amount of soil.

As much as I like peat pellets, not everyone uses them. Some like starting seeds in sterile potting soil or vermiculite in flats or cell packs (pre-divided plastic sections). Then they "prick out" the sprouts and transplant them to individual pots. The advantage of this method is that you don't waste any pellets on duds, and you can focus on transplanting the heartiest seedlings instead of having to thin the plants the way you do with pellets.

Heat and Moisture

Most seeds of plants that are used in witchcraft of European origin don't need supplemental heat to germinate. However, if a seed *does* need bottom heat, there are propagation mats designed specifically for this purpose. I have used water-resistant heating pads set on low as an inexpensive alternative to propagation mats. Propagation mats do use less electricity, however, and are safer.

To use a water-resistant heating pad, remove the cloth cover. Put the pad under the flat or pan containing the pellets and set it on low. I unplug mine whenever I leave the house, just to be on the safe side. Make sure your cat doesn't use it as a lounger.

It takes a while to get the hang of how much water a plant needs. Once they've gotten wet, seeds shouldn't dry out; but too much water will make them rot or encourage the growth of fungus. Some people like to use a mister on their seeds, but I prefer to water them from the bottom instead. Just add water to the bottom of the flat or pan containing the pellets rather than watering from the top. The pellets will draw up as much water as needed. Pour out whatever liquid has not been absorbed after approximately a half hour.

NURTURING YOUR SEEDLINGS

The first leaves of most plants are all the same shape. It's only the second set of leaves, known as the "true leaves," that display the kiddie version of the adult plant's distinct leaf shape. Thus, it can be difficult to tell seedlings apart, until they get their true leaves. This is one reason why it's so crucial to label them.

Strengthening

You can strengthen your newly sprouted seedlings by setting a small, gentle fan to blow on them. The slight movement of the seedlings that this causes helps to strengthen their stalks, but it will also dry out the soil faster, so keep an eye on moisture. Another way to strengthen seedlings is to gently brush the tops with your hand every day. This helps to set up and create a means of communication with the seedlings as well.

Sun and Light

Most seeds do not require direct sunlight to germinate or to grow. In the wild, seeds germinate beneath the protection of their parents, which provide shade. Shop lights are great for germinating seeds. Keep the fluorescent tubes about one inch away from the tops of the leaves. You can also put your seedlings by a window that does not receive direct sunlight; just make sure to rotate the container every day.

When your seedlings appear, they need to be exposed to direct sun slowly so they don't get scorched and die; this is called "hardening off." Start out with an hour or so of morning sun and gradually work up to a day. I usually put my seedlings on a covered patio out of direct sunlight. After they've been out there for several days, I start moving them to full sun, if that's what they need. If they start to get leggy (long stalks with no leaves except at the top), this indicates that they need more sun.

Damping Off

If seedlings are not thinned and/or are given too much water, you may come to them one day and find them all keeled over or with thin spots on their stalks. Then they slowly die. This is the result of too much water and not enough ventilation. It's called "damping off" and is caused by a fungus. Once seedlings show this behavior, they are goners and cannot be saved. This is one of the primary reasons why you should always reserve some of the seeds in your seed packet.

You can help prevent damping off by watering with liquid kelp solution or with tepid chamomile tea (which is also good for fungus gnats). But the best way to prevent damping off is to use scissors to cut down all but the biggest seedlings of each pellet, don't overwater, and be sure to provide ventilation (a fan).

Learning how much to water is among the keys to successful growing; more plants are killed by overwatering than anything else. The soil should be kept the consistency of a moist cake, instead of sopping wet. Use weight to judge whether watering is needed. Lift your pots or flats to gauge their weight before and after you water. You will soon get the hang of knowing, just by the heft of the container, whether the plants need to be watered or not. Looking at the surface can trick you into thinking that they are fine—at least, that's been my experience—but hefting them consistently tells the truth.

Potting Up

When roots start to emerge from the bottom of your peat pellets, it's time to pot up. Get some good-quality potting soil or make your own from equal parts of peat moss, compost, and perlite. Select pots for potting up that are a finger's width wider than the pellets. Whenever you pot up over the course of a plant's life, don't choose a pot that is too much bigger than the pot the plant has just outgrown. If there is too much room between the roots and the bottom of the pot, the roots won't be able to reach water.

The height of a new pot should be one third the height of the plant that you're repotting. If you have many plants and need pots, nurseries often give them away. You can also buy pots online very cheaply. Wash pots before using them to help get rid of insects, especially slugs and aphids. Washing the pots will also help prevent the spread of plant diseases. It's not necessary to add bleach to the water to control plant diseases.

Throw some potting soil in the bottom of the new pot, then place the peat pellet within it so that the top is even with the top of the soil you add. Tamp down the soil a bit, kind of tucking it around the pellet without making it too tight. If you cover up the stem, it will rot (with the exception of tomatoes). Do cover the edges of the peat pellet, however, because they can wick water out into the area.

Moving Your Seedlings Outdoors

Once the weather is sufficiently warm and your seedlings have become juvenile plants, you can plant your babies directly in the ground outside, if that's what you want to do. You can prepare an entire plot by double-digging or tilling, by incorporating compost, and so on.

Or you can just treat the ground like a flower pot, digging a hole and filling it with good potting soil. This works fairly well in areas where the soil is very sandy or nutrient-poor; clay soils are nutrient rich. The point of preparing the soil is to get rid of grass and tree roots, as both will steal almost all the water and nutrients from the soil and leave nothing for your herbs. Your witching herbs will grow more happily if they do not have to compete with other plants for air, moisture, or nutrition.

In the fall, I cover the transplanting areas with flattened cardboard boxes, which I then cover with hardwood mulch (not dyed). Over the course of the winter, the grass beneath the boxes dies and the boxes themselves become soft. In the spring, you can easily dig down into the mulch and put in your transplants without too much effort. This beats the heck out of tilling or double-digging every spring.

When you put a plant in the ground, tuck in the soil and then water heavily (this is called "muddying in"). This is supposed to drive out all the unwanted air pockets. It makes the top of the soil sink, so just top up with a little more soil and gently firm. Cover with a nice mulch—hardwood is best; eucalyptus or cypress will work; cedar or pine will kill your plants. Leave a space about the width of your finger between the plant's stalk and the mulch. The mulch will help prevent weed seeds from germinating and moderate the soil temperature.

Fertilizing Your Seedlings

Foliar feeding is the only kind of fertilizing that I do. This involves using a hand-pump sprayer filled with a mixture of liquid kelp solution and fish emulsion. The latter really stinks, but boy do plants (and cats) love it. You can purchase it at the same sort of stores that sell liquid kelp. You can use liquid kelp solution at any stage, but I don't begin using fish emulsion until the plant is past the seedling stage. Pump sprayers work better for this than spray misters.

When the birds are singing in the morning, plants are most ready to accept nutrients through their leaves. Mix up the fertilizers according to the packages and spray the undersides of the leaves. If your plants are inside, play music that has high notes in the morning to get the plants ready for feeding. You can spray as often as the label recommends; alternatively, you can dilute more and spray more often. I usually spray once every week or two with a more dilute mixture, because foliar feeding makes me really look at the plants, helping me notice issues before they get too out of hand.

GROWING PLANTS INDOORS

It's not that hard to grow leafy plants inside under shop lights, but flowering and fruiting require much more energy from the plant. And that energy is something they make from sunlight. The witching herbs that I have gotten to flower dependably indoors are henbane and mandrake. I have not tried any of the more high-powered grow lights, so I can't make any recommendations on that score. I use cheap fluorescent shop lights to carry plants through the winter.

An enclosed sun porch is an excellent place to grow plants inside. This kind of situation provides them with plenty of air. Because heated indoor air is very dry in the winter, misting plants every day really helps. I grow my plants in my basement during the winter, because it is very cool down there and has plenty of air circulation.

WORKING WITH THE MOON

You can use the phases of the moon to organize various garden tasks. When the moon is waxing (its right-hand side is lit):

- From New Moon to Half Moon, plant annuals or crops that will be harvested for their tops and that don't produce what we think of as fruit.

- From Half Moon to Full Moon, plant annuals that have seeds inside their fruit.

When the moon is waning (its left-hand side is lit):

- From Full Moon to Half Moon, plant roots and bulbs, perennials, trees, and shrubs.
- From Half Moon to New Moon, perform garden chores other than planting, especially pruning.

Avoid gardening on the Full or New Moon. Celebrate instead.

ACCEPTING RISK

This book begins with poppy because poppy is all about risk. It thus teaches a very worthy first lesson for any gardener. Without being willing to take risks, you cannot garden. Gardening requires that you invest work now for what you hope will bye a positive outcome later. If your actions in the garden do not produce the results you anticipated, the lesson learned from the loss is worth almost as much as what is achieved by success. To be a gardener, you must learn to accept loss and move on.

CHAPTER THREE

POPPY
The Charm Bag

P oppy is a good witching herb for the novice gardener because it's an annual, which usually means the seeds are easy to germinate. Poppy produces a profusion of fairly tough seeds that are small yet big enough to handle and are very vigorous. So from the point of view of the gardener, poppy is almost always a safe bet.

This magical herb has been grown in many kinds of gardens, not only because of its beauty and ease but also because of its usefulness to human beings for medicine and food. This native of the Near East (from the Middle East up through Turkey and Iraq) has been cultivated for three millennia and harvested for four or five. There are records of its use in Mesopotamia, ancient Egypt, Greece, and Rome. Some believe it evolved naturally from a wild cultivar, but others think that humans deliberately developed it. I think it may be a little bit of both. At any rate, poppy has bound up its survival with that of human beings so tightly that you never find it growing in the wild today.

THE SECRET LIFE OF ANNUALS

Poppies are annual plants, meaning their entire life cycle occurs in the time period of one year. (We'll discuss biennials and perennials in later chapters.) Annuals go from seed to seedling to plant to flowering and fruiting (producing seed) in twelve months or less; then they die. Compared to biennial plants, which live for two years, and perennial plants, which live three or more years, annuals are in a hurry. They've got a lot to do in a single year. The seed must germinate and the seedling must root. True leaves must be produced to gather additional energy for supporting the hard work of flowering. Then those flowers have to be pollinated in order to make seeds for the following year.

Unlike biennials like clary sage or perennials like belladonna, annuals like poppy reproduce only by seeds. They do not engage in vegetative propagation (making more plants by non-sexual means, like roots that have arms easily broken off or creeping rhizomes that will, if separated from the plant, go on to make an identical twin or clone of the plant that produced them). Annuals reject nonsexual reproduction, so they are much more sexual than perennials. With annuals, sexual reproduction through seeds takes up all the plant's reproductive energy. A flower is already a sex organ of a plant, but annual flowers are all there is for the plant's reproduction. That makes the flowers of annuals (as opposed to those of biennials and perennials) especially appropriate for potentiating sex magic and for spellwork involving any kind of fertility.

Annuals like poppy are the socializers of the plant world, much more willing to mix it up with the community and to gamble on their interactions with their environment than perennials are. In contrast, there is a lot of self-sufficiency (and perhaps self-absorption) in the kind of asexual reproduction through creeping or fragile roots that biennials and especially perennials engage in. I always think of them as a little bit like that cranky old man down the street who wants you to stay the heck off his lawn; these plants don't look for a lot of interaction with others.

It's true that some annuals are what is called self-fertile—the ovary and the pollen-producing parts of the flower are close enough and ripen near enough in time for the plant to pollinate itself and produce seeds without any outside help. But most annuals do rely on others. Perhaps the ovary and the pollen are very close to each other inside the flower, but don't ripen at the same time. Or perhaps the ovary needs pollen from another plant and can get that through the help of the wind, but more likely if it's carried into the flower by an insect. Imagine the kind of trust implied in the fact that a plant needs nonplants to make its seeds—its own children—and that annuals that are not self-fertile depend entirely on other species for reproduction. Annual flowers live by the kind of perfect trust that we humans only talk about.

Annuals also know how to get along—they have to modify themselves in order to appeal to the other species (bees, beetles, flies, or even birds and mammals) that they need to produce seeds, their children. So right away we see that annuals have to be more in tune with other species than biennials and perennials do. They are right in the middle of a large community that they depend upon for the lives of their children. They make flowers with strong scents to guide moths and flies. They have petals with landing pads and runway "lights" visible to the ultraviolet vision of bees. They have succulent fruits that signal their ripeness with appetizing aromas so birds and mammals will eat them and thereby distribute the seeds (which are ripe when the fruit is ripe), ensuring the spread of their children over the Earth. Even those animals that take a bite of a fruit and then cast it aside and take another are not wasting the fruit. They are giving the seeds a chance to germinate immediately instead of taking a ride through their gut first.

Clearly, annuals must modify themselves to entice all those others whose help they need to reproduce. They must therefore be much more involved with their community than the typical perennial. Annuals are creatures that thrive in a diverse community. And their interaction with that community also means that their children contain much more diversity than the vegetative production of offspring characteristic of perennials. The advantage of sexual reproduction is precisely that there's a much bigger chance of genetic variety, since the influx of the genes of other plants helps ensure that a group of genes doesn't become weakened and lost. The genetic treasure is preserved with sexual reproduction, even though all the genes are not used all the time. With vegetative reproduction, by contrast, recessive genes will always be just that. Only a duplicate is possible, not something new and different. So diversity in, diversity out with annuals.

We humans are not out of the loop here. Gardeners and farmers go out of their way to nurture certain plants and help them reproduce. That we have, since the invention of agriculture, tended to favor and nurture herbaceous (nonwoody) annual plants as our primary source of food probably says something about us. The Mercury energy of plants that "hurry up and produce" appeals to us. We seem not to have the patience for slow-growing Saturnian plants and their contemplative and self-absorbed nature. We want results now, and the straightforward and straight-ahead annuals provide that for us. In this way, they have modified themselves to bring about certain actions from us, as well as from bugs and birds and other mammals.

If perennials are basically Saturnian by nature, annuals, by contrast, are primarily Sun. Annuals grow and flower along with the growing strength of the sun and its rise in the sky during the year. And as the sun weakens toward the end of the season, annuals finish the business of making seeds and proceed to die. Such a strong connection to Sun means that, typically, annuals will not do well during the winter. The sun is not in the right place or of the right strength for annuals when it is in the grip of winter darkness. Starting annuals much before spring, therefore, is not productive. While the seeds may germinate, they will not do well. You can see this especially if you start another batch of the same annual seeds at a later time in the spring; the later batch will germinate more strongly and produce healthier seedlings that quickly overtake the earlier batch. Indeed, annuals are much more Sun than many other plants, even when their characteristics may be more clearly influenced by other planetary energies.

LORE

Despite being an annual, and therefore Sun, poppies have traditionally been connected to the night as well. The ancient Greeks portrayed all the night-associated deities holding or decorated with poppy flowers—Nix, goddess of the night; Thanatos, god of death; Hypnos, god of sleep; and Morpheus, god of dreams. The Romans called the god of sleep Somnus. The Swedish botanist Linneaus, who developed the system of Latin plant names still used in the West, based the poppy's species name, *somniferum*, on Somnus. The god of sleep (Hypnos for the Greeks; Somnus for the Romans) is Death's cousin. This deity is often portrayed as a somewhat cherubic, black-winged boy sleeping on the head of a lion (a good symbol for the Sun, over which night triumphs). He usually holds poppy pods or a horn of poppy juice or poppy tincture in oil that he pours over the eyelids of sleepers. He is often depicted with a lizard or reptile (chthonic animals) beneath him.

Yet poppy's associations are not as simple as plain literal death; it also has a connection with agriculture. The deities who rule over death also rule over the wealth that comes from the earth, whether in the form of crops or minerals and metals. Perhaps this is why, in European cultures, Death is often portrayed as a reaper. Just like wealth buried underground, the true nature of death is hidden from us. The horn of the god of sleep is echoed in the fruit-filled cornucopia that Hades is sometimes shown holding or even emptying on the ground. The goddess Demeter, an agricultural deity, also rules over the Eleusinian Mysteries, which were said to help initiate triumph over death or learning about the afterlife. The connection between agriculture, death, and the Underworld is very powerful—even without touching upon the Greek mythology associated with Demeter and her daughter Persephone. Remember that Demeter's grief for absent Persephone brought the night of the year (winter) into being, and that Persephone was one of the very few able to travel to the Underworld *and* return.

For the Minoans, Demeter ruled not only grain but also poppy. Poppy was very widely cultivated for its nutritious seeds, which, mixed with honey, were made into cakes. But it was also valued for its opium, which was used as a euphoric and visionary drug.

Since, in other streams of magic, poppy is sacred to night-associated goddesses like Lilith and Hekate, it's not surprising that poppy's planet is the Moon. The plant's milky white sap (or "latex"); the roundness of its fruit (the pod), which is often covered with a translucent white bloom when fresh; and the damp, earthy, cool scent of its flowers, the scent of the Earth breathing out its night-time dew—all point to the Moon's influence.

Poppy and Childbirth

In 19th-century Tuscany, poppy was sacred, not only to the night and all its rites but also to Laverna, the goddess of thieves and imposters.

Laverna resembles Hermes in so many aspects of her character—she is a trickster, thief, and master of disguises—although some identify her with Diana. This may seem contradictory, but consider that Diana rules the Moon, and the Moon rules the night, when thieves operate most freely. It is said that Laverna's worshippers used poppy to ease childbirth, but in fact, the poppy may have been used to deaden the pain of childbirth and make it easier for the child to be taken from the mother (perhaps to Laverna's temple) while she was still under the plant's influence.

In his book *Aradia, or The Gospel of the Witches*, Charles Leland gives a full description of a rite to Laverna that was practiced when a woman had to hide a pregnancy that would cause a scandal if it became known. The rite involves the use of a fume consisting of "paura" and "concordia." He argues that "paura" is not *herba della paura* ("fear herb," or *Stachys recta*), but actually a play on the word for poppy (*Papaver*). I think he was on the right track. Here's an excerpt from the description of that rite, which Leland says is quoted from Virgil, although he gives no source:

> Then when the time came for the suppliant to be delivered, Laverna would bear her in sleep during the night to her temple, and after the birth cast her into slumber again, and bear her back to her bed at home, and when she awoke in the morning, she was ever in vigorous health and felt no weariness, and all seemed to her as a dream.[1]

This sounds as if the poppy may have been used to sedate the mother during birth and then make it easier for the baby to be "spirited away" to be raised as an orphan or to be allowed to die from starvation—as was common practice in Victorian baby farms, where unwanted babies were given to a "nurse" who deliberately let the baby starve to death—or to be killed outright. This practice resonates with the belief that the smoke of a fume containing poppy can function as a path for the newly dead to travel to the Underworld.

··

⇌ *Twilight Sleep* ⇌

During the Victorian period, poppy was often combined with the unpredictable belladonna to furnish a hypnotic, pain-killing drug used in childbirth and referred to as Twilight Sleep. This was later refined to simply a couple of alkaloids from these plants.

··

Poppy and Ritual Magic

Poppy was also used in ritual magic. The medieval European magician Agrippa gives a formula for a "suffumigation" that combines poppy, hemlock, henbane, mullein, red sandalwood, and sagapenum[2]. He writes that "spirits and strange shapes" can appear in the smoke of such a fume and that, if smallage (celery seed) is added, spirits will be chased from any place. He doesn't identify which part of the poppy plant should be used, however. The seeds do have a traditional purpose when burned, which we'll discuss below. But, although some latex sticks to the outside of the seeds, they themselves don't contain any. Burning other plant parts or pods would therefore be more potent in terms of releasing the plant's alkaloids.

··

☠ *Warning: Hemlock is sedative (to the point of paralysis!) and henbane combined with poppy causes sleepiness, with a possible tendency toward hallucinations. So if you use this recipe, do not burn it in a closed room.*

··

Thus Agrippa's suffumigation may have had physical as well as magical action. But the poppy seeds are a part of this formula because of poppy's connection with the Underworld and those who rule it. This means that, if you are working with spirits of the dead, poppy seeds can be a very convenient incense that can substitute for more involved formulas or ingredients that are more difficult to obtain. Because poppy is connected with dark goddesses like Lilith and Hekate, it also works well as a general incense for them, or as an ingredient in oils dedicated to them, making a nice substitute for other more highly baneful herbs typically associated with them, like belladonna. With poppy seeds, you can have your baneful and safely eat it too.

Poppy and Divination

Poppy's strong lunar connection makes it an especially good choice for divination. And, in fact, it has historically been used for that purpose. For instance, in Tuscany, witches put poppy leaves on hot coals and read the answers to their questions in the flames' shape and size. A similar type of divination was practiced in which the crackling and popping of burning seeds became the voice of prophecy.

Other forms of poppy divination incorporate dreaming—appropriately, considering its lunar rulership, as dreamwork is often thought to be dominated by the Moon. One Tuscan rite involves making a hole in a dried poppy pod, shaking out all the seeds, and inserting a piece of paper upon which is written the witch's question or wish. The pod is then put under the pillow of the dreamer, who, before going to sleep, recites: "*In nome del cielo, delle stelle, della luna! / Fate mi face il sogno secondo . . .* " ("In the name of heaven the stars and the moon! / May I dream and that full soon see . . . ") and then states his or her wish. The future is then revealed to the dreamer.

PRACTICE

Dried poppy latex, known to us as opium, has been used by humans since antiquity to induce sleep or dreams or to help us disregard physical or emotional pain. But opium well illustrates how the Moon, which has a reputation in Western magic for passivity and weakness, is in fact as powerful as any of the other classical planets. Moon power is evidenced, not only in the sleepiness and dreaminess that opium use can induce but also in the passivity of addiction that results from chasing this plant (passivity being a negative Moon trait).

Still, poppy does not lie in wait for us, snapping us up into its clutches. Rather, we chase the passivity of addiction until we find ourselves mired in it. It is as if we see a swamp, struggle headlong toward it, and get stuck there. We then craft every aspect of our lives to honor the force of poppy's Moon, while withdrawing more and more from the rest of the world. We surrender to its tidal pull.

Risk vs. Recklessness

We who practice magic must know ourselves well. That self-knowledge must include an awareness of our own susceptibility to the undertow of passivity. If we know our limits, we don't swim in the riptide. There is so much more to experience than oblivion. When we blame the poppy for enslaving us, we refuse to face how hard we worked to forge our own chains.

I think our contemporary attitudes of passivity are reflected in our sometimes addictive relationship with poppy and in our perception of poppy as a deadening, rather than a visionary, drug. We've come a long way from the Minoans. I've even heard those who use more currently fashionable euphoric plants in their practice deny that poppy has any euphoric properties. The difference, in my opinion, is that poppy is dangerous—unlike euphorics like peyote, which, while illegal, is safe. Not only does poppy open a gate for those seeking addiction, its side-effects can kill.

Poppy is a good example of how a plant does not have to be typically baneful—for instance, ruled by Saturn—to be dangerous. Poppy's bitter, milky white blood has the power to cause suffocation; it acts on the center in the brain in charge of breathing. This is why poppy has traditionally been taken medicinally in small amounts to soothe a cough, whether as a pea-sized ball of opium or as codeine in cough syrup. A tea made from one dried pod, which has much less power than a fresh one, can be sufficient to cause breathing difficulties. We can see how the Moon rules over the darkness of death, as well as shedding light on the hidden.

Poppy demonstrates its willingness to accept risk by depending on animals for its reproduction and by wholeheartedly throwing its lot in with humans to the point that it no longer grows in the wild. We, in turn, flirt with risk with this plant because of its legal status—much as the practice of magic has generally been illegal in the past and, in some places, still is, even constituting a capital crime in some countries.

If we trifle with this plant, we also risk the snares of addiction. In the same manner, we risk various snares in magic. Most of them, like addiction, are problems of our own making, arising more from the shape of our own personalities than from the wiles of demons or the punishments of karma or the Three-Fold Law. What poppy has to teach us as magic workers is to accept risk without being reckless. If we truly feared risk, we would never practice magic at all, yet we cannot be reckless in our Craft. The adage, "Don't raise up anything you can't put down," applies not only to spirits but also to our own vanity or pride, which can trip us up and cause us to make harmful errors.

A final danger from poppy arises from the fact that, although it is perfectly legal to buy, sell, or possess poppy seeds, actually growing the plant is not legal in the United States or in Canada. However, gardening magazines regularly advocate poppies as valuable additions to the garden, and most seed companies sell a variety of *Papaver somniferum* seeds, especially the peony types. I have, as of the time of this writing, been unable to find evidence of anyone who has gotten into trouble for growing poppy as a garden plant. So don't worry about it, but don't slit any pods either.

I see poppy's blending of Moon qualities with Sun adoration as instructive. If you go all daylight or all nightside, you cut off an enormous realm of experience and knowledge, in essence mutilating your magical practice. We all know Bunnies of Light on the one hand, and Darker than Thou types on the other. Either type may well practice magic, but they will accomplish less than half of what they could if they were willing to risk working on both sides, blending them with the wholeheartedness and trust that is poppy.

If you want to be reckless with your freedom and health, just slit some poppy pods, harvest and dry the latex, and consume it. This approach is in keeping with a lot of what I see going on in relationship to popular entheogens; it's all about the alkaloids.

I believe this comes partly from the perspective of allopathic medicine, with its concern for "active ingredients." Allopathic practice, which relies on drugs and physical interventions to treat or suppress symptoms, generally rejects a holistic or contextual approach to healing. In the case of poppy—and a number of other baneful plants—this approach can be very dangerous. The latex, present throughout the plant except in the seeds (although they can be coated with it), affects the respiration center and causes sleep. Take too much and you can suffocate, *especially* if you fall asleep. Furthermore, from a legal perspective, slitting poppy pods is considered the equivalent of manufacturing a controlled substance in the United States.

I don't usually rely on Jungian approaches to working with the Divine, but I like what the author of *Dionysos: Archetypal Image of an Indestructible Life* (Princeton, 1996), Carl Kerenyi, has to say about employing *pharmakon,* using the old Greek word. He points out that, generally, when a substance becomes necessary to attain a visionary state, it means that the underlying culture has lost the knowledge of how to attain that state without the use of a *pharmakon.* He cites the Native American peyote culture as evidence. I will say more about this in later chapters.

Poppy and Dreamwork

Poppy's ability to stimulate dreams can be utilized by tincturing petals in alcohol to make a dream scent. Due to the delicacy of the petals, a white wine may be the best choice for this. If you want to use vodka, try potato vodka—it is much creamier than grain vodkas and potatoes are Moon. Lightly sprinkle the mixture on the hair before sleep. In the Sabbatic tradition, poppy has been infused in wine together with warming herbs like cinnamon and cloves to make a dream tincture. If you do this, however, I suggest that you take it by the drop, as this tincture is very close to laudanum. Poppy is also a traditional component of flying ointments or lifting salves, which are reputed to help magic workers attain the dream state necessary for traveling to nighttime Sabbats.

≋ A Pricey Cocktail ≋

Thomas Sydenham's 1669 recipe for laudanum contained the following ingredients:

> *1 lb sherry wine*
>
> *2 oz opium*
>
> *1 oz saffron*
>
> *1 oz powder of cinnamon*
>
> *1 oz powder of cloves*

Saffron greatly potentiates opiates and so can make them even more dangerous. I do wonder if real saffron was used in this recipe, however, given its cost. Today, one ounce costs about $140!

Poppy's bitter alkaloids (which are the plant's warning to us of its power) are known to counteract the alkaloids present in some baneful ingredients of flying ointments, like henbane. This goes far toward explaining how witches of the past could balance the antagonism between belladonna and poppy. Belladonna widens the pupils; poppy causes them to contract and to become "pinned." The trick is to achieve a balance—a normal-looking pupil size, in other words. However, without the firm backing of a practice-based tradition, you certainly should not go about cobbling together flying ointments from belladonna and poppy.

I also believe it is very important for modern-day practitioners not to use plants as a crutch to attain particular states. This smacks of the dangerously one-sided approach of allopathic medicine, where plants are drugs rather than guides. We also have to keep in mind that those who ingest a lot of alkaloids are often unable to perceive the effects of smaller amounts because they develop a tolerance for them. A much safer vehicle for dreamwork can be made from small amounts of the poppy seeds, as in this chutney.

Dreamwork Chutney

1 tsp white poppy seeds

1 tsp grated coconut or coconut powder

Dab of ghee or butter

Pinch ground cumin

Pinch turmeric

1. Mix the poppy seed and the coconut with a just enough water to make a paste and set aside.
2. In a frying pan, melt the ghee until it clears or the butter until it is just melted.
3. Add cumin and turmeric and mix. Take the pan off the heat right away.
4. Leave the mixture in the pan until its color changes, then add to the poppy seed and coconut paste.
5. Stir and let stand for 5 minutes, then add salt to taste and eat on some crackers or a little rice one hour before going to bed.

Poppy as a Magical Tool

In Tuscany, a gold amulet shaped like a poppy pod has traditionally been worn to attract wealth, perhaps because of the extreme fertility of the plant and the great number and vigor of its seeds. This practice, combined with the shape of a poppy pod itself, made me think of using a pod as a charm bag, only, rather than inserting objects into the pod, I drop essential oils into the "vents"—the little windows that run around the side of the poppy underneath the rays. Not all poppy pods have vents, but the essential oils can also be dropped into the center of the rays and allowed to run gently down inside.

A poppy plant typically produces four to five pods, but if you use plenty of fertilizer and pinch back the side branches of the poppy plant so that it puts all its energy into one stalk and one pod, you can harvest a good-sized pod that will make an excellent scented charm bag when dried. It can also serve as a fine object for the altar that can focus variously on fertility, abundance, dream divination, or contact with the dead, depending on the scents used. For fertility, choose lunar scents like star anise, lotus, white rose, or camphor. For a charm bag dedicated to dreamwork, choose clary sage and chamomile.

Let's consider the pomegranate for a moment. I've often been struck by the similarity in shape between the pomegranate fruit and a ripe poppy pod. It's interesting that Demeter, who rules agriculture, holds poppy pods, while her daughter, Persephone, is associated with the pomegranate, six seeds of which she ate—either by the trickery of Hades, or perhaps willingly, in order to be "forced" to remain free of her mother's rule and exert her own power as co-ruler of the Underworld. Consider that these two deities are referred to generally in the Homeric poems as "mighty Hades and dread Persephone." "Dread" is not a term usually applied to a helpless victim.

⟫ Kidnapped Brides ⟪

In ancient Greek culture, bride kidnapping was often a way for couples to marry when their social positions or families would not allow it. As long as the bride maintained the fiction that she was taken against her will, the family's "honor" was not damaged, and the marriage was considered valid. Thus, couples often secretly arranged for the bride to be kidnapped.

The pomegranate's rind and seed capsules are blood red, the color of life, and full of juice. The "blood" of poppies is white, as are the seeds of white-flowered poppies. Poppy seeds are dry compared to pomegranates. The poppy signifies fertility and thus life due to its many seeds; but it also represents death through the ingestion of its latex. This is a contrast to the rejuvenating quality of red, blood-like pomegranate juice. It is quite interesting that Hades is associated with the poppy pod with its white, semen-like latex and Persephone with the womb-like pomegranate, red with menstrual blood and plump seeds. Hades rules over the dead, but is also connected to the riches hidden beneath the earth, including those of germinating seeds.

The poppy is just as double-edged; its fertility is indicated in the large number of its rich, nutritious seeds (hidden beneath the globe of the pod as seeds are hidden beneath the soil) and its white latex can cause death. It is thus a good match for the pomegranate, with its blood-juicy seeds hidden in its ovary. In fact, I have always wondered if the pomegranates mentioned as decorations of the high priest's garment in the Temple of Jerusalem—which persist today as *rimmonim* on the Torah scrolls in modern synagogues—were really poppy pods.

In my research in the dusty tomes of folklore for this book, I stumbled upon an excellent instrument for using poppy seeds in a description of rites dedicated to Hades and Persephone, Hermes in his role as conductor of souls of the dead, Hekate, and the Eumenides. In ancient days, during difficult times or problematic situations, certain particularly implacable gods were worshipped by sacrificing black animals that

≋Holy of Holies≋

In the Temple of Jerusalem, there were two separate altars—one for the sacrifice of animals and another, much closer to the Holy of Holies, for the sacrifice of incense. The incense altar provided an alternative to the killing of animals. Certainly present-day magical practice generally prefers the burning of incense to the taking of life. And although some will insist that killing is the more "traditional" sacrifice, clearly, it is not more traditional than burning incense.

were killed, not at altars, but on low mounds of earth. The blood was allowed to seep into the ground, since these more truculent gods typically lived in the Underworld. As a substitute for killing animals, however, people also made cakes of honey, "meal," and sometimes poppy seeds, which were not eaten but simply burned as a sacrifice. I thought a cake like this offered a good opportunity to work with poppy safely and with the Underworld. I knew already that, in India, a chutney made of poppy seeds is eaten on a cracker before going to bed to promote sleep. That implied that cakes made of the seeds could have usefulness as an instrument in dreamwork. Here is a recipe for cakes that can be eaten.

Papaver Chthonios Cakes for the Living

> *¼ lb (125 g) butter*
>
> *⅛ cup (25 ml) honey*
>
> *½ cup (125 ml) poppy seeds (try white seeds for use during a waxing or Full Moon, black for use during a waning or New Moon)*
>
> *1⅓ cups (300 ml) almond flour*
>
> *Greased cookie sheet or one lined with baking parchment*

1. Preheat oven to 325°F (160°C).

2. Melt the butter and honey together in a small pot (not too hot—you don't want to boil the honey or let the butter brown).

3. Pour in the poppy seeds and gently warm and soften them. Add the almond flour and mix well. If you are using any incantations, now is the time to say them.

4. Roll the delicate dough into balls and flatten them into moon shapes on a baking sheet that has been greased with coconut oil or lined with baking parchment.

5. Bake 10 minutes, or until the edges just begin to turn golden (baking too long makes them taste burned).

6. Let cool on the cookie sheet; they're very delicate.

7. Eat a couple before bed on an empty stomach. The effects are subtle, but useful for dreamwork.

Almond is a lunar plant and the flour is not difficult to find. It is thus in keeping with the ancient origins of this cake. Butter is also Moon. Honey is not Moon, but does have that great bee connection, bees being messengers from the Underworld and, in some cultures, considered to be the souls of the dead.

Since burning meal smells a lot like burnt toast and so has many distracting associations (to me), I changed the recipe for the cakes for the dead that were burned to appease difficult deities of the Underworld by substituting myrrh for the meal. This resin has long played a part in preparing the dead. It was, for instance, the favored agent in mummification and the preservation of corpses generally, and thus represents one way the living can honor the dead (by not mistreating the body). It also hints at immortality (the mummification connection). Myrrh also makes a nice symmetry with the honey of the Cakes for the Living, as both of them are considered Mars. And to me, myrrh smells like the void.

Here is my recipe for cakes to honor the dead—not for the living to consume. The combination of honey and powdered resin can be very difficult to remove, so either have 95 percent alcohol on hand for cleaning up afterward or use utensils and vessels where permanent stickiness won't matter.

Papaver Chthonios Cakes for the Dead

4 oz ground myrrh

A few tbsp dark red wine

¼ cup dark honey

1 oz black poppy seeds

1. Dampen the myrrh with some red wine and let sit in a closed jar overnight. You don't want it wet, just slightly moist. This removes much of the bitterness and makes the myrrh very sweet and wonderful.

2. Boil the honey to remove some of the water or the cakes will become moldy. The honey will foam, so keep an eye on the pot and turn it down to a simmer.

3. Add the poppy seeds.

4. Cook the honey and seeds for a bit, and then pour over the ground myrrh and mix well.

5. Before the mixture cools too much (and thus becomes impossible to remove from the pot due to hardening), form into crescents about the size of the last joint of your thumb.

6. Dry on low heat in a dehydrator or on a rack if your climate is dry, but not in the sun.

7. Store in a tin or jar, but use them soon. Even dried poppy seeds have a tendency to decay (how appropriate!).

8. To use, light a couple of charcoal tabs and place a cake over them. This incense is good for honoring the dead, the deities who rule over them, or the spirits who work with them.

POPPIES IN THE GARDEN

Annuals like poppies may be short-lived, but because of their fast energy, they tend to be much easier to grow than biennials or perennials. Annual seeds can hardly wait to germinate and don't typically demand all the coddling of special temperature fluctuations and pH and whatnot that are typical of perennials. Poppy seeds are an especially good example of this. The tough coats of poppy seeds protect them if they are thrown out into the snow, keeping them warm until spring, when they crack open obligingly before there is much competition. Their life energy is also shown in how long they remain viable; living poppy seeds have been found in the pyramids of Egypt. A high percentage of poppy seeds will germinate even if they are handled poorly, which is quite a contrast to lots of other seeds whose germination rates decrease if they have to deal with too much warmth or light.

The vigor that poppy seeds show is also seen in poppy seedlings, so it's very important to thin them or the seedlings will compete so strongly with each other that all will be harmed. The best time to plant poppy is, of course, during a waxing moon, when the moon is drawing up energy from the ground and encouraging top growth. Poppies like cool weather and, to me, this suits their Moon identification. So start poppy seeds when it's cool—either very early in the spring (the seedlings can stand a little frost), or in the fall when days go below 80°F (27°C). Just make sure that your climate will allow ninety days before a freeze so that the plants have enough time to flower—up to 120 days if you want to collect ripe seeds from some of the varieties bred for hot climates. If you're only interested in getting flowers from poppies and not pods, you can shorten that time a bit to ninety days.

Sprinkle the seeds thinly on the planting medium (see chapter 2). Barely cover the seed with soil about the thickness of a coin. When planting, you can either ask Hekate to watch over her sacred plant or simply direct your love and caring toward the seeds, imagining them as your children whom you protect and cherish. Temperatures at planting time should be 60–65°F (15–18°C). These seeds don't like heat. The closer to 80°F (27°C) at germination, the fewer poppy seeds will germinate. They should germinate in ten to twenty-one days. If your weather is too warm at planting time, but you know it'll be cooling off soon, put the seeds (soil and all) in the refrigerator for a week or so. When you take them out, they should germinate quickly. They won't germinate inside the refrigerator, however—they need (indirect) light for that.

More than most plants, poppies can suffer severely from over-crowding. The best way to deal with this is not to overplant. That's easier said than done, however—I myself have a very heavy hand when sowing. Try to sow only a very few seeds per pot, cell, or pel-let—say, five. Most people plant more like fifty or a hundred per pot, because they don't really believe the seeds will germinate, and because they get so many seeds in a typical packet, which gives them the idea they should all be used up. Most seeds, including poppies, store very well in a jar in the fridge, so you can always save extra seeds for other times, or share them or trade them with others.

I make it a rule for myself never to plant more than half the seeds in a packet. That way, I don't end up with too many plants if they all germinate. And, if there is a problem, I get another try at growing, because I have backup seeds. If you find that you have overplanted and your seedlings are jostling each other and growing as close together as grass on a lawn, be cruel. Get out the scissors and cut off their heads, leaving two to three seedlings per pot. Three is nice, because it's a magic number; but two is good as well, because it's easier to break the planting in half when it comes time to pot up or transplant outside.

Now, I know you're thinking you should just let all the seedlings grow, and may the best plant win. But two things happen when you do this. First, there may not be enough food, water, and light for everyone, so all the seedlings will be stressed. Just like baby people, plants that have a malnourished childhood are generally weak and prone to sickness when they grow up. You'll notice, for instance, that the seedlings' stems become longer and thinner, weaker and paler, as each seedling competes for light. They waste a lot of energy compet-ing that they could be using to build stocky, healthy bodies.

The other possible result of not thinning is called "damping off" (see chapter 2). In this case, the seedlings don't even make it to a weak adulthood. Instead, you go to water them one morning and find them all bent over in a bow to death. They have succumbed to fungal disease, unable to resist it because they were too crowded and stressed. They won't survive this, no matter what you do, and usually will be dead within hours.

So thinning, which does cause the death of a number of seedlings and which seems terrible, is actually beneficial, because it allows the plants that remain a good chance to make it to a healthy adulthood. I do hate to do it, however, and that's why I just plant a few seeds per pot. Whenever I thin seedlings, I think of the figure of Death on the tarot card. The horseman mows down people with his weapon of mass destruction, the scythe. But the scythe is also a tool of harvest. Just as Death represents regeneration as well as the ending of old things, so does thinning. So when you think of thinning, think of the tarot's thirteenth trump.

After hardening off, transplant your poppies to a sunny area with rich, moist soil (see page 24). As devoted as they are to the sun's doings, they will not be happy in shade. The poppy usually gets two to three feet (60–90 cm) tall. You should set them out nine to twelve inches (22–30 cm) apart in rich soil and full sun.

The poppy hurtles from germination to maturity (flowering and pod-formation) in ninety days, which is quite fast. It has taproots, which tend to extend more deeply and straighter down than other types of roots. This indicates a stronger connection to what is beneath the ground and to what is deeply hidden than you may find in a lot of other plants. Poppy reaches deep and pulls up what it finds hidden, bringing it into the upper regions where we can see it. As the taproot reaches down, the upper part of the plant forms a "rosette" of leaves that spreads out in a circle from the plant's center like the rays of the sun—or, in this case, the moon. These leaves lie close to the ground, as if demonstrating this plant's affinity with what lies beneath. The plant hangs back a little, just like a cat gathering energy for a leap.

When the plant has grown a sufficient number of leaves to support flowering and fruiting, the leaves in the center of the rosette lift themselves skyward. Then, suddenly, a hairy stalk comes from the center, as if the leaves were hands pushing it up. In some poppy species, these hairs are actual thorns. In *P. somniferum*, however, Mars is clearly overcome by Moon. Up until this point, the poppy's growing structure is similar to that of the Underworld plant extraordinaire, the mandrake. The difference is that the mandrake does not ever form lengthy stalks for its flowers. They are almost stalkless, demonstrating thereby that plant's greater affinity with the Underworld.

At the hooked end of the stalk, a fuzzy bud watches the ground as it rides upward, keeping in touch with the source of its strength and knowledge. The bud points up and cracks open when it's ready to do Sun work. You begin to see the incredibly sensual creased silk of the petals inside, giving a hint of the power the flowers can give to sex magic. Then, usually the next morning, the flower shines in the sun with newness, exuding the fragrance of earth. It has four (or eight) petals surrounding a thick ring of stamens. I have seen bees joyously dragging themselves around this ring to pick up as much pollen as possible. I have often wondered whether it is the purple blotches that attract them—bees have a special fondness for blue or purple markings on flowers—or whether the scent of earth has something to do with it. Bees do use their sense of smell to distinguish various flowers, and they are certainly a highly chthonic animal.[3] Each plant gets four to six flowers, but each is on its own stalk—which is unusual. Most herbaceous plants (plants with non-woody stems) develop several flowers on each stalk. Poppy highlights its flowers with their dedicated stalks.[4]

In keeping with fast annual energy, poppy flowers usually last only a day or so. You come out to find the petals crumpled on the ground, the ovary standing naked and proud as it takes center stage in the plant's life, looking much like a miniature mature pod. Each ray on the top of the ovary represents a wall of a chamber inside that contains the embryonic seeds growing in groups. I believe that the number of rays is related to the number of visits the ovary receives from pollinating insects like our chthonic friends, the bees. A single pod produces about 1,000 seeds.[5]

If poppies are stressed, they produce a flower and fruit while very small. This is called "bolting." I have seen a poppy bolt when it is only a hand's-length tall from being in a too-small pot. Too much heat, too little water, not enough light, poor soil, too many rocks, disease, insects, small pots, not enough nutrients, uneven treatment (lots of water and then nothing for too long)—all of these can cause bolting in poppies and some other plants (spinach, brocs, etc.). The variety of poppy and the condition of the seed don't control this. A stressful growing environment is responsible.

Plants that reproduce sexually have children with more variation. This is a real advantage for the human gardener and magic worker. Alchemy teaches us to work with plants in our own environment, preferably ones we grow ourselves, rather than with those that come from other places. This is because the alchemist can then imbue the plant with personal energy, as well as learn about it in depth and in its own context. The relationship between alchemist and plant is also strengthened by the fact that both are experiencing the same local, seasonal, and celestial energies; in a sense, they grow together and meet the same environment. They are thus tailor-made to help each other.

Workers of magic can take advantage of this same strengthening relationship when they grow their own herbs. If you grow annuals for magical use, collect the seeds and plant them the following year instead of buying new seeds from plants grown elsewhere. Not only does this mean that you get basically free seed, but also more plants will be produced with more of a variety specific to your environment. The plants that succeed best will be not only those that can deal best with your soil, your growing methods, and your level of attention to watering but also those most in sync with your personality, your energy, and your magic. Every year, your relationship with these plants will deepen. The plant will hold up its end of the bargain as best it can by producing more and more energetic plants that *want* to work with you and to help your magic. This is the "food" that these plants will make for you on a spiritual plane.

If you grow more than one variety of poppy and want to save seed for replanting, keep in mind that the poppy's appreciation of diversity extends to its sex life—poppy varieties are very happy to cross-fertilize. This means that, if you've got a luscious Black Peony growing in the same garden as a pristine Swansdown, the seeds you harvest from each plant will produce not only Black Peony and Swansdown but also single-petaled purple flowers, perhaps with fringe; double white flowers, perhaps without fringe; and plain single-petaled white-and-lavender flowers—lavender especially, because that's the dominant type, the sort of default poppy. The more you collect and reseed from your own poppies each year, the more the children of those plants will come together to lavender.

You can ensure that your plants and seeds come true in a number of ways, however. You can plant only one variety each year (nice in massed plantings, but not so massed that your neighbors get suspicious). You can separate varieties by at least two miles (as far as a bee can fly)—not a possibility for most of us. Or you can exclude other pollinators and do the pollination yourself. This allows you as a witch to come into especially intimate contact with the plant.

If you want lots of seeds and a larger pod, you can help the plant along by brushing along the stamens with a feather, a paint brush, or a cotton swab as a pollen-grabber. Be sure that you move the pollen powder toward the center of the flower onto the lips of the ovary. If you want to preserve a particular variety, choose the healthiest example. As the buds get ready to open, check them early each morning and, as soon as they point up, cover them with a small bag. The muslin ones used for charms or the synthetic organza bags that you can see through but that don't block light, air, or water both work well. Tie the bag closed lightly but securely. You're just keeping bees out. Check the bag every day and, as soon as the flower opens, rub the tip of your pollen-grabber around the circle of stamens. Then dab the lip of the ovary gently with the pollen. If you are doing this with more than one variety, make sure you use a different pollen-grabber for each variety. Then gently cover the flower again.

The petals may well fall off as you follow these steps, but that's not a problem. Usually the petals fall and the stamens start to wither as soon as the ovary has received the pollen and is cooking up some babies. When the petals have fallen, you can take the bag off. Even one single pod will provide you with plenty of seeds for planting the following year.

The seeds of other plants can be used in other ways. You can even create your own varieties this way by deliberately mixing the pollen of two different varieties—transferring, for instance, the pollen of a Black Peony to the ovary of a Swansdown and vice versa. Or try crossing two plants that you have imbued with two different kinds of energy or two different magical tasks. The following year, the seeds from those plants will give you a range of flower types that you can then further refine in following years.

To get the best poppy children, select a plant for which you feel the strongest affinity. You can also deliberately work with a particular plant from seedling stage, feeding it energy or guiding it to a particular task you want accomplished. You can give the seedling energy by holding your hands over the plant, palms facing it, and pushing out excess energy to it. In this way, you not only nurture the plant; in effect, you "imprint" it with your energy, so that it will be especially suited to your magical purposes. Remember to open yourself to the plant as well, so it can touch you if it wants to.

Instead of using your hands, you can also use your Third Eye. I like this method because it emphasizes the two-way aspect of the relationship we can have with our plants. We beam energy out to a plant, making it the apple of our Third Eye. But in return, we (hopefully) have our Third Eye opened by the plant's energy and spirit. This is one of the oldest ways in which humans have interacted with plants—choosing plant friends that will be especially protected and nurtured. Since poppy is a Moon plant, it can be especially helpful to work with it on a night when the moon is high and bright, especially if waxing. The sight of moonlight on your own garden is powerful in its own right, and a balm to the spirit.

Poppies can be used as cut flowers, but they require a bit of fuss. They should be cut before they ever open completely—just when the buds are cracking open, but before the petals have come out. Cut them early in the morning with a sharp knife or very sharp, small shears. Make the cut at a slant. When you cut a poppy stalk, you immediately see the white latex that has made this plant beloved by humans all over the world. You can either dunk the stem into ice water right away or hold it in boiling water (ouch!) for thirty seconds. Alternatively, you can sear the end of the stem with a flame for fifteen seconds, until the latex turns black (the latex will close the stem end if it isn't burned off). To make them last, put the flowers in warm water and cover them gently with waxed paper for a couple hours. Then they will be ready to display and should be good for four to six days. If you add a tablespoon of sugar and ¼ teaspoon of bleach to a gallon of water and use that for your flowers, they will last longer. Or just use two parts water to one part tonic water or lemon soda. Flowers need sugar, so no diet soda for them!

Poppy pods are one of the few plant parts you can let dry on the plant. They will eventually turn brown and hard and have more than a passing resemblance to the moon, complete with dark splotches. You can cut the stalks with a pruner.

You can also cut the stalks once the pod begins to turn brown and hang it upside down from the ceiling. This is helpful if you have a rainy season in the fall that might make for moldy pods. Some pods have vents that allow the seeds to be shaken out. If you're drying them upside down, do it in a bag. Other pods have closed vents and so act as a storage container for the seeds. To get at them, you have to crush the pod. When you do, you can see the various internal chambers that correspond to the rays on top of the pod.

CHAPTER FOUR

CLARY SAGE

The Mouth of the Prophet

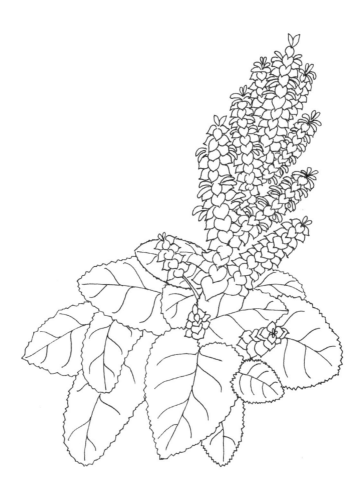

Clary sage has a very different growing cycle from the annual poppy. Rather than devoting all of its energy to end-of-life reproduction (flowering, making seed, and then dying), it takes two years to flower and produce seeds, which is why it is known as a biennial.

THE SECRET LIFE OF BIENNIALS

A biennial's life cycle is not centered on the sun like that of an annual. As the sun rises higher in the sky before Midsummer and the days get longer, annuals grow and flower. When the sun begins to lose power and become lower in the sky and the days get shorter, annuals make seeds and die. Biennials do nothing of the sort. Unlike the solar focus of an annual, clary sage and other biennials attune themselves to the dark as well as the light. In their first year, they generally concentrate on growing a rosette of flat leaves that are designed to take best advantage of the sun. Rather than rising toward it, however, biennials funnel sunlight down into their roots, building a strong tie to the earth that will bring them comfortably through the cold and dark of the winter that annuals never know. Because biennials plan for winter in this way, we can think of their nature as prudent, as opposed to the rather headlong rush of the annuals.

Biennials also spend a good part of their lives appearing to be dead—typically, all upper parts look dead—but still living underground. That they so ably store energy for winter and withdraw to under the ground shows us that we can learn about the Underworld from them. They know a world that generally isn't familiar to annuals. What's more, biennials can withdraw into the Underworld and return safely. Such knowledge is of great value to magic workers.

In the spring of their second year, biennials like clary sage climb out of the safety of the Underworld. Leaving behind the rosette form, the funnel of sunlight, they raise stalks. These are often tall in relation to their first-year height, with leaves of various sizes as opposed to the mostly uniform leaves of the rosette stage. These stalks also carry the blooms that produce seed. It is almost as if two different plants are presented to us: a sun-funnel that pulls solar energy down into the Underworld, and a reserve plant that banks on the solar capital it has built to rise up to meet the sun.

Thus, while annuals are quite straightforward as plants, biennials know both the dark and the light in a way that annuals do not. Because their life experience is so much more extensive, biennials have a much more complex spirit than annuals. They travel between the dark and the light and take from each, which gives them a dualistic quality that annuals do not have. What we can learn from a biennial is therefore quite different from what we can learn from an annual.

Although clary sage is a Moon plant in its effects upon us, some believe that biennials have a fundamentally Martial quality, as Mars has a two-year orbit. After it is conjunct with the sun, Mars appears to move widdershins (against the sun; counterclockwise) for a year. In the same way, a biennial does not reach for the sun in its first year like an annual. Instead, it holds itself close to the earth as a rosette, building reserves to keep it safe during the winter.

In the second year of its orbit, Mars marches across the sky in a sun-wise direction (deosil). Similarly, biennials become more solar-oriented in their second year, putting up a stalk with flowers and often more leaves that reach for the sun. However, the flowers of biennials are generally not sun-shaped, as are those of many annuals. They tend to appear more often on stalks, as with henbane, mullein, and motherwort. It thus seems that perhaps the solar energy possessed by biennials is influenced by Mars, implying a hidden, but deeply protective, quality in them. So, for instance, if clary sage is useful for prophetic work, we might expect that its spirit will not allow us to be completely naked out there in the ethers; it offers us some protection on the ride.

Moreover, biennials show us that the Underworld is not just a place of death. It can also be a space for gathering energy and knowledge that enable a return to the world beneath the sun. They garner and husband sun energy, and then expend it in a glorious burst that creates the beauty of flowering and the fruitfulness of seeding. Clary sage, for example, can help reveal the hidden and guide us if we want to journey to the Underworld. As clary sage is ruled by the Moon, it offers its revelations through dreams and visions. As a witch, you can bring these into the light of day, where, through your actions, they can be helped to flower and fructify.

LORE

For clary sage, the dualism of biennials comes through in the contrast between what it seems to be—how it presents itself—and what it actually is. Clary sage has a long-demonstrated ability to go about in disguise and so can teach us the use of "glamours"—false appearances, usually cast by Faeries, that affect the sight, making things look different from what they really are. This is why clary sage is considered a "glamourous herb," from the Scots word *gramarye*, the archaic meaning of which was "sorcery."

Clary sage has, for years, been confused with another sage that was used to remove foreign objects from the eye because of the mucilaginous nature of its seeds. Various references can be found—all apparently copied from each other—saying that clary sage is also known as clear-eye, *Godes-eie*, seebright, *oculus Christi*, *gallitritum*, Goody's eye, and scallewort. However, these names actually refer to *Salvia verbenaca*, which has seeds coated with a gluey substance that, when soaked in water, helps clear the eyes. I don't believe that clary sage seeds have this property, as they contain plenty of essential oil, which isn't at all soothing to the eyes.

In fact, as far as I can tell, clary sage has rarely been used in any medicinal way. Its "clary" is not the clarity of physical sight, but of other ways of seeing—of second sight and of the ability to pierce the veil of a glamour, which, according to folklore, occurs when a bewitched person rubs something *on the eyelids*, not in the eye. I think this reveals the real use of clary sage.

Clary sage performs a number of other "glamourous" tasks that further underscore its nature. It has been used to adulterate wine to make it taste as if it were made from muscatel grapes when it isn't. It remains a frequent component of faux ambergris (amber) formulations, as well as of vegetable musks, bestowing an ambergris scent on substances that do not actually contain any ambergris.

Clary sage has properties similar to regular sage (*Salvia officinalis*), but without the toxicity of thujone or the propensity to cause skin irritation. In that way, it is a sage that is not sage. It greatly potentiates alcohol—it was added to beer to increase its inebriating qualities in the Middle Ages before the use of hops became common. In England, up until at least the early 20th century, it was still being grown in cottage gardens to give an extra punch to herbal wine. In other words, when combined with alcohol, clary sage acts as if it is an alcohol itself, yet it isn't an alcohol at all. In all these ways, clary sage demonstrates its ability to mask itself, to cast a glamour upon those who encounter it, and reveals its willingness to teach us how to see true.

But now a little craziness.

Clary Sage and Lunacy

Even though poppy is a Moon plant and has Moon effects, we can see Sun's influence, not only in the fact that it is an annual—a Sun follower—but also in how straightforward it is. There is no trickery in poppy. Its latex is bitter precisely to let us know that ingesting it will have an effect—perhaps deadly. It never pretends to bear a healthy fruit, as belladonna does. It is straightforward, like the rays of the sun, not a trickster. Moreover, Sun-like poppy's germination and cultivation, although involving some legal risk, is physically direct and simple. Throw the seeds on the snow in winter and they will come up in the spring. No finagling or special treatments are needed. The speed and force of Sun is also shown in the burst of annual flowers and their brevity. Poppy flowers, for instance, last only a day.

Even the shape of poppy flowers, with their corona of stamens and rayed ovary, is Sun-like. In contrast, biennial flowers are slower—they take longer to appear (in the second year of their growth cycle) and last longer once they do.

Now contrast the annual poppy with biennial clary sage. Poppy and clary sage are both Moon plants and share certain Moon characteristics, but the Moon nature of clary sage is completely different from that of the poppy. In its action on the body, poppy focuses on sleep and sleepiness. It slows things down. This Sun-focused annual sleeps at night and encourages the same in its users. And what is a poppy pod but the poppy's final gift before it goes to the sleep of death?

If poppy is aligned with the New Moon in its ability to induce sleep and perhaps death, clary sage is connected with the Full Moon that drives two- and four-footed animals a little bit crazy. This walker between two worlds that enjoys disguises focuses on the lunacy side of Moon. With clary sage, night is not the time for sleeping and sedation, but for activity and euphoria—for greeting the Lady of the Hunt and dancing in her train. It is, in fact, one of the only euphoric herbs found in temperate areas, and its ease of growth makes it an obvious choice over inebriating New World tropicals. Just as the plant, during the night of the year, is busy beneath the ground preparing itself to break through the earth once again in the spring, so it offers that kind of Moon energy to magic workers.

The breaking through in this case is to insight, intuition, understanding of dreams, and knowledge of the future. The dualistic properties of clary sage are well exemplified when it is combined with alcohol (not a good thing to do in large quantities with this herb, as it can result in a horrific headache). It can either greatly increase alcohol's ability to stupefy, or it can induce a frenzied exuberance. For me, this fits with the aspect of the leaves, which are as wrinkled as the hand of an elder, and with the sense one gets from the plant of something juvenile (that duality again). Oddly, just as the Moon plant poppy deadens pain, clary sage can help people with pain in a completely different way—by raising their spirits enough to be able to deal with it. It also regulates estrogen and so has another completely different connection to Moon than poppy, which tends to damp down hormonal processes.

✖ *Warning: Although clary sage is basically nontoxic, it should not be used in the presence of estrogen-promoted cancers, because it can encourage the uterus to produce hormones.*

PRACTICE

The scent of clary sage is very relaxing; it lowers heart rate and blood pressure. It helps relieve pain and even has aphrodisiac effects. A good way to use it for those purposes is to put it in a muslin bag or a large tea infuser and soak it in the tub. Outside of that, clary sage is a good scent fixative, famous for its mildly ambergris fragrance (you will get more of this from the leaves than from the whole tops). It does not have the camphorous nature of other sages, although, strangely enough, it does contain some of those latter-day demons—alpha- and beta-thujone.

Clary sage does have a very few uses in herbal medicine, but the primary and most important role of clary sage for witches is as an aid to dreamwork. I have found it to be absolutely ace for this purpose, with none of the nasty hangover of a more typical dream-assistant like mugwort. Clary sage does not bring on more dreams by keeping you half awake, as mugwort does. Instead, it works as a sort of key to a deeper level of dreaming, where prophecy can occur. We have a signature for prophecy in the shape of clary sage's flowers. In contrast to the Sun-wheel aspects of poppy flowers, the clary sage flower looks like a speaking mouth—the mouth that speaks prophecy.

A relatively easy way to engage with clary sage's dream aspects is through a tincture.

Witch's Tinctures

Probably everyone reading this has made a tincture at some point, but I want to cover some of tincturing's lesser-known possibilities, like using different menstrua— water, alcohol, vinegar, and wine.[6]

Water is best for working with plant materials that have been mortified by drying and pulverizing. It helps the dried bones of an herb to rise again. But consider: A tea relies on water with the addition of heat to bring about the release of herbal goodies. Teas tend to be made quickly and are not preserved—they steep for a maximum of fifteen minutes and are consumed within a day. Speed is important with a tea, because water is not a preservative; it just promotes change—that is, putrefaction, the Black Crow of alchemy. That is good if you are making wine, but otherwise generally not very beneficial.

By contrast, a tincture is slow. Tinctures generally don't involve the addition of heat, and the tincturing process occurs over hours, days, a Moon cycle, or weeks longer. With that much time, you need to delay the putrefaction process that water would otherwise initiate. That's why tinctures almost always involve alcohol as well.

Alcohol is better at extracting alkaloids and their salts—always popular with witches—as well as essential oils and their aromatic components. It won't dissolve cane sugar, minerals, or gum. That means you can use 95 percent alcohol to tincture even cheap dragonsblood and yet produce a very high-quality product. Alcohol leaves all the gum, which smells just like burning tires when it's combusted in incense, on the bottom of the tincturing jar. You can strain that out and then either let the alcohol evaporate to get pure dragonsblood resin, or use the tincture itself as an incense dressing. Don't be surprised if you try this with cheap dragonsblood and find great gobs of gum on the bottom of the jar!

Water mixed with alcohol is one of the most time-honored menstrua in herb work. But there are other possibilities that were more popular in the past and now have been mostly forgotten, except in some herbal practices. Wine vinegar, apple cider vinegar, or rice vinegar (without all the sugar and additives) can be useful as a menstruum, especially if you want to change the pH of the mixture, which can affect the color of fruit tinctures (more on this in chapter 14). Vinegars turn alkaloids into their salts, making them much more available to the human body. However, how well they do this varies with the percentage of acetic acid in the vinegar. This can be problematic if you are looking for a bit more predictability when dealing with very dangerous alkaloids, although it is always difficult to talk about predictability in plant work. The same species of plant, for instance, can have a different level of alkaloid depending on a number of variables—soil, sun, moisture levels, competition from other plants, stressors like bug predation or disease or crowding, and which part of the plant is harvested when. Some people use the seeds to try to standardize a "dose" or attempt predictability, but seed size varies dramatically as well, depending on how the plant grew that season.

Store-bought vinegars can be of some help here, because their acidity level is standardized. However, keep in mind that much that is sold as wine vinegar is just grape juice with industrially produced acetic acid added to it. You can get real wine vinegar from gourmet shops (I buy mine by the gallon) or make it yourself, in which case the acidity will not be predictable. When you tincture plants containing dangerous alkaloids, standardized vinegar is safer.

Apple cider vinegar is more reliable if you get the cloudy variety. I have great suspicions of clear apple cider vinegar and believe it to be a concoction of apple juice and industrially produced acetic acid, similar to the cheap wine vinegars out there. Don't use distilled white vinegar. It is an industrial product that is only good for cleaning things.

Vinegar tinctures are excellent for banishing, especially in mist form, and were once used as fresheners in sick rooms to banish miasma. If you want vinegar to preserve your tincture, the menstruum must be pure vinegar (no added water). If you want it for its ability to extract the most alkaloids, make your menstruum from 35 percent water, 10 percent vinegar, and 55 percent alcohol.

Wine is a time-honored menstruum that is no longer used in pharmacy because a wine tincture won't last indefinitely. Wine does not have a high enough alcohol content to prevent the putrefying action of its water. If it includes preservatives, it will "go off" in a generally unpleasant way, like an oxidized oil. Without preservatives, it will tend to turn into vinegar. Chose white wine, since it has far fewer tannins than red wine. Tannins (which usually give a dry-mouth feel, like oak or very strong Darjeeling tea) cause alkaloids to fall out of the solution of your tincture and lie on the bottom of the bottle. This means that, unless the bottle is shaken religiously before each use, the last few doses could be deadly. So avoid tannins in tinctures. A fortified white wine like sherry is a good choice. Fortified wine, brandy (distilled wine), and other high-water-content menstrua are good for tincturing dried herbs that don't bring their own water to the tincturing process.

In terms of distilled spirits, 151 rum (75 percent alcohol) or cane spirits (43 percent alcohol) are made from plant juices and so are especially fitting when you are tincturing leaves and flowers. Consider that other spirits may work better for other plant parts: potato vodka for roots, grain vodka or 95 percent alcohol for seeds, brandy or fortified wine like port or sherry for fruits, and rum or cane spirits for leaves. Personally, I tend to use 95 percent alcohol frequently, because it is so fast. In alchemical terms, it is the Mercury of the plant world, and it shows its Mercurial nature by the speed with which it can work on its own (away from water) and how quickly it will fly (evaporate off, in this case). Higher-proof alcohol will dissolve the waxy and oily parts of the herb that would not be extracted by water. For herbs especially high in essential oils, like sage, higher-proof alcohol will get more of the aromatics out.

Something else to consider if you are going to dilute your alcohol (which you should if you are going to use 95 percent alcohol) is using wine as the diluent. Wine is more acidic than water and can thus extract different substances than plain water and alcohol can. It can substitute for vinegar without giving the tincture a sour taste. In my experience, white wine is an excellent diluent for a strong clary sage tincture.

Generally, the best time to make a tincture is when the herb in question is in bud or has just begun flowering. In my experience, the phase of the herb's growth cycle is more important than the phase of celestials like the moon or the zodiacal signs. However, you can get lucky sometimes and combine them.

Some people believe that herbs must be chopped up finely before tincturing. I do not. I base this on the writing of Isaak Hollandus, an alchemist who asserted in his treatise on making the Plant Stone that, if you can smell a plant while processing it, its vitality and soul are being destroyed. We also know that the cut edges of plant material respond to the injury and sudden exposure to air by producing different chemicals than are present in whole leaf. One way you can get around the cutting or chopping question is just to use a very high-proof alcohol. This will break down cell walls and even the water will be pulled out of the herb. Higher-proof alcohols do indeed act quite differently from lower-proof spirits like brandy or rum, even though they can be much higher proof than vodka, which is often held up as the tincture base *par excellence*, but is much more watery.

Another way you can get around the chopping issue is by cutting the herb while it is beneath the surface of the menstruum. This can be a bit clumsy, but sharp scissors stuck into the jar will work. This allows you to use a lower-proof alcohol and even perhaps a bit of vinegar, which can be helpful in some herb tinctures. Freezing can also break down cell walls (think frozen spinach) and tends not to harm the plant's volatiles. Finally, some people put the herb in a (hopefully glass) blender, cover it with menstruum, and chop it that way. I generally leave the leaves and flowers whole.

To make an exceedingly strong tincture, reinfuse it with fresh tops every day for three days, and then every month at the appropriate phase of the moon during the growing season. This will give you a strong tincture that has a range of properties from the plant at different stages in its growth. Another approach is to strain the marc (plant material) out of your tincture and then use that to tincture again with fresh material.

Clary Sage Tincture

Harvest clary sage when the flowers begin to appear, preferably on a Monday (Moon day) when the moon is waxing or full—although you can also see what comes of harvesting on the New Moon, since that implies digging really deeply into dreams. The best time to harvest the flowering tops is in the morning for highest essential oil content. You can use the entire above-ground parts of clary sage, although some people use only the flowers. The leaves are much more powerful, in my opinion. Harvest after the dew has dried, and try not to harvest when it has just rained, which adds a lot more water to the plant's flesh.

Cut or pull the leaves and flowers off the stalks; generally, stalks are good primarily for making powders rather than tinctures, macerated oils, or ointments. They have a lot of wood in them that prevents them from being extracted very well, so put those aside for drying and grinding into powder.

I use the "folk" method for tincturing this herb: Put the (whole) fresh herb into a jar and cover. Add one finger's breadth of your menstruum of choice. The best menstruum for clary sage is 151 rum, cane spirits, or 95 percent grain alcohol.

1. The green goodness of the clary sage will be released into a strong menstruum pretty much within twenty-four hours—less with higher-proof alcohol like Everclear, where even an hour may be sufficient.

2. The herb will turn dull and even slightly crisp in high-proof alcohol, as the menstruum extracts all the water and water-soluble goodies from the herb.

3. Strain without pressing the marc in order to obtain a clear tincture.

4. If you don't mind cloudiness, press the herb. In my opinion, however, patience pays off here, just as in jelly-making.

5. Bottle and keep the tincture in the dark or expose to the Full Moon periodically to charge. Eventually, the green tincture of clary sage will turn olive and then amber, but will still be good.

☠ *Warning: 95 percent alcohol always has to be diluted before being ingested. It is extremely drying and can ulcerate your esophagus. Always label your tinctures when you use 95 percent alcohol, so that no one accidentally ingests them straight.*

For safety's sake, you can mix tinctures made with 95 percent alcohol with something else once they are extracted. A good partner for clary sage tincture is rose water in equal parts with the alcohol. The result will be the alcohol strength of a strong brandy. Take one tablespoon diluted in a small glass of white wine or warm water right before bed on an empty stomach. However you choose to dilute a 95 percent–alcohol tincture, the result should have an alcohol strength of at least 25 percent so that it does not spoil in your cabinet. It is nice to combine the use of this tincture with a mugwort dream pillow, but it is in no way necessary.

Clary sage aids in creating very vivid, divinatory dreams and helps with their recall, but because it is so good at casting a glamour, be careful not to mistake a mundane visual for a great revelation—or vice versa. Keep in mind that the "clary" of clary sage is all about seeing clearly—distinguishing between the false and the true, the amber and the ambergris.

CLARY SAGE IN THE GARDEN

It is best to start the seeds of clary sage or any other biennial when the days are getting longer—during the first half of the year—and when the moon is waxing, if possible. Still, if you start biennial seeds in the fall, you can sometimes get flowering in the following first full year. Since clary sage originated in dry and rocky soils in the mountains of southern Europe, it does best where the soil is not too rich or too wet. Even though it is a biennial, like many of that tribe, it can live longer than two years—perhaps up to six.

Some people don't like the smell of clary sage's leaves, so you may want to site your planting away from a patio; others think the leaves smell pleasantly of grapefruit. I personally haven't noticed a smell unless the leaves are crumbled or torn, in which case the scent recalls a woman's sweat, making it a good basis for a vegetable musk in incense and magic oils (thus the "muskiness" of clary sage, Sweat of Our Mother). Otherwise, the scent is just herby and kind of medicinal. Clary sage is usually "deer proof"; they don't seem to like oddly textured leaves, and clary sage is a bit fuzzy. The flowers can be dried (cut them just before blooming).

Since clary sage is in the mint family, it can be pretty aggressive in spreading around the garden, so put it in a place where its exuberance won't be a problem—like areas bordered by pavement or grass, where unwanted plants can just be mowed down. In the rocky clay of my upstate New York garden, this herb has not spread much at all and, in fact, I have to replant it every few years.

Grow this plant from transplants. Unlike poppy, whose seeds are vigorous enough to germinate simply if enough of them are tossed on the ground, clary sage and all the other plants in this book need help and protection to get established in a witch's garden. Yes, once they are there, they may well reseed if they are happy and if that is their nature. But reseeding means that literally hundreds or thousands of seeds are tossed away by the plant to get just a few children. We don't usually have that many seeds. And besides, helping seeds grow is part of our work as witches in the green world. It isn't that difficult, but it does take attention and that most Saturnian quality, patience.

Just barely cover your clary sage seeds with potting soil, and they should germinate in two weeks if kept at room temperature. Once the seedlings come up, harden them off and set them out in the garden in full sun after all danger of frost is over. The first year of its growth, clary sage forms a rosette of leaves—they spread out from the center low to the ground. The second year, stalks bearing mint-like pink, lavender, blue, or, in some varieties, white flowers shoot up. These stalks can be twenty-four to thirty-six inches (61–91cm) tall. In keeping with the dual, guising nature of this Moon herb, most of the flowers are actually not flowers at all, but specialized leaves called "bracts." You'll notice that they're a bit stiffer and dryer than the average petal. They act as beacons or guides to pollinators, leading them to believe the flower is much larger and thus has more nectar than it really does. And here we see how well a glamour can work, because it is precisely because of the bracts that clary sage has been grown in gardens, especially today, when the place of this herb in magic has been all but forgotten.

A typical temperate-climate plant, clary sage is hardy down to –20°F (–28°C; zones 5–9). It is tough enough to prevail against most plant diseases and bugs without any help.

CHAPTER FIVE

YARROW
Tail of the Werewolf

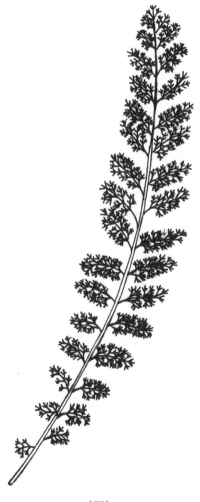

Y arrow has been cultivated in Europe since the Middle Ages for medicinal purposes, in particular for dressing wounds. This gives it a kind of obverse correspondence with Mars, who rules war. Although it was often used in love magic in the British Isles, it was traditionally taken to war because of its ability to stanch bleeding and its association with the warrior Achilles, who first used it to stanch blood and whose name was applied to its binomial, *Achillea millifolium*. Yarrow was still a part of the U.S. Pharmacopeia from 1836 to 1882, and was used to treat battle wounds during the Civil War. Stonecutters and carpenters also kept yarrow handy for dressing injuries.

This connection to wounds, and thus to the skin, shows a Venus influence, which is strengthened by the historical use of this herb in British folk magic for love charms and love divination. But I think yarrow's use in war—definitely a Mars task—and its ability to stop the flow of blood reveal an unexpected depth to this herb.

Yarrow is a perennial. That means that it can take two seasons or even more to get to the point of flowering and producing seed, but from then on it will blossom and fruit for some years afterward— although not forever, despite what the word "perennial" implies. Any plant that lives longer than two years is called a perennial, but the length of a perennial's life varies quite a bit. Most herbaceous perennials—those that do not have woody parts and are not grass (all the perennials in this book are herbaceous)—live seven to nine years, but some trees can live for millennia. Yarrow and perennials similar to it thus experience a very different relationship to both the Underworld and the sunlit world from what other plants do.

THE SECRET LIFE OF PERENNIALS

Annuals germinate, grow, flower, and produce seeds in the space of a single season; biennials take two years to accomplish that work, although it's not uncommon for them to live longer if they're in a happy situation. Perennials, on the other hand, can live for much longer. They thus have much more of an underground life than annuals and biennials. Furthermore, perennials know their way around under the ground in ways that the other two types of plants do not comprehend.

Perennials use various means during their time beneath the soil to strengthen themselves, build reserves for future use, and propagate. They can send white stems complete with vestigial white leaves through the soil to colonize new areas. Because they're underground, we think of these structures as roots and call them *rhizomes* and *stolons*. They also create underground storage tanks that we humans often like to eat (tubers). And they can pierce the Underworld with a spear-like tap root, rather than traveling through the ground horizontally with a rhizome or stolon.

Tap roots often have arms and legs, like the mandrake. These limbs seem to exist, not only to charm us but also so that, when the root is pulled up, some will break off and remain in the ground to produce clones of the plant. It seems that this type of reproduction, which involves traveling, takes much less plant energy than reproduction through seeds. It makes sense, then, that the slow, Saturnian perennial makes use of low-energy reproductive strategies like this.

What does it mean for us that perennials do not rely on making seeds to reproduce as much as annuals and biennials do? Making seeds is a risky business involving a lot of trust on the part of the plant—for instance, the trust that pollinators will appear. Perennials don't bother with that kind of trust. They just go ahead and make more of themselves with no outside assistance. If I chose tarot cards to represent the different types of plant life, I would select The Sun for annuals, The High Priestess for biennials, and The Hermit for perennials.

What is the tarot Hermit looking for? Not buddies, not a crowd, but something that will further his own enlightenment, an expansion of his consciousness. I see this as the perennial's quest as well, with the same sort of self-reliance and lack of interest in the great, crowded world of variety. The perennial has Hermit business below the ground: digging, burrowing, traveling in the night of the Underworld, going where The Sun and even The High Priestess cannot or will not go. Perhaps part of the reason why so many witching herbs are perennials is because witches sense this plant group's Hermit nature.

Reproducing through seeds is a gamble, but has the advantage of allowing for expression of the complete cache of genes that the plant carries. It favors adaptation, variation, and risk-taking. Annual plants generally make good charms for gambling or for protection in urban environments, since they have mastered these. That doesn't generally happen with the vegetative reproduction of perennials. Instead, what you see is what you get. They reproduce themselves, not as a motley crowd, but as individual duplicates.

"Making more me all the time" may sound kind of selfish, but perennials break down the very concept of the unique individual. Consider: What happens to a plant's self when it is divided, as may happen to a yarrow plant in its third year? You can dig up the crown, rudely split it apart with garden forks or even rip it apart with your hands, and plant the two different clumps in two parts of your garden or in two different hemispheres. They will grow. But are they still the same individual? Do you have one individual in two different places? Or do the two clumps, by being separated, somehow become two different individuals? Personally, I wonder if plants produced this way—by dividing the crown, or breaking arms off a tap root, or even rooting a cutting—have a consciousness that extends to all the parts of itself, no matter where they may be. In effect, do all the clones share one mind or a collective soul?

We are not advanced enough in our communication with plants to know this, one way or the other. But it may be worth trying to make use of the possibility in magical practice. For instance, if a group of magic practitioners separated by distance encouraged vegetative reproduction in a single plant and then shared the clones, could they amplify the power of the plant through long-distance communication if they worked with it at specified times?

The offspring of plants that reproduce through seeds are each as unique as any mammal's offspring. Perennials can also reproduce through seeds, but seem not to favor it. Nor do they engage in the same level of risk-taking or trust as annuals and biennials, although they do not reject it completely. After all, perennials build parts of themselves that they know full well may be broken off and eaten, or lost to disease or killed through lack of water or nutrients. They gamble that, even if some part of them is broken away, that part will continue to grow, which permits the experience of a different part of the world, a different perspective on their environment.

Areas prone to fires, desert droughts, or harsh winters—environments that would kill an annual or a biennial—are usually not problematic for perennials, as their vibrant underground life seems to make them much stronger. Their toughness is also demonstrated by how much more difficult it is to germinate a perennial seed than that of an annual or biennial.

Sometimes, perennial seeds can't germinate until the seed has gone through some weathering that leaches out germination inhibitors—snowmelt, for instance—or that scratches entries for water into a very tough shell—sandstorms, or fluctuations of heat and cold, or even the acid and grit of a bird's gut. This gives an immature embryo time to mature. A number of perennials actually do produce seeds with such embryos. But it's almost as if the perennial's vegetative reproduction has caused them to lose interest in reproducing sexually. Some perennials don't even bother with an embryo in the seed at all, so that the seeds can never germinate. Some annual seeds can literally be tossed on the ground and they will germinate, but I am aware of no perennial seeds that will do this. Perennials are too involved with the Underworld and with their connection to it to put much energy into the sexual world. What this means for a witch is that perennials ought to be first choice when working with the Underworld.

Plants are as influenced by memory as animals. Although we don't know what is going on in the mind of a plant, we can see the results of memory in their form. An annual's form is, for the most part, determined by the present—how much rain or sun they experience or the type of soil they are planted in. They are little influenced by the past, except in terms of the health of the seed itself—what has gone into forming it. Perennials, however, embody their past to the point that it trumps the present. For instance, if the previous year was very dry, a perennial will show the effect of that lack of water, regardless of how much water it receives this year. This is in keeping with their strong connection to the Underworld.

While it's true that the ancient Greeks considered that those who wandered the shores of the River Styx had lost their memory (through the help of henbane, incidentally), memory is crucial when it comes to the Underworld. After all, when we try to connect with that place, it is often because of our memory of someone whose shade is there. It is as if memory were the current that allows us to plug into the Underworld.

When I look at the Hermit tarot card, I see a figure who holds memory and who looks into the past (generally the Hermit is portrayed facing left, where the past is located in our culture). For me, this fits well with the nature of perennials. This means that, if you are working on a spell that is dependent on memory, perennials can be excellent for sharpening memorization skills. They remind us; they reveal secrets of the past; they bring the past into the present— exactly as they return from the Underworld every spring, remembering the previous year.

Biennials usually become taller in their second year, but don't extend outward very much. Perennials, on the other hand, spread. Each year, they claim more ground and make more of everything that is them: leaves, stalks, flowers, fruits, roots. Carl Linnaeus (1707–1778), the Swedish botanist who created the Latin binomial (two-name) system still generally used for plants (and animals), considered that perennials' tendency to take up more and more space was a reflection of a fundamentally Jupiter energy, as Jupiter is considered expansive and is characterized as "standing out" from others—taller, brighter, bigger, stronger. Although he was a scientist, Linnaeus clearly had no trouble recognizing planetary influences.

The more aggressive perennials are especially beneficial for spell-work meant to create lots of something—in particular, duplicates, perhaps even as many as twenty. Because of their ability to travel underground and establish themselves in new places, they are also beneficial for magic involving attack, sabotage, or spying. Moon energy also strongly affects perennials. In the second half of the year, when the Full Moon appears higher in the sky and the sun lower, perennials begin establishing the buds that will be the basis of their growth the next season. By the time the moon is at its height, during the Winter Solstice, perennials are finished bud-building and are in their deepest dormancy.

Perennials start to come back to life, back to the upper world, after the Winter Solstice. It's perfectly fine to cold stratify perennial seeds beginning in fall, but I always wait until late December to start stratifying them (see chapter 2). I find that I get better germination if I go with the plant's clear desire to stay dormant as the moon ascends. Perennials' inherent connection to the moon means that Moon-ruled perennials are especially powerful for work with lunar energies. You get a sort of "double helping" of Moon with perennials that you do not get with annuals or biennials that are Moon-ruled.

LORE

Consider this verse from Scotland describing the use of yarrow for love magic. It starts out like the typical, sappy love charms reproduced in lots of late 19th-century collections of British folk practices. Indeed, many such charms do involve yarrow.

> *I will pluck the yarrow fair,*
> *That more benign shall be my face,*
> *That more warm shall be my lips,*
> *That more chaste shall be my speech,*
> *Be my speech the beams of the sun,*
> *Be my lips the sap of the strawberry.*

But something drastic happens after these first six lines:

May I be an isle in the sea,
May I be a hill on the shore,
May I be a star in waning of the moon,
May I be a staff to the weak,
Wound can I every man,
Wound can no man me.[7]

The requests are no longer about acquiring (Victorian) physical attractiveness, but instead about gaining strength (a staff capable of wounding), solitariness (an isle, a hill, a star), and invulnerability (protection from wounding). This part of the verse may be metaphorical, just like the first part, where the request is for lips like strawberry juice, for instance. An isle in the sea is a refuge; a hill on the shore and a star in a dark sky stand out. Both can be metaphors for standing out from other women and offering men a comfortable port or refuge, even hope.

But what if we don't confine our perspective on this verse to the maidenly? Could it not also be about taking on other forms? If we look at it that way, the strawberry lips and chaste speech have an altogether different meaning—they're a mask, an appearance, a guise. And then we have yarrow, not so much as Venus's eyebrow (one of its common names), but as the tail of the werewolf—the shapeshifter.

Despite yarrow's efficacy in healing wounds, this plant has always seemed more Mercury than Venus to me. First, something about its scent reminds me of Mercury aromatics like celery and dill. Indeed, yarrow shares a number of important fragrant chemicals with Mercury-ruled plants like celery, parsley, cumin, carrot, and fennel.[8] The delicate ferny quality of its leaves also fits with Mercury, as typically the leaves of Mercury-ruled plants are finely divided—like the nervous system, over which Mercury presides. Mercury is a bit of a trickster and is perfectly capable of indulging in disguise. And disguise is where yarrow really comes forward. For instance, this plant is often condemned in North America as a vile and reprehensible, invasive, non-native weed—a foreigner that showed up with the Europeans and that has been helping besmirch a once-pristine environment ever since (sort of like the rest of us).

In fact, however, yarrow was here before Europeans were—just in a different form. *Achillea lanulosa*, the native North American plant, is almost indistinguishable, even by botanists, from *Achillea millefolium*, the European import. Thus, folks ripping out yarrow may well be destroying native plants. Clearly, yarrow has the ability to fool us—and to make fools of us, as many trickster entities are capable of doing. But it goes deeper.

Yarrow and Shapeshifting

Yarrow is known for being polymorphic—taking many forms in one single species. In other words, as a species, it's a shapeshifter. Remember, the Latin name for yarrow's genus, *Achillea*, comes from Achilles, the warrior who was the son of shapeshifting parents. Each of its forms—*Achillea lanulosa* and *Achillea millefolium*—has a different number of chromosomes and a different profile of volatile chemicals (fragrances), depending on the locale where it grew. So, from plant to plant, one yarrow can have not only a different scent but also different medicinal and magical capabilities. If that's not Mercury, I don't know what is!

Now if we go back to that "love" charm, we can imagine that perhaps it is not about either love or war, but shapeshifting—especially considering that, according to Carmichael, Mary Stewart, the dairywoman from Skye whom he interviewed, "knew many occult runes and occult arts." Isn't that precisely the kind of person who would know a thing or two about shapeshifting and be a bit of a trickster herself? Perhaps she offered him a little love charm for his lady readers and gave him part of a powerful shapeshifting charm instead.

On the other hand, this verse may also represent a bit of lost magical knowledge of which Mary Stewart was herself unaware. It would not be the first time that someone who knew something of the occult arts did not know the depth of the information they passed on. When looking at folk magic practices, we must keep our minds open to the possibility that what we are reading (or hearing or seeing) may originally have meant something completely different from what it supposedly means now—although it may be transmitted correctly by the people who engaged in it and by those who recorded it.

We can even see a verse like the one above as a *palimpsest*—something written over something else that is only partially erased. Thus, on the surface, this may be a love charm, one of many yarrow love charms. But perhaps what is glinting through is a shapeshifting charm. In fact, it is possible that a lot of the yarrow "love" charms may actually be yarrow shapeshifting charms that were modified as their original use was forgotten or rejected, even by the practitioners of magic who preserved them in the first place. We see this happening today as practitioners remodel what were traditionally "black magic" rites and spirits, turning them into something that is vaguely Goth rather than truly dark and dangerous.

In the scheme of magical things, love charms or spells for beauty are not usually threatening to the powers that be or the order of things—especially when compared to being able to transform yourself into a hill or a star, or become invisible (which is also implied by these little ditties). Shapeshifting and invisibility, on the other hand, tear at the very fabric of the duly predictable material world we normally take for granted. We all know that those seeking love may engage in a little "shapeshifting," altering their appearance through clothing or colorants or padding. But to go beyond that challenges our concept of reality. Such spellwork strides off into the completely ambiguous (which, I would argue, is the very essence of the witch's world). But a love spell is a clever place to hide a shapeshifting spell. Moreover, that deception is very much in the spirit of yarrow. This is not to say that this poem or chant is evidence that, historically, witches used yarrow to turn into hills and stars. Instead, it indicates yarrow's role in helping witches morph into nonhuman entities—into things much more like the spirits with which they work.

The connection between yarrow and shapeshifting in this verse fits with the plant's ability to change its nature (for instance, in terms of the volatile chemicals it gives off) with small internal changes of gene numbers. What's more, shapeshifting fits with the herb's historical use on the physical level—stanching blood stops what is hidden from being seen, and healing wounds covers the interior that was revealed. For these reasons, consider using yarrow as a shapeshifting aid. Such a skill can be valuable to everyone, but it is especially so in love and war.

Now, you may be saying: "Why are you bringing up a silly topic like werewolves in a serious book about herb magic?" Well, I'd like to convince you that the werewolf is not silly, but an important image for witches working along European lines. We're not talking about Hollywood werewolves here, where an individual turns into a physical wolf and goes off killing folks when the moon is full and the wolfsbane blooms. That is actually a very new conception of the werewolf that was created in popular culture rather than in folklore or magic. The werewolf of popular culture is the product of our industrial modern society. The werewolf of folklore is a product of a traditional society.

Such is the influence of movies and other entertainment that many believe shapeshifting involves physically, materially morphing into an animal, especially a wolf. Originally, however, the word *werwolf* meant someone who knew how to change physical form, not someone who turned into a wolf. In fact, most animals associated with shapeshifting European witches were not even predators. They were mice, butterflies, goats, cattle—in fact, just about anything.

The concept of the shapeshifter who becomes a savage wolf came into being in Europe at the same time that witches came to be viewed as those who meant to do harm—in the mid-1400s. Werewolves and witches became closely connected after that time. This is one reason why the Livonian shapeshifter Thiess baffled his judges at his 1691 trial for heresy. He insisted that, although he was indeed a werewolf, far from preying upon the community, he and other shapeshifters fought battles with magical evildoers to protect the fertility of the community's crops and guided the dead to the afterlife. It's interesting to see how society inverted this, turning the community-protecting shapeshifter into a predatory wolf just as the perception of the witch morphed from healer and helper (an ambiguous figure, since the help requested might involve harming someone else) into a contract employee of the devil bent on harming the community

Traditionally, shapeshifting occurs as a sort of projection that emerges from the witch or shaman when asleep or in trance. It is an aspect of the witch's spirit, a double that a skilled witch can, with practice, talent, and luck, make appear to others in the material world, as opposed to the world of dream or spirit. This is not something beginners can do, since it is a highly complex work that involves developing the skills to dream lucidly, to appear before others who are awake, to seem solidly material, and to mold that appearance into the shape of an animal. It seems clear that the ability to leave the body and appear to others is necessary to those witching practices that involve participating in the Wild Hunt, processions of the dead, or flying to the Sabbat. This obviously goes far beyond love spells, drying up the milk of someone's cow, or locating stolen objects.

PRACTICE

The practice of shapeshifting brings up the same issue that arises so often with the practice of the Sabbat: whether the use of an ointment of some kind—physical help in the form of chemistry—is necessary for achieving particular states or effects in magic. If witchcraft is a craft that is dependent on skill in using its tools, then something like an ointment may help a practice, but it cannot do the actual work. Believing that an ointment can enable you to turn into a literal wolf or fly to the Sabbat seems about as likely as believing that simply holding a hammer will cause a house to appear before the would-be carpenter. We don't expect that a needle and thread will make someone a seamstress or that a brush and paint will make someone an artist. So why would we think that practice, time, and skill are not just as important to witchcraft as they are to dressmaking or carpentry? Magical practice is just that—*practice,* something you do, rather than an object that you make or buy.

Obviously, tools can enable certain tasks or at least make them easier. A screwdriver generally helps you put in a screw better than a butter knife, although you can use a butter knife to put in a screw if you haven't got a screwdriver. Likewise, in witchcraft, you can ask the help of a plant's spirit when you work with an herb for a particular magical task. Yarrow shows, on the material level, what a master it is at shapeshifting, so it makes sense to ask its help when you want to learn how to shapeshift.

The different scent profiles of yarrow are like the different shapes that an individual witch's double can take. You can explore along those lines by growing some of your yarrow in one area and the rest in another and comparing the results. Incorporate powder of yarrow into an incense burned for trance, or put a pinch into the hot wax of a candle lit for trancework. (Instructions for crafting the powder follow.) A dream pillow stuffed with dried yarrow leaves and flowers, or a tea made from them and consumed before bed, can help you acquire shapeshifting skills.

Another way to learn shapeshifting is to bathe with yarrow, but it's crucial to test the herb first on your inner arm to be sure you are not allergic to it. Infuse a handful of fresh or dried flowers or leaves in one pint of boiling water for fifteen minutes. Strain the mixture and add it to a bath. This yarrow bath is gently relaxing and lessens pain and inflammation, which alone may be helpful for trancework. I suggest bolstering yarrow's action along these lines with Mercury herbs like lavender and dill seeds, because the stream of Mercury energy is typically connected to disguise and the acquisition of magical skills. Since, historically, European shapeshifters tended to work at certain times of year, try to select similar times—the equinoxes or the Ember Days—to focus especially on developing the skill of shapeshifting. Since fresh yarrow is not available all year around, dry some plants so you have it on hand when needed.

Drying Yarrow

One way to utilize yarrow is to dry it and turn it into a powder. Although hanging bundles of herbs from the rafters looks really wonderful, it's an invitation to pantry moths. Moreover, I've found that, if I don't use the dried herbs fairly quickly, they get all dusty and lose much of their identity and spirit. So I use an electric dehydrator and dry them at the lowest possible setting for the shortest possible time.

The practice of "garbling," separating an herb's leaves and flowers from the stalks, lets you capture more of the plant's physical and spiritual essence—its essential oil, its sap, and just generally the life of the herb. Typically, you can remove most of the leaves by just zipping your fingers down the stalk from top to bottom. Then dry the leaves and flowers at a low temperature—around 95°F (35°C)—so they stay greener and retain more of their nature.

....

☠ *Warning: Always wear gloves when garbling rue and other herbs that may be irritants. And don't sit in the sun while doing it or touch your eyes.*

....

If you're harvesting green stalks, use secateurs or bypass pruners, which are curved. Or you can use a ceramic knife, which works fine and is neutral in terms of planetary influence (but be careful of its sharpness). Scissors also work on small stalks. For woody or brown stalks, use an anvil pruner, which looks more like a pair of pliers. Bypass pruners and anvil pruners cut in different ways: using the right one will give you clean cuts and ensure that you don't crush or tear the plant. Clean cuts are easier for the plant to heal and are more respectful.

Some people just compost the stalks of their plants once they've stripped off the leaves and flowers, but stalks have good uses. They are excellent for drying and grinding, then incorporating into incense or powders. Save the leaves and flowers for teas, infusions, macerations, baths, and stuffing poppets. Use the powdered stalks for everything else. Snip them into smaller pieces and dry them fairly quickly. Then pound them in a sturdy mortar to help with the powdering process. Grind them in a dedicated coffee grinder or mini food processor with a metal blade.

When drying, remember that you can always halt the process and add some liquid—wine for sweetening or intoxicating spells (or red wine for blood), vinegar for embittering or love-busting spells, salt water for tears of sorrow or joy, or the sweat of love or labor. Toss the partially dried material with some of the liquid as if dressing a salad and let it sit for an hour. Then strain out the fluid and proceed with the drying. You can add tinctures back into an herb this way, either to create an extract (use a tincture of the herb you are drying) or to create a multidimensional herbal ingredient that contains aspects of various herbs. You can also imbue an herb with an individual's essence, either your own or another's, by using personal fluids or by laying small pieces of a sweat-soaked T-shirt or the crotch of unlaundered underwear in the dehydrator tray and putting the herbs to be dried on top of it. This can add an extra dimension to the plant material that is not attainable in other ways.

When the herb is dry (crispy, usually, but not brown), let it cool off a bit before putting it into a storage vessel, so that you are not packing in humidity condensed from the cooler air. You can use some uncooked rice or silica gel packets in the vessel, but herbs are usually fine as long as the vessel has a tight lid to keep out pantry moths and other critters. You can actually keep moths out with a few bay leaves in the top of the vessel; they hate them. For storage, cool and dark is best. And don't forget to label, especially when you've got a powder.

Each herb has its own best time for harvesting, and that time can vary depending on what you are using the herb for and whether you want the part of the herb to be especially strong or not. With yarrow, the flowering herb is the best stage for harvesting. Gently touch the new flowers each day; when they start to feel stiff instead of soft, you'll know it's the time to harvest and dry.

YARROW IN THE GARDEN

For all its experience with the Underworld, the tiny seeds of this perennial plant require surface sowing—instead of burying them, simply press the seeds gently into moistened soil. This is often the case with any sort of small, dust-sized seed; they tend to get lost below the soil surface and rot. Bottom-watering is thus generally beneficial (almost mandatory) with yarrow plants, and especially seedlings, so you don't risk washing seeds away. This means that, rather than pouring water onto the top of the soil, you feed it into the bottom of the soil container. For instance, if you are starting seeds in peat pellets inside some kind of flat or pan, pour the water into the pan and let it seep into the soil for a half hour, then dump out whatever has not been absorbed.

Yarrow seeds prefer temperatures on the cool side of a normal room (62–75°F or 18–25°C). They should germinate in five to ten days. Colder temperatures mean slower germination; hotter temperatures will decrease germination. Many people have the idea (mostly perpetrated by some of the larger seed companies) that a warm humid environment, like that provided by a tray with a plastic top, or even bottom heat and direct sunlight, are necessary to germinate seeds. The truth is that, for many seeds—especially those of the witch's art—a warm, humid environment means death.

Consider how seeds tend to germinate outside in the garden—protected from direct sun and harsh rain by the branches of their parent. The environment beneath the shade of a perennial is more moderated than that around it, but it's far from being a greenhouse. I've found a plastic cover is never useful for seed germination, although bottom heat can be good for tender perennials like tomatoes, peppers, and datura.

Once your seedlings are up and have two sets of true leaves, you can transplant the yarrow babies to full sun and a nice, light soil. Soil that is very rich produces floppy stems. The first year, the plant will make a smallish rosette of feathery leaves that (appropriately) resemble werewolf tails. Their appearance fits with the Airy nature of this plant. Make sure to run your hands over the soft, fine leaves to catch the yarrow's scent; it's one of the pleasures of a witch's garden.

The second year, the rosette of leaves will get much larger and the plant will shoot up a two- to four-foot (60–120 cm) stalk atop which the buds form. Bees, ladybugs, and butterflies enjoy the slightly sweet white flowers that occur in flat groups called *umbels*, because the flowers stand on stalks that keep them all at the same level, like the ribs of an umbrella. Yarrow is hardy in zones 3–10, so most of the United States and pretty far north is fine.

Once it gets going, yarrow will spread by underground runners called rhizomes—you'll see new plants popping up a few feet away from the parent. As is fitting for our first exploration of the perennial plant world, yarrow's roots don't go deep beneath the ground, but instead explore the area just below the surface. This "traveling" can make yarrow a problem for perennial beds, as you'll constantly be weeding it out. However, as yarrow also increases the fragrance strength of the herbs it grows near, there are reasons to leave it there. Still, it's probably best if you can give yarrow its own plot surrounded by grass that is kept mown (it will pop up in lawns). I have grown yarrow backed with tansy as a bright green edging along my driveway, where it formed a nice little mini-hedge.

You can make more plants and improve flowering by dividing yarrow plants in their third or fourth year. In the spring, dig up the crown of a plant, literally pull the clump of its fibrous roots apart, and plant the parts separately.

The leaves of yarrow are especially aromatic while dew is fresh or just after it has rained. In fact, this is one of the few plants whose scent is not diluted by moisture. Its fragrance remains intoxicating when it is dried, and the flowers make a great potpourri ingredient.

Yarrow is a tough plant once it matures; sometimes the leaves will stay green under the snow. Small bits of very young leaves (they are strongly herby!) can be incorporated into salads; but typically, it's the flowering tops that are harvested and dried. Since I like its very herby scent, I have my sun-basking chair next to my yarrow plants.

CHAPTER SIX

RUE
The Subtle Warrior

Herbalists Culpeper and Gerard both considered rue to be a Sun herb, as, medicinally, it is hot and dry and has yellow flowers. Although rue does have strong solar affinities, I think that, for witches, it should be considered a Mars plant. When we think of Mars herbs, thorns usually come to mind. Thorns are not just a defensive weapon, but also a visual warning that approach is unwise—like the stripe on a skunk's back. Thorns are the plant equivalent of the sword of Mars. Of course, Mars can be more subtle than macho displays of sharp weapons. Rue demonstrates how Mars can be significantly less obvious and still be extremely effective.

LORE

What is there about rue that functions in place of the thorns of a typically Martial plant like prickly poppy or cactus? Its "sword" is, in fact, its strong scent, which arises from its irritating sap. How irritating? That depends on the delicacy of your skin and the brightness and heat of the day. In keeping with Gerard and Culpeper, the sun potentiates the fierceness of this plant. For some people, brushing against rue while the sun is shining brightly may feel as if someone brushed a lit cigarette against their skin; if they don't wash it off, it can literally burn them. Yet other people have no reaction to rue's sap. Skin is ruled by the planet Venus, which many Venusian herbs are known to protect. So an attack on the skin seems very Mars to me.

....

≋ *Frogs, Figs, and Caterpillars* ≋

In temperate climes, we lack poison frogs, whose vibrant skin colors advertise their hazard to potential predators. We do, however, have very brightly colored swallowtail butterfly caterpillars that feed on rue. These strong colors warn birds that the caterpillars are poisonous. Their toxicity is increased by eating rue. If rue is unavailable, they feed on parsnip, parsley, celery, carrot, or dill, which all contain bergapten, *the chemical that's the primary cause of the blisters that rue causes for some people in the presence of sunlight.*

Rue is traditionally recommended as an under-planting for fig, the plant with the greatest amount of bergapten. The fragrant fig absolute is no longer in use because of its ability to affect the skin negatively.

....

The chemical that causes the blisters that result from contact with rue is *bergapten*. Its action hints at magical connections indicated by the dependence of Air creatures like butterflies on plants such as rue, not just for food but also for protection. Butterflies are especially noteworthy to witches, as they are among the animals that witches traditionally morphed into to engage in flight, as we saw in chapter 5. The protection that rue offers to butterfly young (caterpillars) implies a protective spiritual quality that rue may offer to witches who are new to flying. I think that hidden substance demonstrates just how subtle Mars energy can be.

Moreover, consider what rue's irritating sap may mean magically. It occurs on the surface, affecting the outer covering, unlike the kind of hazard that might come from a poisonous plant, which is usually an interior danger, causing corrosion from within. Rue presents itself as acting on the exterior, so choose it for protection of property borders, the exterior of the home, and for magic circles or altars outdoors. Expect its magical action in such locations to cause some damage to trespassers, especially those who appear in the daytime. Do magical workings asking for rue's protection during the day, especially when the sun is shining and at its highest to obtain the strongest effect.

As a subtle warrior, rue lets us know through its scent and the unusual bluish color of its leaves that it should be noticed. That blue tint can be considered the plant equivalent of the poison frog's bright skin or the swallowtail caterpillar's bold stripes. As its bluish color has a light waxy coating (known as "glaucous" in the plant-nerd world), rue is, in fact, occasionally considered a Moon plant, which fits with its sometime association with Diana.

It is striking how various plants signal the intensity of their life's blood with bluish leaves. Poppy's blue tinge points to its narcotic, bitter white latex. Wormwood's intense bitterness is indicated by its silvery blue tinge. Rue's blueness signals its caustic, bitter nature. It contains the same substance that is in the bitter white pith of citrus peels, to which it gives its name, "rutin."

Working with Unfriendly Plants

Working with energy is an important part of magic. Some energy has the power to harm, like the sap of rue, but that doesn't mean we shouldn't work with it or that the plant has a negative character we must avoid. People regularly work with fire, which can destroy entire cities. Rue is nowhere near as dangerous. Just take precautions when handling it (wear gloves, don't work in the sun). The same holds true for plants that possess more potent dangers than rue and that are likewise important to witches, like the baneful herbs addressed later in this book. You need to be cautious, not frightened.

☠ *Warning: If you are fearful of a plant, don't work with it. Mushroom gatherers know that fear can exacerbate a reaction to a poisonous mushroom. I think the same applies to the baneful herbs. If a potentially harmful herb makes you feel uncomfortable, don't work with it; just learn about it from books and the experiences of others. Gradually, you can decide whether you want to go further. That said, there is no requirement for any witch to work with baneful plants. You can work with the rose for the rest of your magical life and not be any less of a witch than someone who has buckets of belladonna and wolfsbane around. Remember: It's not the tool; it's what you do with it that counts.*

Nor is it necessary to withdraw entirely from growing a plant that may cause you harm. You can just heed this particular aspect of it. Learning to work safely with plants is as much a part of wortcunning as learning which plants are good for protection or banishing. You can come to understand how to guide the plant's energy in a way that you want it to go—for instance, by using it to keep animals (including the two-footed kind) out of certain areas of your yard.

The ability to determine which precautions are necessary to work with a plant is part of the experience and learning of a mature witch.

I have seen how those who are fairly new to magic tend either to refuse to work with potentially harmful plants, or else discount that harm entirely. Mature witches—and by "mature" I mean in learning, not in years, because there are as many old fools as young ones—can work around a potentially harmful plant without being either reckless or paralyzed by an excess of caution.

PRACTICE

Rue has been recognized in various parts of the West as protective and purifying. As an example of its ability to purify, in English law courts, the floors were strewn with rue because it repelled vermin, plague, and "jail fever," another name for typhus (which is generally spread by lice or fleas). In Morocco, one variety of rue (*Ruta montana*) is traditionally burned as a cleansing smoke inhaled to get rid of illness-causing spirits. In the Muslim world, it is used to keep away demons (*jnun*) and frequently turns up in rituals meant to purify an area of such entities, as well as in protective charms to keep them away. It is also worn as a protective amulet, since it keeps off the Evil Eye.

Like many Martial plants, rue has historically been considered effective against the bites of mad dogs, poisonous insects, and snakes. Infused in water, it makes a good sprinkle for people who are troubled by spirits. As a strewing herb, it can help purify a sacred space that has been profaned.

One notable aspect of military forces and this Mars energy is their external sameness—the use of uniforms, for example. We can see this tendency to external sameness in rue's use in Italy. There, a magical illness called "Fright" (*scantu*) causes a condition where parts of the body feel out of proportion with the rest—too big or too small, for instance. Healers confronted with this disease measured the various body parts with a string to check the proportions. If the proportions were off—if the externality of the individual was not symmetrical or uniform—they cut up the string, put the pieces on the joints, and prayed. Then they told the victim to burn the strings and drink *centelvo*, which is usually composed of rue (*Ruta chalipensis)* in alcohol.[9] I would not be surprised if this were *grappa con ruta*—that is, grappa into which a sprig of rue has been dropped; the brew was judged ready when the sprig turned white. Rue, then, helps make things uniform. For that reason, consider it for use in situations where you must hide in plain sight or blend into the uniformity of the crowd for the sake of subtle Mars protection.

The Cimaruta

Italy is the home of the *cimaruta*, an amulet in the shape of a hand-like branch of rue that keeps away the Evil Eye. The word literally means "sprig of rue" in Italian. In Naples, the area where this type of charm is most popular, cimarutas are typically made of silver, the quintessential Moon metal. You can consider making your own from a three-branched rue stem when it is podding (make sure to dry it thoroughly first). A cimaruta may be worn around the neck or hung on a wall to provide protection. As rue is itself such a protective plant, various protective charms are attached to its branches so that they can augment one another. A favorite charm to include on a cimaruta is a crescent moon, and several of the charms traditionally hung on a cimaruta have lunar associations—for example, a key.

....

≋Cimaruta Charms≋

According to the magician Agrippa, perhaps the most influential writer of Renaissance esoterica, the first talisman of the moon is dedicated to opening locks. In herbal lore, the most famous lock-opener is the moon-wort fern. Many cultures perceive that it is Moon, traditionally envisioned as a gatekeeper who aids the diviner, who seeks access to other times or places through the Gate of Dream. In tarot, The Moon is considered a gate (the birth canal). In the guise of her alter-ego Jana, the lunar goddess Diana—so important to Italian folk magic—opens and closes the Doors of Night. Perhaps the concept of the moon as a gate originates with her. Other symbols typically included on a cimaruta are a flower (that may be shaped like a rue flower), an animal horn, a rooster or eagle, and sometimes a snake.

....

A cimaruta often contains balanced male and female symbols: lock and key, rooster and crescent moon, flower and horn. The stem that holds these charms is not leafy, but rather of the type that carries the seedpods—in other words, this amulet is the stem of fruition, in contrast to a leafy stem, which is about becoming or building. The sprig should have at least three branches, perhaps because three is often considered a magical number, although others believe that this harkens back to the three faces of the goddess. The number three can also symbolize female genitalia.

Subtle Protection

Rue has been grown as a low hedge and, in that manner, can function well as a Martial protector of your home. Dogs and cats don't like the smell of this herb, so if you have problems with dog-walkers allowing their companions to leave souvenirs in your yard, consider planting a rue hedge with a buffer zone of French marigold, especially the *Tagetes minuta*, which has tiny flowers. This allows the scent of both plants to repel animal trespassers, but not expose those who are very sensitive to rue's potentially caustic sap.

Here again, we see how Mars can be subtle in terms of defense. It is the scent of the rue that animals don't like. Likewise, some people intensely dislike the scent of marigold. Scent is the closest our material world comes to a manifestation of spirit on the molecular level. The *Zohar* considers scent to be the food of angels. In fact, many mages provide spirits with the smoke of incense as an aid in their materialization. Rue's scent is not in the angel-food category, however. Instead, it is the scent of warning.

Yet there is nothing bullying about this plant spirit, which offers us a lesson: Witches are subtle warriors, not wielders of brute force. They don't break the lock; instead, they use the key. This is unlike the kind of brute force normally associated with Mars energy. It is a more sinuous power, like the snake on the cimaruta.

Witches, like rue, do not have to show their thorns or be bullies. True, some delight in yelling things like "Death to you!" if someone corrects their spelling online, or putting a death curse on a wedding photographer who takes lousy photos. Instead, a witch can work on a spiritual as well as a material level to fend off attack. In my experience, many witches tend to start off a bit loud and bombastic; but with maturity in the Craft comes quiet confidence—the subtle warrior, the hand of fruition.

A very common use of rue in witchcraft is as an important ingredient in Four Thieves' vinegar. Here's a recipe that can be used for warding, but not for ingestion.

Four Thieves' Vinegar

> *2 oz lavender tops*
>
> *1.5 oz each of rue, sage, mint, wormwood, and rosemary (leaves)*
>
> *½ oz clary sage or chamomile (leaves or flowers)*
>
> *¼ oz each of cinnamon, clove, garlic, and calamus root*
>
> *1 gallon of red wine vinegar*

1. Add all the ingredients to the vinegar.
2. Let sit, covered, for a month and a day.
3. When the time is right, strain out the herbs.
4. Use the vinegar on doorways, cracks, and corners to keep things out.

The dried leaves of rue are also good for adding to candles and incense for honoring Mars energies, or for censing your Black Knife (traditionally, a steel or iron blade used for magical bloodletting) or any iron or blood-connected magical tool. But you can have your Four Thieves' vinegar and a powder, too, if you save the stalks.

Making Powders

Many of the powders sold to practitioners of magic are composed mainly of talc, which is problematic because it is a known carcinogen. Another common ingredient in commercial powders is called wood flour, finely ground up wood of unknown source—so it could be "pressure-treated" wood (i.e., poison). Why mess with these ingredients when you can make your own powders? Moreover, since an excellent main ingredient for homemade powders—and a traditional use of plant material in old-fashioned pharmacy—is stalks, they demonstrate a witch's thrift. You can strip off the leaves of a dried plant and reserve those for teas, strewings, stuffings, vinegars, waters, or even incense. But you can keep the stalks to make powders.

Stalks are the bones of a plant; this analogy appears as far back as the Greek Magical Papyri. One witchcraft practice distinguishes between Living and Dead Bones when it comes to plants; I find these categories useful. Living Bones are green stalks, those that are living when they are harvested. When dried and ground, Living Bones make powders embodying the plant's more positive or friendly aspects.

Brown stalks—those that have gone through a winter or have turned brown because the plant experienced drought or disease—are considered Dead Bones. Dead Bones evoke the plant's more negative aspects (hostility, aggressiveness) or may simply be used in more negative magic. To make your life a little easier, cut the plant bones up before you dry them. Use secateurs for Living Bones and an anvil pruner for Dead Bones. Even though Dead Bones are already dried, they may have dew or rain on them and should be put through the dehydrator to crisp them up. Plant material is easier to grind when it's crispy dry.

You can take this further by "mortifying" Dead Bones in several ways. You can perform what is basically a Black Toad operation using decay. This was the first stage in alchemical transformation, during which most of the impure aspects of a substance are destroyed by rotting or fermentation. To do this, wet them and seal them up (the smell of such an operation can be pretty atrocious). Think of the possibilities of various liquids used in the wetting—wine for deadly intoxication, urine for destruction, vinegar for sharpening or souring.

Another way of mortifying a plant's qualities is to heat the bones until the plant material is blackened, turned to ash, or even calcined (when the white, caustic, alchemical salt of the plant is all that's left). To mortify with heat, put the Dead Bones in a little roasting pan in the oven at 450°F for half an hour or so. This can also be done outside on a fire. Some people use a torch lighter or even a propane torch. You can then add the resulting mortified bones to other items like incense or oils. They also make a good foundation for a magical powder.

You can tweak a powder by adding other bones, Living or Dead, and also by tossing the powder with essential oils and/or perfumes to modify or amplify the plant's energy. You can also add any items that don't work well in incense because they are noncombustible or smell bad when burned, like mint or orange peel. And you can play with noncombustible ingredients like iron oxide (brick dust, for Mars energy), glitter, mica, metallic powders, mineral powders, rocks, dirt, or pigments. You can see how wide a range of possibilities you have beyond the basic dyed sawdust you so often find being sold in foil packets as condition powders in occult shops. Better tools help make better magic.

A powder needs an appropriate vessel, even more than an oil, a water, or an incense. The vibration, if you will, of a powder is more subtle and more easily disarranged. Since only a fairy-sized pinch is necessary for dressing candles, clothing, tools, or other objects, a small vessel is usually adequate. A used antique jar makes a good container—just cense it first with the purifier of your choice. Mugwort is nice for this—it's everywhere; it's a witch's staple herb; and it's a traditional friend of flame in herbalism.

Here are a couple of rue recipes that you can tweak to make all sorts of powders. The sanctification powder can be used for purifying or sanctifying ritual spaces; the hexing powder is good for cursing those who seriously deserve it, or for very Martial protection from ongoing attack.

Rue Sanctification Powder

Living Bones of rue

Living Bones of mugwort

Living Bones of vervain

Lemon verbena or lemongrass essential oil

Frankincense resin, ground or in essential oil form

1. The best time to make this powder is at noon on a Sunday during the height of summer.
2. Grind the bones and the frankincense (if using the resin) together. Be careful not to grind too long, because the frankincense will heat up and get sticky.
3. Add the essential oil(s) and put in a clear jar.
4. Let sit in the sun for seven days, preferably from Sunday to Sunday, for optimum power. If you want to make this as an incense instead of as a powder, increase the frankincense resin so that it is half the recipe and use dried leaves instead of stalks.

Rue Hexing Powder

Dead Bones of rue

Dead Bones of wormwood

Dead Bones of mugwort

Lemongrass or its essential oil

Myrrh powder or myrrh essential oil

Iron oxide—choose black for hexing, red for war

1. Make this powder at night during a time when the sun's power is decreasing (fall, winter).

2. Starting it on the New Moon and harvesting it during the following dark of the moon or creating it during a solar eclipse adds extra power to this powder. The idea is to arouse the plant's negative energy as much as possible. If the planet Mars, the master of attack energy, is visible in the night sky, all the better.

3. You can further mortify the bones by roasting them, or you can just grind them, engaging in a good bit of pounding while doing so to increase the added energy. Mix with essential oils or myrrh and iron oxide powders. Seal in an amber or dark-colored jar and keep in a dark place.

RUE IN THE GARDEN

The best time to plant rue is under the sign of Aries, as this Mars-ruled sign signals the beginning of spring in the Northern Hemisphere. If you intend to harvest the tops of the herb, start its seeds during a waxing moon, if possible. Rue's connection to the Sun is demonstrated in its manner of germination; it must be surface sown. This involves wetting the planting medium, sprinkling the seeds on top, and gently tamping them in with your fingertip. Don't let the soil dry out. Bottom watering keeps the soil moist without washing away the seeds.

Rue especially enjoys germinating in peaty soil, so this is a good occasion to use peat, either as pellets or as a loose seed-starting medium. Always moisten peat before you try planting anything in it, because it resists water when it's in a dry state. That's why it's important not to let peat dry out. A good way to wet peat for seed-starting is to heat some water—not to boiling, just hot—and add some kelp. Pour this mixture on your peat pellets, then plant when everything has cooled. The hot water helps the peat absorb the moisture faster.

Rue seeds germinate in seven to twenty-eight days (interesting, that last number's connection to Moon!). This time frame indicates how close rue still is to the wild, where staggered germination is both normal and advantageous. This is not the kind of seed that comes up all at once, like a highly domesticated plant. It's easy to make more rue by starting cuttings, however. It also reseeds prolifically, so dead-head the flowers if you don't want it to spread by seeds.

Rue is a perennial in temperate climates and likes full sun and dry, rocky areas. But make sure to water it adequately while it's getting established. It becomes eighteen to twenty-four inches (45–60 cm) tall. Mature plants should be spaced fifteen to eighteen inches (38–45 cm) apart. Dogs and cats avoid this plant, as do deer, rabbits, slugs, and other garden predators. Some people with pets who are not the sharpest claw on the paw put rue in a pot and hang it from a fence, rafter, or windowsill to ensure their pets don't go running through it. (My cat just avoids it.)

Rue is a host plant for the boldly colored caterpillars of the black, yellow, and giant swallowtail butterflies. They also like parsley, dill, fennel, Queen Anne's lace, and bishopweed. Rue is also home to the babies of a little parasitic wasp that is very helpful to have in your garden, because, as an adult, it ferociously hunts obnoxious veggie-chomping caterpillars.

Be careful where you site your rue, however; you don't want folks who are sensitive getting a burn from brushing against it. On the other hand, consider it as a border plant if you have frequent trespassers. Keep in mind, however, that it is an allelopathic plant, meaning that it guards against others so well (again, subtly) by releasing substances into the soil that other plants can't grow near it. This property can be positive or negative, depending on whether it is used as a tool or viewed as a mere aspect of the plant to be managed.

The best time to harvest rue is in the spring. Harvest the tips before flowering, unless you are gathering the plant for luck in business, in which case, harvest after flowering. Remember to wear gloves.

CHAPTER SEVEN

HYSSOP

The Asperger

Recently, someone remarked to me that she thought that, some-times, people used the rarity of an ingredient in a historical spell as an excuse not to use that spell. I think she's right. But if you do want to work a spell with a difficult-to-find component—like lion's skin or lark's brains—you can learn from a plant like hyssop that it's quite possible to make viable substitutions. Practitioners of magic have been doing this for millennia. In fact, the Greek Magical Papyri contains a list of substitutions of herbs for animal bits (*PGM* XII:401–404).

LORE

A large number of books on magical herbalism refer to the men-tion of hyssop in Psalm 51:7 as justification for its use in magi-cal purification—"Purge me with hyssop till I am pure; wash me till I am whiter than snow." This reference, in turn, points to a purification ritual described in an earlier biblical book, the Ritual of the Red Heifer found in Numbers 19:2–19. This ritual is the true origin of using hyssop as an asperger in magic, since it actu-ally describes asperging, the practice of sprinkling a congregation, space, or objects with a purifying liquid to cleanse it of evil spirits or negative influences. Other mentions of hyssop in the Hebrew Bible do not. It also gives some interesting clues about the identity of the hyssop used.

The Ritual of the Red Heifer describes how scarlet wool, cedar, and "hyssop" are burned with the ashes of a red heifer (a female animal, and thus more identified with blood in the Bible). The ashes are added to spring water and a hyssop branch is dipped into it. This water is then sprinkled on people or objects to purify them. This may be a priest or another person, their belongings, or their home—any-thing that has been rendered impure by coming into contact with a corpse, a grave, or human bones.

With the exception of the hyssop, all of the items in this ritual have the color red in common. It makes sense in this context, then, that the herb mentioned should be hot or at least warm, and perhaps have red flowers. But the hyssop familiar to most of us, which I will call "our hyssop"—*Hyssopus officinalis*—is camphorous, or cold. Its default flower color is a cool blue. So perhaps "common blew-flowered Hyssope" is not the hyssop that is referenced in the Bible.

In fact, historically speaking, our hyssop doesn't grow in the Middle East, which excludes it as an ingredient in the Red Heifer ritual or any other biblical use. The hyssop in the Hebrew Bible is *Origanum syriacum*, which I will call "biblical hyssop"; it is still used today as the primary ingredient in a Middle Eastern spice blend called *za'atar*. Biblical hyssop has pink flowers, an oregano-like taste, and a warm scent. Even the leaves are different from those of our hyssop. They're fuzzy, an advantage in low-moisture environments, because the fuzz helps the plant hold onto what little water is available in its surroundings, especially dew. Biblical hyssop thus fits perfectly with the rest of the warm, red ingredients of the Red Heifer ritual.

So, if we are justifying the use of hyssop as an asperger in magic based on its use in the Bible, we are using the wrong hyssop. Does this mean that, during all those centuries when European witches and mages used our hyssop (*Hyssopus officinalis*) for aspergers, nothing was actually purified, because they were doing it wrong?

On the contrary. We know from practice that our hyssop does indeed purify on the material plane, in the same manner as biblical hyssop.[10] Europeans used our hyssop materially and spiritually in ways similar to biblical hyssop—for instance, as a purifying medicinal herb for driving disease from the lungs. Like a number of other plants in the mint family, our hyssop has a strong Air nature and has been used for respiratory cleansing. In 16th-century England, our hyssop was strewn on floors that were difficult to keep clean—for instance, those made of dirt or uneven brick. This use continued in Colonial America.

Whenever a plant is helpful for purifying or driving out pests and pestilence on the material plane, it's likely that it will also be useful to purify and drive out spiritual pests. We see this with *Hyssopus officinalis.* For instance, our hyssop repels envy, just as it repels fleas and disease germs. In fact, volume 8 of John Baptist Porta's 17th-century book on natural magic cites hyssop as helpful in turning away the "witchcraft of envy." It was a part of 17th-century protection charms in England and, in Wales, bunches of hyssop were hung on the inside of school doors to protect the children from charms. The herb was placed in coffins, along with rue and wormwood, as a symbol of repentance in England, probably based on the reference in the psalm.

Our hyssop (*Hyssopus officinalis*) was used to get rid of noxious spirits and to purify an area of their verminous infectiousness. We can see that a body of practice involving various sorts of purification on the material plane was built up around our hyssop, much as a body of purification practice was built up around biblical hyssop (*Origanum syriacum).* To use our hyssop in place of biblical hyssop is, therefore, not a simple substitution based on name alone or on a hunch or even on personal gnosis. The different characteristics of these two plants show that a substitution in magic can bring in almost the complete opposite energy of the original ritual ingredient—which is fine, as long as there is a similarity in how it works on the material plane (and, by extension, on the spiritual plane), and there is support for its ritual use by the community. Hyssop is thus a good example of how magical substitutions can be made, even for ancient magic, and still be very effective. This example should give us the confidence to make substitutions ourselves when necessary.

Something to consider with purification is that it can come either through warmth or through cooling. Both our hyssop and biblical hyssop are aromatics that drive out germs and bugs. One is warm; the other is cooling. But both work to purify. So we can conclude that no single elemental quality holds the patent on purification. It can come through any of them, thus further opening up the possibilities for substitutions.

Substitutions in Magic

Contrast the substitution of our hyssop for biblical hyssop with the common substitution of American mandrake (*Podophyllum peltatum*) for European mandrake (*Mandragora officinarum*). Like biblical hyssop and our hyssop, these two plants have the same common name. And, like them, they aren't in any way related. While this substitution does have community support, the working actions of American mandrake and European mandrake are not at all the same (see chapter 1).

European mandrake root is a deliriant and hypnotic, like its relatives henbane, belladonna, and datura. Historically, it's been used as a sedative, an anesthetic, and even as a painkiller. By contrast, American mandrake root is a purgative and cathartic, causing violent vomiting and diarrhea. Since inducing purgatives were once considered generally beneficial in American botanical medicine, American mandrake root had a minor place in the formulary. But it was never used for fertility, painkilling, sedation, or anesthesia, as European mandrake was. In other words, these two plants have never had similar material uses.

⇒ Oops! No Tea for Me ⇐

Some years ago, a customer of mine bought some American mandrake root and then called to ask how much she should use in a fertility tea. I said: "None!" and explained that, if she did, she could end up in the emergency room for dehydration from severe diarrhea. She claimed she had been advised by a local "herbalist" to drink a tea made with mandrake to help her get pregnant. I explained the difference and advised her to let this "herbalist" know how wrong she was. In the United States, herbalists are not credentialed by any independent entity, so some end up prescribing a violent purgative for infertility. Perhaps those who do should be given of a dose of their own medicine!

The true similarity between American and European mandrake—and what won American mandrake its name—does not reside in the roots (the most important part of European mandrake from a magical perspective) but in the fruit. Both plants bear small, golden, fragrant, tasty "apples" that are not toxic. Substituting American mandrake root for European mandrake root in magic is pointless, because there is no parallel between the roots and their actions on the material plane. However, if you are making a fertility charm and don't have access to ripe European mandrake *fruits*—which are a good choice for historical reasons and are still used in this way in the Middle East—ripe American mandrake fruits are an excellent substitute. On the material level, the ripe fruits of American and European mandrake are similar in that they contain small amounts of active ingredients and can be eaten safely. Both their appearance and their physical action are similar, so they can be substitutes in magic.

Clearly, in order for a magical substitution to work well, a mere similarity in name—European mandrake root and American mandrake root—is insufficient. Some similarity on the material level, whether in appearance or activity, has to exist for the substitution to be considered. Moreover, the material action should be supported by some kind of communal, cultural use of the herb in question. Our hyssop works as a substitution for the hyssop of the Bible because of the similarity in material actions, and because of its acceptance in magical practice built up by communities.

Hyssop entered into magical practice in the West because of its imagined biblical connection. But it proved to be helpful enough in practice that its use continued in spite of that connection in later times. Today, when the Bible no longer has a strong hold on Western imaginations and when it is no longer imposed on people—when, in fact, many in the magical community have a strong dislike for all biblical references—our hyssop is still used.

PRACTICE

Solomonic magic bases the practice of asperging on the biblical reputation of hyssop, but extends it to include other familiar cleansing plants, which further supports the concept of logical substitutions in magic. Thus aspergers are made from hyssop, vervain, fennel, lavender, sage, valerian, mint, basil, and rosemary bound to a hazel branch by a thread spun by a maiden. Many of these same herbs are ingredients in absinthe (or Pernod or Chartreuse), of which hyssop is an ingredient.

⇒ How to Make a Hyssop Asperger ⇐

To make an asperger from fresh hyssop, simply cut a small handful of the aerial parts of the plant (best when it is in flower) and tie them together with a cord of your choosing. Embroidery thread makes a nice choice, since it comes in a wide array of colors in small amounts and is readily available at craft and sewing stores.

In my experience, all cleansing plants are aromatic—and not necessarily sweetly so. They usually have an herbal, rather than a flowery, scent. Most purifiers in Western culture have a somewhat camphorous nature. Aromatic herbs that are purifying on the material level—antiseptic, antifungal, antiviral, or antivermin—can typically be counted on to be purifying on the magical level as well, as we can see from the list of Solomonic asperger ingredients.

Our hyssop is not all cool Air, however. It is also warming and slightly stimulating. Its scent raises blood pressure, causes sweating, and lowers the seizure threshold by increasing the electrical activity in the brain. I think its relatively gentle warming quality is why Culpeper deems it an herb of Jupiter. In other ways, our hyssop has no Jupiter aspects. It's not tall or bold; its fruits are not nourishing; and it doesn't have yellow flowers. However, its medicinal action (and perhaps what was considered its connection to biblical lore) gives it enough Jupiter influence to satisfy Culpeper. To my mind, our hyssop's slight warming property also makes a neat occult connection to the outright warming of biblical hyssop.

Warning: The essential oil of our hyssop contains a high proportion of chemicals known to lower the seizure threshold in humans and other animals. For most people, this is not an issue, but for those who suffer from seizure disorders, it can be dangerous. Be careful, because you may not even know that you have such a disorder. Moreover, these effects don't have to develop into full-blown seizures to be an issue. I've had the experience of working carelessly with camphor, which is contained in hyssop and has similar chemical components, and it was very unpleasant—a horrible jittery, shaky, cold feeling, with tremors that lasted for hours. The essential oil of Hyssopus decumbens, however, does not contain the camphorous element that is dangerous.

By contrast, Agrippa considers our hyssop to be a Moon herb. As the coolness of its scent is so lunar, this makes sense, even though the plant bears no watery fruit and does not especially enjoy growing near water—both considered qualities of Moon plants. In fact, our hyssop likes a dry growing environment. The dryness preferred by this mint (a plant family that usually likes lots of water) is reflected in the combination of scents in hyssop's fragrance and taste—like a mixture of cool mint and warm sage.

Purification and Binding

Camphor, which is strongly present in hyssop flowers, has a reputation for being antisexual or anaphrodisic. Nonetheless, hyssop is often implemented in binding love magic. An example is described in Fernando de Rojas's 15th-century novel, *La Celestina,* which describes a charm used by Saint Martha, who famously bound a dragon that was menacing the town of Talarçon:

> To the mount of Talarçon you went and beheld the live serpent;
>
> With your hyssop of water you sprinkled it and with your holy girdle you bound it and delivered it to the people.
>
> Just so, deliver my love to me, and if he loves me not, let him love no one else.

There's plenty of phallic binding here, even though this charm was cast by a woman over a man. Its binding nature and all-or-nothing attitude seem to have characterized love magic in the past just as in the present. In his study of medieval magic, *Forbidden Rites*, Richard Kieckhefer regards this type of magic as responsible for medieval society's "aversion" to magic on account of its coerciveness—a connection relevant in post-modern society as well. The driving out of the noxious serpent and its binding through hyssop is very akin to purification (which drives out) and, in this spell, to the "purity" of loving no one at all should the spell fail. The coolness of hyssop is utilized to freeze the target. We see here the dark side of purification and hyssop's double-edged power.

Like other magical operations, purification can protect or mutilate, cure or cripple. It is a question of perspective and degree. I am sure we have all known folks who engaged in purification to the extent that they were almost imprisoned (bound) by it and it became, for them, a destructive force. There's an unsuspected ambivalence to purification—and to hyssop—that has something in common with the ambivalence of magic itself, which can help or hinder.

In magic, the decision must often be made to do one thing or another, and to recognize that, often, either choice will involve the other as well. Surely gardening teaches this. After all, the difference between a witch's garden and the wild is that the garden is a place of intention, of choosing—not only which plants will grow but also which will be discouraged or even destroyed. Things don't just happen there, as they do in the wild. Instead, witches work in the garden to bring about certain results and not others, guiding the garden's energy just as they guide other magical workings by creating conditions that encourage particular results. It's about acknowledging your will and putting it into action rather than just waiting around to see what turns up. Just as the garden is a place of both nurturing and destroying, purification can be used to drive out the bad, or to bind and freeze.

The double-edged sword of magic scares a lot of people, including many witches. But it is quintessential to witchcraft. We can see this ambiguity in all the plants that are described in this book, which work for good and for ill on both the material and spiritual planes. It is not all one or all the other. Even a rose has its thorns.

Essential Oils

The positive and negative aspects of purification reflected in our hyssop (*Hyssopus officinalis*) are also demonstrated in a tendency I often meet among magic workers today to prefer hyssop essential oil over hyssop tincture or hyssop hydrosol, or even a bundle of fresh hyssop from their own gardens. I am frequently told that hyssop essential oil, especially if used straight on the skin, is magically "better" or more authentic than other forms of hyssop. However, hyssop essential oil is not especially "authentic." For one thing, our hyssop's essential oil is not the same as that of biblical hyssop. Moreover, hyssop essential oil reveals the negative side of purification.

Remember that an essential oil is a highly modified version of the plant, as heat and water are normally applied to extract essential oils during distillation. This means that some components of the plant are destroyed and new ones created. I have encountered people who have mocked my concern about what I consider the careless use of essential oils, saying things like: "It's just an herb." An essential oil is not just an herb. It's a modified, highly concentrated extract of some of an herb's components. Its strength and uniqueness should be respected.

Hyssop essential oil is at least one hundred times more concentrated than the fresh herb, and it is in a form that penetrates the body very quickly, in a way that the herb itself or less concentrated extractions do not. As an experiment to demonstrate this, mix up a few drops of essential oil in some carrier, like olive oil, and rub it on the bare souls of your feet. It will take only seven seconds for you to breathe out its scent.

People have experienced severe convulsions from using the essential oil of our hyssop, but there has never been a report of this happening from using the whole herb or its tinctures in sensible moderation.[11] Essential oils are wonderful for making scented magical items. They are nicely compact and readily available. They're safer and more magical than synthetic fragrance oils. But you must be wise and informed about their use.

There are several other ways to take advantage of our hyssop's purifying powers. An asperging liquid can expel negative spirits and ghosts, or help keep out unwanted people. You can put it in a spray bottle or use it as a floor wash. Herbed vinegars have been used for centuries in Europe to protect from various negative influences like miasma, fleas in living spaces (not on animals), and germs. Herbs with high amounts of camphorous scent like hyssop or rosemary, as well as garlic, are especially effective—for instance, as used in the famous Four Thieves' vinegar.

Here is a recipe for a purifying vinegar based on a 19th-century recipe. This vinegar should not be ingested or put on animals or children, largely because of the essential oils it contains.

Hyssop Asperging Vinegar

1 oz dried rue

1 oz dried or fresh hyssop (fresh is better, focus on the flowering tops)

1 oz dried or fresh vervain (fresh is better)

16 oz red wine vinegar

Quart jar with a tight-fitting lid

Fresh hyssop asperger (bundle of hyssop tops)

1. Wait to harvest the hyssop asperger until the liquid has been prepared.

2. Infuse the first three herbs in the wine vinegar in the jar for a moon cycle.

3. Whether you put it out in the sun or not depends on what sort of use the asperger will have. If you want to affect primarily solar spirits, do an infusion under moonlight. If lunar spirits, infuse with sunlight. Leave exposed all the time to affect all sorts of spirits.

4. Strain and then filter through a coffee filter.

5. Asperge with a hyssop bundle, dipping the branch into the fluid and flicking it around. The filtered liquid can also be put into a sprayer or mister, or added to water to serve as a floor wash or a ritual bath.

....

☠ *Warning: Do not put this vinegar on animals or children. And be sure to wear gloves when garbling the rue. Never garble it in the sun and avoid touching your eyes.*

....

Since herbs in the mint family, like hyssop, generally smell quite bad when burned, they are not good candidates for incense. However, it's possible to have your hyssop and a fragrant incense, too. Just tincture the herb, then dress the other dry incense ingredients with the tincture. Dry the mixture until it is barely moist, then use. This can be done to add any herb to an incense. Here's an example.

Red Heifer Purifying Incense

Fresh hyssop

A fortified red wine, like port or Fortissimo

Cedar chips

A bit of red wool yarn (synthetics smell bad when burned)

Glass or ceramic jar

Ceramic knife

1. Roughly chop the fresh hyssop and cover with fortified red wine. Use the folk method for the quantity, covering the fresh leaves with menstruum up to a finger's breadth above the top level of the herb. This tincture is beneficial for purification magic of all sorts.

2. Let sit overnight, then squeeze it out and strain. The used herb can be placed in a compost pile or, if you have enough, dried to make a mortified herb powder, since the herb has already had its goodies extracted. Repeat these steps with fresh plant material to make an extra-strong tincture.

3. Cut up the red yarn and add to the cedar chips.

4. Use the red wine hyssop tincture as a dressing for the cedar chips and yarn, tossing them with fluid as if you were making a salad.

5. Let them sit in a jar overnight and then drain off any extra fluid.

6. Dry the mixture on a low setting of your dehydrator or let air dry.

7. If fresh hyssop is unavailable, dress the cedar chips with essential oil of hyssop—just a few drops per ounce of dry material—then put in a lidded jar and let sit. The longer the better with this kind of dressing.

HYSSOP IN THE GARDEN

Like many plants, hyssop responds to the stresses of strong sunlight and dryness by producing more protective aromatics. Hyssop that grows in moist rich soil or in shade will not be as highly scented as hyssop that grows in drier, sunny conditions. So if you are interested in the highest amount of aromatics in your hyssop, consider the site when you are transplanting. Hyssop is a nice addition to medieval or cottage gardens, but also grows well in rock gardens, which are closer to its native Mediterranean habitat.

Since hyssop helps to keep some pestiferous bugs away, like aphids and cabbage moths—it's that purifying thing again—it's a good candidate for the border of a vegetable garden, especially a cruciferous one. Other plants that produce more alkaloids in similar conditions, like belladonna, will be much more potent, since the increased alkaloids serve the same function for the plant as increased essential oils. They keep off predators—at least the buggy kind—and, conversely, attract humans who will save their seeds and reproduce them.

The best time to harvest hyssop tops is in the morning when the dew has dried off. Choose a time when the moon is waxing and the flowers are just forming, typically around Midsummer for this plant. Harvest the stems just before the flowers open if you want them to open after harvest and last longer in your bouquet. Harvest on the Full Moon for maximum energy.

Because its camphorous aspect is fairly strong, hyssop is one of those herbs that can be gathered in bunches, tied loosely together, and dried by hanging upside down in a warmish place that has good ventilation to carry off the plant's moisture (not in the kitchen with all the food vapors). When the herb is dry, garble it and store the leaves and flowers in a dark container. Reserve the stalks for crafting powders or incense.

Our hyssop is perennial throughout the temperate zones of North America (zones 3–9). It gets eighteen to twenty-four inches (60 cm) high and forms a small shrubby plant that's very nice for the borders of paths, where its fragrance can be released by brushing against it. The default color of the flowers is a violet blue, but some plants will naturally produce pink or white flowers. Hyssop varieties have been developed that are dependably pink or white.

Bees and hummingbirds love the tiny blooms of hyssop, which appear in mid-summer. It's a great plant for containers and window boxes, and can even be pruned into mounds. It doesn't expand much.

It does some self-seeding, but maxes out at about an arm's length in width. It does not send out underground runners like some perennials do, which is why it can be grown in pots. You can divide it in the spring if you want more plants.

Hyssop seeds germinate well using the baggie method (see chapter 2). Or you can start the seeds more traditionally by just barely covering them with seed-starting mix. To get seedlings ready to set out when it's sufficiently warm, start them ten weeks before the last frost in your area. They take three to four weeks to germinate at room temperature, showing the typical perennial germination slowness, especially compared to annuals, which usually germinate in just a week or two. Transplant to sunny, dry areas. I have my hyssop in a semishaded, dry perennial bed, and it has proven its toughness, blooming nicely every year with no attention at all.

CHAPTER EIGHT

VERVAIN

The Restless Dead

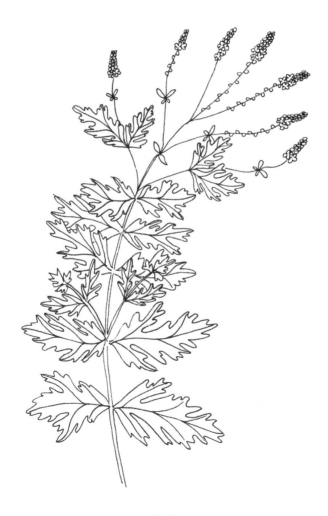

O ne of the things that vervain teaches us is how plants are capable of many layers or types of energy. The mosaic of various planetary attributions accorded to vervain forms an image that reveals great secrets of past magic and points a way to the magic of the future. As beginners at magic, we do well to remember simple magical herb associations like using vervain for protection, love magic, and Druidic initiation. But as we mature in magic, these definitions cease to be enough. We can perceive that a plant is much more than just a few properties. We can begin to wonder if those different properties are linked in some subtle way and if, as a whole, they point to a hidden truth about an herb.

LORE

When you work alone, as so many of us do, you have no one who can pass on secret lore that might allow you to skip some of the untangling necessary to discover the lore of magic herbs—although even those who do work with others don't necessarily have access to secret lore. You must instead combine study with practice, brainpower, and the guidance of the spirits.

Vervain provides us with an excellent example of this process. This herb has properties that belong to Venus, Mars, Jupiter, Mercury, and Sun (Elemental Fire). Let's see how these aspects are connected and how they point to occult knowledge about vervain.

Vervain and Venus

First of all, vervain has Venus aspects. This is apparent in its relationship to birds—especially pigeons or doves, quintessential Venusian creatures. In fact, in England, vervain was once called "pigeon's meat" because they reputedly liked to eat it. Vervain is identified as "pigeon's grass" in *Gerard's Herbal*.

The Greeks also considered that pigeons were especially fond of vervain, so in ancient Greek, the name for vervain and the name for pigeons have the same root, which comes from the Hebrew word for flying, *parack*. A reference in *The Memoirs of Sir Isaac Newton's Life* by William Stukeley suggests that vervain's connection to pigeons came about because it was used with the sacrifice of pigeons at Midsummer, a very important time for this herb, as we shall see.[12]

Venus herbs are generally considered helpful in treating skin ailments, and sure enough, vervain is good for that. An 18th-century English pamphlet prescribed vervain for scrofula (a tubercular infection of the skin of the throat), advising that the herb be hung around the neck and allowed to rest against the skin. However, Venus also rules over women's reproductive organs. Culpeper recommends that vervain be picked in the Venus hour to "remedy all the cold griefs" of the womb.

Vervain likewise demonstrates Venus inclinations in love magic. These may be elaborate, including prayers for favor, as well as acts of purification with water and fasting. But love magic connected to vervain can also be as simple as rubbing the herb between your hands, wiping them on your mouth, and then kissing the person you desire.

Oddly enough, vervain is also reputed to suppress sexual desire (anti-Venus or anaphrodisiac). It was believed in Early Modern England that, if a man gathered vervain before sunrise on the first day of the New Moon and drank its juice, he would not experience lust for seven years. I wonder if this reflects some earlier use by magical practitioners, given the history of this herb's association in various cultures with magic and the frequent requirement of sexual abstinence prior to magical ritual. One group of people that might need an anaphrodisiac would be priests, some of whom were also practitioners of magic. This charm also recommends a time for picking the herb—before sunrise on the first day of the New Moon—that has much in common with that recommended for picking vervain by the Druids or "magicians" of Gaul.

Traditionally, the darkness of the New Moon is a fallow time when nothing is planted. This spell takes advantage of that fallowness and hopes to extend it to seven years of fallowness of sexual desire—no "plowing" or "planting" will occur during that time.

Vervain and Mars

Darkness is an important factor in some other vervain work as well. There is also a strong connection between vervain and the Dog Days, the time in the depths of summer when Sirius, the Dog Star, is above the horizon. Sirius once rose with the sun from early July to early September in the hottest time of year. In honor of the star, the Romans called these the Dog Days, which for them ran from July 24 to August 24. Both the Romans and the ancient Greeks believed that the proximity of the Dog Star and the sun was responsible for the excessive heat. At that time, the rise of the Dog Star came just before the Summer Solstice—that is Midsummer, later known as the Festival of St. John. In ancient Greece and Rome, it was during the Dog Days that men's virility was believed weakened and women's passions "unnaturally" heightened, to the point where women were actually perceived as dangerous(!). Consider how damaged virility and heightened female sexuality fit perfectly with the uses of vervain under Venus for sexuality.

Paradoxically, despite vervain's connections to Venus, this herb does not appear typically Venusian. It lacks lush flowers (its flowers are very small) or a sweet fragrance (although the leaves have an herby scent). Furthermore, it also has some very Mars qualities related to blood and iron, the planetary metal of Mars. For example, according to English folklore, it stanched Jesus' wounds. Wound-healing is usually an occupation of Venus, but vervain's focus is on dealing with the flow of blood rather than healing a clean wound. The task of stanching blood not only associates vervain with blood, that most Martian of substances, its action is also especially helpful in battle, where Mars is supreme.

Vervain's link to iron, the Mars metal, is even stronger. On the Isle of Man, infants were protected from theft by fairies with vervain and iron, while Bohemians believed that, if a gun's flintlock was soaked in vervain water, the gun would be very accurate. They also believed that vervain that had been touched to a St. John's bonfire could snap iron.

This Venusian herb's identification with Mars reminds us of the goddess Aphrodite and her husband Hephaestus, the divine patron of blacksmiths—the mistress of love was literally close to the weapon-maker. A German folk name for vervain is *Eisenkraut* (iron wort). In Germany, it was actually used as an herbal quench by blacksmiths, those masters of fire who work the metal of Mars. Herbal quenches go back to antiquity. Hot metal is often quenched in water or another liquid to bring down its heat after working, and blacksmiths added various herbs to these waters to increase their effectiveness. Moreover, in addition to their work with metal, blacksmiths, throughout history and in many places around the world, have simultaneously functioned as herbal healers of both animals and people. It's likely that vervain's use as an herbal quench in metal working is the source for other beliefs about vervain and iron.

According to Pliny (23–79 CE), there were male (upright) and female (recumbent) versions of the plant. I have grown vervain for years, however, and mine stands up. These versions are now considered separate species, but the difference may account for the association of vervain with iron and war on the one hand and healing and fertility on the other—although Pliny states the two plants have the same effects. Agrippa, who considered it an herb of Venus, recognized Pliny's distinction between the two vervains and assigned the upright version to Taurus (ruled by Venus) and the recumbent version to Gemini (ruled by Mercury).

Iron conducts electricity. While the ancients did not possess electricity, they did notice the affinity of lightning for iron. Thus the connection between vervain and iron extends to lightning. In Normandy, vervain was gathered on the Eve of St. John's Day or St. John's Day itself for house protection against physical threats like lightning and thieves, but also spiritual threats like sorcerers and demons. According to Pliny, it was used to cleanse the altars of Jupiter, god of lightning. Pliny explains that the Septemviri, priests who prepared and arranged public feasts dedicated to Jupiter on September 13 and at games and other public occasions, carried vervain. In Germany, it is associated with Thor, who uses lightning as a weapon.

Vervain's association with iron, that most magical metal, points to its value as an aid in magic—it was bound to the ceremonial swords used by sorcerers to draw magic circles for protection from demons in European grimoire magic. Pliny called it the most popular herb in sorcery. One French nursery rhyme mentions it as a divinatory herb.

However, vervain's most popular traditional use was to chase out demons. Combined with either dill or St. John's wort, it was used to banish witches, demons, and even the devil himself (in England, at least). Certainly ordinary folk believed in its protective powers. A Welsh charm describes hanging it around the neck or drinking its juice before bed to prevent "nocturnal goblins and terrible sights and dreams." It's interesting that this is almost the direct opposite of its use in other arenas—for instance, causing divinatory dreams. Clearly, vervain has a long tradition of magical use.

Vervain and Mercury

Vervain enables magical tools and, in that way, helps make magic itself possible. In other words, vervain is the path to the goal. Along these lines, sorcerer Aleister Crowley identified it as an herb of Mercury, whose force assists the acquisition of magical skills. And, of course, Mercury is in charge of luck, which is also mentioned by Charles Leland in his 1899 publication *Aradia, or The Gospel of the Witches.* Leland claims that vervain was especially favored by the witches of Tuscany. Like rue, it was considered not only protective but lucky as well. In fact, in this excerpt, it almost seems to stand in for magic itself:

> *I rise in the morning by the earliest dawn, [perhaps when neither*
> *the sun nor the moon were in the sky]*
> *And I go forth to walk through (pleasant) vales,*

All in the mountains or the meadows fair,
Seeking for luck while onward still I roam,
Seeking for rue and vervain scented sweet,
Because they bring good fortune unto all.
I keep them safely guarded in my bosom,
That none may know it—'tis a secret thing,
And sacred too, and thus I speak the spell:
"O vervain! ever be a benefit,
And may thy blessing be upon the witch
Or on the fairy who did give thee to me!"
It was Diana who did come to me,
All in the night in a dream, and said to me:
"If thou would'st keep all evil folk afar,
Then ever keep the vervain and the rue
Safely beside thee!"

Not only is the herb itself lucky; with vervain as a tool, you can make magic and thereby create your own luck. This fits with vervain's part in purifying a ceremonial magician's sword and, as described later in this chapter, its role in the preparation of the Hand of Glory.

Vervain and Sun (Elemental Fire)

The depth and range of vervain's planetary influences does not end with Venus, Mars, Jupiter, and Mercury. Among the most interesting aspects of vervain is its connection to the trinity of Elemental Fire, Midsummer, and the Dog Days. The Edwardian folklorist Folkard says that Persian Zoroastrian priests, who were worshippers of fire, used vervain when approaching their altars. He also writes that they "smeared the body over with the juice of this plant" to have wishes granted, to reconcile enemies, to win friends, and to cure diseases. Many of these actions are Mercury tasks. On the one hand, this sounds a lot like Pliny's description of how the Roman priests dressed Jupiter's altar with vervain, except that lightning is changed into fire. The use of vervain as a body wash to achieve magical ends is interesting, especially in light of the root of the original name for this plant is the Hebrew word for flying.

There are many more connections between vervain and Fire. In England at Midsummer, people decorated themselves with mugwort or vervain and cast the herbs into the fire to cleanse themselves of ill luck. Sir James George Frazier tells us, in his iconic book *The Golden Bough*, that in Spain, vervain was gathered at sunset on Midsummer Eve and made into a facial wash to be used the next day; although, Frazier does not explain the purpose of the wash. I suggest that perhaps such a wash might be used to aid in divination.

The Feast of Saint John the Baptist typically coincides with Midsummer, corresponding to the Summer Solstice, the day when the sun is at its maximum height. Vervain is one of the "Herbs of St. John," which include St. John's wort (*Hypericum perforatum*), hawkweed (*Hieracium pilosella*), orpine (*Sedum telephium*), mullein (*Verbascum* species), the *Artemisia* plants wormwood and mugwort, and mistletoe (*Viscum album*). A number of these are Sun herbs. Most of them have yellow flowers—perhaps to be expected from a Sun plant, although vervain's tiny flowers are pale pink. However, the Druids thought that vervain's leaves resembled the oak's, a primary Sun plant. So perhaps, in the face of that identity, the color of the flowers was not very important to them.

Vervain's Irish folk name is "lion's foot" and, of course, the lion is a solar animal. Vervain's solar associations are specifically connected to its use at Midsummer. Which came first—the Sun connection or the Midsummer connection? That's unclear. However, vervain does bloom in July, so the connection may have been made by the plant's own growth behavior.

Vervain in Ancient Times

Pliny describes how vervain is used by "the magicians." Some writers interpret "magicians" here to mean Druids, but Pliny only mentions the "Gallic provinces" in the previous sentence, so he may have meant Druids or solitary witches or someone else; we don't know.

What's important to us, however, is that he describes how these magicians follow a particular ritual to harvest the plant. According to him, they believed that it should be picked around the time of the rising of the Dog Star (a Fire time), but when neither sun nor moon is shining (an anti-Fire time)—recall here the opening of the excerpt from Leland. Before harvesting the herb, honey or honey-combs (products of the bee, a creature of Mars) are given as an offering to the Earth.

Pliny's "magicians" first drew a circle around the plant with an iron implement (the Mars metal again), then harvested it with the left hand. I believe the left rather than the right hand is used when harvesting herbs to signify the intended use as magical rather than mundane—that is, not for cooking or medicine or strewing. Each part of the plant was dried separately in the shade, the different parts apparently having distinct magical uses.

Compare this ritual of picking to Folkard's description of how Druid priestesses harvested this plant. Under a Full Moon at midnight, they threw a looped string over the plant, the other end of which was tied to the big toe of a virgin, who walked away and thus pulled out the plant, which the senior priestess gathered in a cloth. This very much resembles the manner in which mandrake was supposedly harvested (more about this later). This ritual also has many more Moon indications than Sun.

In England, vervain is associated with Sirius, the Dog Star—possibly because of its use in bonfires during the Dog Days. The Dog Star rises just before sunrise, making that a good time to harvest vervain according to these strictures. But vervain has even more canine associations. Carrying it allegedly prevents dogs from barking at you. It was also recommended for the bite of mad dogs, typically a Mars type of protection.

····································

⟹ *The Hand of Glory* ⟸

Vervain was part of the process of making the Hand of Glory. Accord-ing to Le Petit Albert, *a grimoire published in Lyon in 1782, the Hand of Glory was an actual hand chopped off a hanged man and then treated by various means—including drying in a pot of salt, salt-peter, and long pepper during the Dog Days, and drying in an oven heated by vervain and fern. The gruesome product was then used as a candle that purportedly rendered its carrier invisible or paralyzed those who saw it.* Le Petit Albert *claims that these were used by bur-glars. And indeed, if I saw a flaming hand floating down the hall, I too might be paralyzed.*

····································

PRACTICE

One odd little recipe notable to modern witches combines vari-ous aspects of vervain—its association with solar herbs, its protec-tive abilities, its ties to iron, and its use as a body rub. This 1696 recipe calls for combining *Unguentum populeum* (see below), ver-vain, and hypericon (St. John's wort), which are heated with a red-hot iron—yet another connection with iron. This unguent is then rubbed on the spine or chest to protect a person from evil gossip.

····································

☠ *Warning: Anything containing poppy or henbane or nightshade can be psychoactive and hallucinogenic. These herbs can all cause drowsiness and vivid nightmares. So be sure to use this ointment in small amounts until you are certain of its particu-lar effects on you.*

····································

Unguentum populeum

> *1 part dried leaves of white or black poppy (depending on the particular country)*
>
> *1 part belladonna*
>
> *1 part white henbane (which is not as strong as black henbane)*
>
> *1 part black nightshade*
> *40 parts fat (usually hog's lard, although moderns can use any vegetable oil)*
>
> *8 parts bruised popular buds*

1. Bruise the leaves and moisten them with an equal amount of alcohol (95 percent would be a good choice here). Let stand for one day in a closed jar.

2. Add the fat and gently heat for three hours.

3. Add the poplar buds and simmer over a gentle heat for 10 hours. Strain and cool.

Unguentum populeum has been in pharmacy since its creation by the Alexandrian pharmacist Nicolas De Myrepse in the 13th century, so it may well have been available to our Early Modern ancestors already made up. That may explain why two herbs are added to it separately. Notice that the addition is made in a way that would minimize the risks of botulism from incorporating fresh herbal material into fat (using the red-hot iron to boil off the watery parts). Making this in a crock pot set on high may be more efficient, removing each herb as it is exhausted. Older recipes for this unguent have more ingredients, by the way, but these seem to be the most important.

At least one formula for this unguent recommends that the freshly harvested poplar buds be held in the lard until summer (these function as a preservative). This unguent was applied for spot pain killing, as in arthritis, sore nipples, hemorrhoids, and cancer. It was not intended to be smeared all over the body, but no doubt people tried it to see what would happen. I think that, in that case, the unguent would have had much more powerful effects than simply topical pain killing. It could cause hallucinations and it certainly would encourage drowsiness, which in turn would lead to dreams. And given the reputation of solanaceous plants used at toxic levels for causing extremely vivid nightmares, it is likely that, at lower levels, these plants could encourage vivid dreams. Of course, poppy is likewise known for its connection to sleep and can cause vivid hallucinations as well. The formula including vervain and St. John's wort is especially interesting, given the references to the Druids using a vervain tincture smeared over the body for magical purposes. The recipe says it's for preventing evil gossip from harming the person who uses it, but by itself, *unguentum populeum* seems a very good candidate for witches' flying ointments.

Flying Ointments

We must ask first, however, whether flying ointments ever actually existed. Moreover, were they ever really necessary, especially for a practiced witch? Claude Lecouteux, a historian who specializes in Northern European pagan practices and magic, argues that practitioners of magic in medieval Europe were of two sorts—what he calls professional magicians, who practiced magic for a living, and occasional practitioners or amateurs. He believes that the professionals knew how to enter into trance without the use of any herbal aids, whereas people who only occasionally engaged in witchcraft needed herbal assistance to achieve the out-of-body experiences and deep trances that seem to characterize European witchcraft. We're talking about flying to the Sabbat, or entering the Underworld, or guiding the dead, or joining in the Wild Hunt. Yes, we're talking night travels.

Vervain may well have been a component of a flying ointment (and a very old one at that), given the root of its name ("flying"). The mention of the Druids smearing their bodies with its juice for magical purposes, its medicinal applications to the nervous system, its protective function against nightmare, and its incorporation into a psychoactive unguent that had magical powers all point to this use. The possibility is enticing and frankly makes me wonder how much of vervain's tie to Midsummer is due to that being a particularly good time for group flying to occur. Indeed, that particular time of year is good for these rites because of the warm weather, the availability of herbs at their peak, and the fact that Midsummer is a kind of pause in agrarian work. The garden is all in and growing, but is not yet ready for harvest. The animals have all had their babies. There's a bit of lull as plants and animals rest from the heat. This seems to be an excellent time for outdoor magical activities.

There is a lot of "movement" with this herb in terms of its uses—a kind of flickering back and forth. We go from birds (a Venus animal) to fertility magic (a typically Venus task). But vervain can also be a rather Hekatean anaphrodisiac because of its connections to the New Moon and thus the Underworld. And indeed, Hekate was often involved in love spells in ancient Greece.

The animal most associated with the goddess Hekate is the dog (Dog Days). So we have vervain's connection to Sun/Fire/Midsummer, but also to Mars/Blood/Iron—and thus, for good and for ill, associated with healing as well as attack. To bring things full circle, vervain is also used for luck, which is ruled by Hermes, the god of the winged (flying) feet, known for his speed but also as a teacher of magic. It may, therefore, be associated with flight, both in terms of its original name(s) and in terms of its uses in witchcraft.

Unlike the witch's favorites in the nightshade family, vervain doesn't contain any tropane alkaloids, but it does contain iridoids, which are precursors of alkaloids in the body. One of these that was once a standard in botanical medicine is verbenin, which was used as an epilepsy remedy. Remember that vervain seems to raise the seizure threshold—just the opposite of hyssop. Its flowers and leaves also contain verbenalin, another iridoid, and both these substances are considered nervine, tonic, sedating, and neuroprotective.

Clearly, vervain is an herb that bears much more testing in all the various ways it can be used. For instance, it is worth trying a tea made from the dried leaves, since this has been shown to increase dreaming. A good dream tea can be made with one to two teaspoons of dried vervain herb in one cup of boiling water. Let the herb infuse for fifteen minutes and then strain. This herb has little toxicity, but it should still not be used by pregnant women.

To find out what it may have been like for those who smeared their bodies with the juice of vervain in order to have wishes granted, reconcile enemies, win friends, or cure diseases, make a bath of a handful of fresh leaves or a few tablespoons of dried vervain. Put these in a muslin bag and allow it to infuse in the water before bathing. It's best to try this during the waxing moon, perhaps before engaging in ritual work or sleep for dreamwork.

☠ *Warning: Don't drink vervain in a tea or use it in the bath if you are pregnant. For anyone else, I suggest doing a test on your arm first, because some people find vervain, like many aromatics, irritating to the skin.*

To make a protective house wash, soak the dried herb in equal parts in 40 percent alcohol (brandy, vodka). Strain and then add to a bucket of water. Pay particular attention to doors, thresholds, and windows. You can use this same recipe to make a tincture if you let the herb soak for two weeks and then strain. In that case, one to two teaspoons (5–10 ml) is considered a dose.

A very simple but effective way to work with vervain is to make a folk tincture of the fresh leaves using 95 percent alcohol. Strain and, shortly before bed, put a dab of the tincture on the back of your hand and briskly rub your hands as if washing them. Then go to sleep. This herb produces very vivid dreams without the hangover that mugwort can cause. Like many herbs, it loses effectiveness if used too often. I think this shows that vervain has great possibilities as a flying herb and one that has very little toxicity at all.

VERVAIN IN THE GARDEN

Start vervain in the early spring—preferably at a time when the Moon is waxing, since you will eventually be harvesting the tops. Just barely cover the seeds. They like cool room temperatures—60–70°F (18–21°C)—and should germinate in three to four weeks.

After the seedlings are up and have at least their first set of true leaves (what looks like the second set of leaves), transplant them to an area with full sun (but of course!) and rich soil, spacing them twelve to twenty-four inches (30–60 cm) apart. The first year, the plants will form a rosette of leaves and may put up a stalk or two of flowers, but they don't come into their own until the second and third years, when they will send up rather weedy-looking flower stalks eighteen to thirty-six inches (45–90 cm) tall. If you are harvesting leaves, cut them before the flowers open. If possible, do it in the traditional way.

This herb will reproduce from cuttings, but it's actually fairly easy to germinate for a perennial. To harvest the seeds, wait until the flowers are done and then carefully test the seeds for ripeness every couple of days. When the tiny pods are dry, gently run your thumbnail along the stalk and gather the chaff and seeds in a pot held right underneath the stalk. The seeds are shiny in comparison to the chaff and a bit heavier, so shake the gatherings a bit to get the seeds to the bottom, then carefully blow aside the chaff and scoop up the seeds with a bit of paper.

Vervain is hardy down to –25°F (–32°C; zone 4), but doesn't like the humid heat of the South. I've found that it can be overwhelmed by more aggressive herbs like mints or mugwort, so give it its own space.

CHAPTER NINE

MUGWORT
Fire

Mugwort, sometimes called dreamwort, is one of my favorite herbs. Its leaves have a pleasing shape, and the whole plant has a nice herby fragrance. Tear a leaf of mugwort and smell the deep, musty, herbal smell. It makes me think of the back room of a mythical apothecary—the scent of herbal knowledge.

Mugwort is easy to grow, even in challenging dry, rocky areas where other herbs may be unhappy. Practically no insects or diseases bother it and, because it's tall, it produces a lot of plant material in a relatively small area. It's extraordinarily effective at aiding dream recall and has little toxicity. Historically, it has been deemed extremely protective against pestiferous spirits in a variety of cultures.

Like vervain, mugwort is associated with the festival of Midsummer in a number of areas from China to Europe. But if vervain is the daytime herb of Midsummer, mugwort is the night side—a Midsummer Night's dream herb.

Mugwort is proof that we don't need to resort to exotic plants from South America or Africa for dreamwork. There are all sorts of native mugworts that are well worth trying, like *Artemisia douglasiana*, which grows out West. In fact, I have wondered whether mugwort's very commonness and familiarity are not a means for separating the wheat from the chaff in terms of witchcraft. Perhaps not recognizing the value of ordinary mugwort and preferring expensive exotics of doubtful purity that cannot be grown (and thus known) in temperate climes indicates a fault or lack in a practitioner's own personal magical "equipment."

To my mind, practitioners of witchcraft are distinguished from the average ceremonial or ritual magician not only by their willingness to use what is readily available but also by their recognition of the value to be found in the common and everyday. Among herbs, you can hardly get more common and everyday than mugwort.

The other side of this coin is that, in my opinion, the powers that work through witchcraft are not coy. They don't hide in faraway countries or demand that we spend a lot of money to acquire admittance to their presence. They are "easy"—and easy to get. I think this very ease can devalue items like mugwort for some people. It reminds me of the hints found in alchemical texts about the identity of the starting material for making the Stone—this mysterious-seeming, never-named substance is described as common and everywhere despised. At least one alchemist has posited that that material is ordinary dirt.

Thus alchemists don't need to send to faraway places at great expense for the starting material for the Stone, but through work and reliance upon innate skills and the help of the spirits can find the right kind of dirt nearby. Witches experience the same generosity of the natural and spirit worlds with mugwort, an eye-opening, road-revealing herb that does not give us the answer, but shows us a way we can develop the skills necessary to get the answer—through dreams.

LORE

Mugwort's commonness recalls for me the alchemical Secret Fire. Mugwort can be that Fire for witchcraft. It has certainly had Fire associations in spades throughout history and in various cultures. For instance, in China, mugwort is incorporated into the initiation rituals of Buddhist monks. A ball of mugwort and fat is placed on the monk's shaven head and lit. The flame leaves a scar. I am not sure if it is that link to Fire that explains its use in the Buddhist initiation, but I wonder if this ceremony recognizes mugwort's effects on dreaming, which can certainly open the Third Eye.

Mugwort in China

Mugwort is a favorite herb in Traditional Chinese Medicine, especially in connection with Fire. Some have argued that *moxibustion*, the burning of mugwort fluff for medicinal purposes, is connected to a more ancient Chinese practice of burning mugwort to drive away bad luck and demons. In China, mugwort is mixed with fat and burned to evoke helpful deities.

As recently as World War II, it was a popular custom for people in China to pick mugwort before dawn on the fifth day of the fifth month (this is the Summer Solstice, known in China as Double Five) and make it into a bundle with calamus root, an herb with strong Sun associations. The bundles were then tied together with a red paper band and hung on either side of the main door of the house. They were meant to expel poisonous airs or influences and to ward off diseases arising from an excess of *yin*, which is composed of energies that are aligned with Earth, Moon, darkness, Water, space, matter, and rest.

Mugwort and calamus are considered very *yang* herbs because of their scents. Yang is the Fiery force that both opposes and balances yin; it's associated with heaven, Sun, light, Fire, time, energy, and activity. The very yang/Sun quality of these herbs fits with how mugwort so much lightens sleep that all dreams are remembered. Mugwort is like the sun's shining in the dreamworld.

Mugwort and Elemental Fire

Mugwort's Fire association comes through its connection to the Summer Solstice—the festival of Midsummer known as St. John's Eve, with its attendant bonfires. Mugwort was a part of St. John's fires all over Europe and North Africa. On the Isle of Man, mugwort is called *Bollan feaill-Eoin* (John's fease-wort). People gathered it on Midsummer Eve and made chaplets for themselves and their animals to protect against witchcraft. It was worn on the coat or cap on both May Day Eve and St. John's Eve. In France, mugwort was named after John the Baptist, the saint whose feast is held on Midsummer, and was worn to protect health. In Germany, it was worn and also thrown into Midsummer bonfires. In Morocco, *Artemisia alba*, or white mugwort, whose scent is very similar to our mugwort, was a Midsummer fumigant. It is still commonly encountered as an essential oil.

⇒ Thunder and Lightning ⇐

Thunderstorms can usually be counted on at Midsummer. These feature another Fire manifestation—lightning. In China, mugwort is connected with the thunder god. In France, it protects against thunderstorms.

Mugwort and Artemis

There is a curious Fire/Water, male/female, yang/yin thing going on with mugwort that appears in various cultures. Look, for instance, at the way mugwort—which, in different places is connected to Fire—is also connected to Moon, from the lunar goddess Artemis to its physical effect of helping one remember dreams. This hints at interesting possibilities in terms of interactions between vervain and mugwort. Does mugwort help us remember the vivid dreams that vervain tea can engender? This is an area ripe for witches' experimentation.

The goddess Artemis can function as the center of a web of mugwort activities, from protector of women in childbirth to Moon work like dreaming. Artemis evolved from a mugwort, and thus her name was used to create the name of mugwort's genus, *Artemisia*. I imagine it is in honor of her birth plant that the festival of Artemis at Ephesus—also known as Artemision—was connected with mugwort. The herb was ingested as part of that festival during the Full Moon, affecting the ability of her devotees to recall their dreams. I do not know if dreaming was part of the rituals at Artemis at Ephesus. It may have been that mugwort was ingested to cause wakefulness, which, after a day or so, can definitely open someone up to supernatural entities that might otherwise be missed. Such wakefulness may also serve to potentiate any ritual drinks that contain alcohol or other psychoactive substances.

Artemis, of course, was associated with Moon and with feminine biology. She protected women in labor, and the herb helped in delivery.

She is the female dark (yin) to Apollo's male light (yang). Later, in some contexts, she was conflated with another lunar goddess, Hekate.

PRACTICE

Midsummer unites the two halves of the year, as well as dark and light. Mugwort, an herb honoring a Moon goddess, was used on Midsummer in connection with the fires of that festival, to unite the dark and the light when sun time and moon time were equal— when Artemis and her brother Apollo stood side by side. An interesting project for that purpose is mugwort jelly made with natural apple pectin (apple being Apollo's plant). For a ritual item, which is what this is, mugwort and apple pectin are Artemis and Apollo, the perfect Midsummer combination.

Midsummer Mugwort Jelly

> *3 lbs (1.5 kg) granny smith (green) apples*
>
> *6 cups (1.5 l) water*
>
> *2 cups (500 ml) white wine*
>
> *2 tbsp (30 ml) chopped fresh mugwort leaves*
>
> *2 cups (500 ml) sugar*
>
> *6- to 8-quart pot and fine mesh sieve (or a few layers of muslin or cheesecloth)*
>
> *First, make pectin from the apples. You can use a pouch of liquid pectin from the store, but I like making my own so I know exactly what's in it (and it makes me feel more connected to our ancestors).*

1. Chop the apples up—peels, cores, and all—and put them in the pot with the water. Boil, stirring occasionally until the apples fall apart, about 30–40 minutes.

2. Strain the apple mash, pouring it through the sieve (or jelly bag or whatever you're using) into another pot. Resist pressing on the apple mash if you can, because the juice will be nice and

clear if it goes through at its own speed. (You can stir it a bit.) It should be strained in less than an hour, leaving you with a little over 5 cups (1.1 l) of juice. This is the apple pectin. Four cups of homemade apple pectin equal about one pouch of liquid pectin from the store.

3. You can throw the mash out or compost it. Or, depending on how thrifty you are, you can put it through a food mill to remove pits and core pieces, then add a little sugar to make apple sauce. If you have extra pectin, you can throw it into a cake or a quickbread to make it brown. Combine the wine and mugwort and bring to a boil. Take it off the heat, cover, and let it sit for 20 minutes.

4. Strain the herb out the same way you strained the apples. If you're using a jelly bag or coffee filters, wet them with wine before pouring the infusion through. It takes about 20 minutes for the infusion to strain, leaving about 1.75 cups (423 ml) of mugwort-infused wine. You can squeeze a bit more out of a jelly bag if you're on the short side.

Now make the jelly. Before you start, put a saucer in the freezer for testing the jelly to see if it's ready.

5. Put the herb infusion into a pot and stir in the sugar. Bring to a boil while you stir. Don't stop stirring or it will burn and stick. It should get to the point where it's boiling so hard that you can't stir it down.

6. Pour in 4 cups of apple pectin and bring back to a boil for 2 minutes. Take it off the heat.

7. Test for consistency by dropping a small glob of jelly on the plate you put in the freezer. It should show wrinkles when you run a finger or spoon through it, but it won't be firm like store-bought jelly. If it shows wrinkles, it's done.

8. Process jars of jelly in a boiling water bath for 10 minutes, or just store in the fridge until using.
This recipe makes about four 4-oz (125 ml) jars.

This is not the kind of jelly you want to put on a peanut butter sandwich. Instead, spread some on a buttered cracker before bed. The butter fat helps you absorb the goodies from the plant. You can use this same recipe for all sorts of herbs. I've been wanting to try combining clary sage and mugwort into a jelly myself.

In cultures as far apart as China and Britain, mugwort has protected against witchcraft, demons, and bad luck. The Chinese believed that it kept devils off; similarly, Anglo-Saxon leech books claimed that it "puts to flight devil-sickness."

≋ Woden's Herbs ≋

Mugwort is one of the Nine Herbs of Woden that appear in the Anglo-Saxon Nine Herbs charm against poison. These are given as:

* *Mucgwyrt—Mugwort* (Artemisia vulgaris)
* *Attorlaðe—some identify this as cockspur grass* (Echinochloa crus-galli) *and some as betony* (Stachy officinalis)
* *Stune—Lamb's cress* (Cardamine hirsute)
* *Wegbrade—Plantain* (Plantago species)
* *Mægðe—Mayweed* (Matricaria)
* *Stiðe—Nettle* (Urtica dioica)
* *Wergulu—Crabapple* (Malus sylvestris)
* *Fille—*(Thymus vulgaris)
* *Finule—Fennel* (Foeniculum vulgare)

Christianity perceived attack by elf-shot and flying venom as demonic possession (*deōfol-seōcnes*), which mugwort, along with mandrake and periwinkle, can protect against. Likewise, in Britain, leech books advised folks to hang mugwort over the door of a home to protect it from these supernatural attacks, just as was done in

China. So mugwort seems peculiarly able to evoke similar responses from different cultures.

Mugwort has a particular connection with protecting eyesight. In Great Britain, a wreath either worn on the head or looked through at the Midsummer bonfire preserved eyesight. This is interesting in connection with the use of mugwort for clairvoyance or divination through dreams.

In mugwort, we have an example of how a practice that may once have been sacred devolved into simple love magic. A man reports how, in 1694 on Midsummer (St. John the Baptist's Feast, Jun 24), he saw twenty women on their knees "weeding." He found out they were looking for the coal of mugwort root, which could be found only at noon on that day and which they then put under their beds to dream of their future husbands. This coal was really "the old hard black root of the mugwort."

I have grown mugwort, and I have never seen this root, so I think this story is apocryphal. What's interesting to me is the implication here that an activity that was formerly part of serious magic has devolved into a love charm. This is reminiscent of the yarrow love charms mentioned in chapter 5, and implies that simple folk love charms may be a container for descriptions of older, more powerful magic operations.

The fact that mugwort is connected to activities and times similar to those of vervain may have to do with its psychoactive properties or growth patterns. Vervain usually blooms at Midsummer, which seems to account for at least some of its connections to that festival. In North America, mugwort blooms in the fall (mine usually do in late September to early October); but in England, it begins blooming in July and continues through September. Certainly mugwort is good and high by the Summer Solstice, however, which is the best time for harvesting.

Mugwort and Dreamwork

Before using mugwort for dreamwork, consider exactly what you want from the dreamwork and from the plant. Try to pose your question in the most succinct way possible before asking the herb to guide your dreams to an enlightening stage.

One problem with mugwort is that, while it will indeed help you remember your dreams, it will help you remember every scrap of your dreams, including all the unimportant junk. In this way, it works as a dream herb much as it works as a denizen of the garden—all over the place all the time. Another down side of mugwort is that, although it is not toxic, it does seem to work by keeping you half-awake throughout the night. I have found that it takes me several days to "recover" from a mugwort evening. Also, witches should be aware that mugwort loses its power the more frequently it is used. It is best to confine its use to once every two weeks at most, or it loses its effectiveness. To me, this recalls the way some chemicals that have the opposite effect—to cause sleepiness, like melatonin or tryptophan—work for a while and then seem to stop.

Mugwort leaves are excellent for teas, dream pillows, curative and protective baths, smokes, stuffing poppets, and making dream jelly. You can extract the fresh herb (leaves and flowers) into 25 percent alcohol at a proportion of one part herb to one part alcohol. Add a teaspoon of the tincture to a small cup of warm water and drink before bed for dreamwork. Some people find a dream pillow stuffed with dried mugwort leaves is effective. Most commonly, however, mugwort is drunk as a tea shortly before bed. Add a tablespoon of dried herb to a cup of boiling water and infuse for fifteen minutes, then strain and drink.

MUGWORT IN THE GARDEN

The best time to start mugwort seeds is after the Winter Solstice when the moon is waxing, because you will be harvesting the upper parts of the herb. Mugwort seeds are small and need to be on the surface of the soil to germinate. This shows how "weedy" plants relate to the activity of humans and other animals. Seeds that need surface sowing have been designed to germinate after the soil they are in is dug up—"disturbed," in gardening language.

If you want to stimulate the germination of seeds that fall around an established planting of mugwort, do a little surface cultivation around the plants with a claw or hoe. You can do this in a ritual manner, incorporating requests for help from Underworld entities in your work (bringing to the surface). Consider this in relation to perennial mugwort's need for an annual winter nap in the Underworld. We can think of this plant and other surface sowers like rue, wormwood, tansy, mints, and tobacco as being expert at moving between worlds. I also enjoy the lesson that mugwort seeds teach us. Here's a tiny, dust-sized seed that grows into a large, aggressive plant. Size means nothing about power with mugwort.

Most perennials come back stronger after a winter spent in the Underworld. Mugwort comes back like gangbusters, always increasing its territory. This aggressiveness is in line with how it interacts with the human body. In fact, there is nothing subtle about this herb. At the same time, however, mugwort does not send as many chemicals through the ground as its cousin wormwood, which can stunt the growth of neighbors. (Likewise, biologically, wormwood's components are quite rough on the human body.) Mugwort can send enough, however, to deter the germination of other seeds. That said, I grow these plants in a bed with other aromatics like yarrow, tansy, and feverfew, and everyone seems to get along fine. It may be a different story for nonaromatic plants. Mugwort can overwhelm other plants physically rather than chemically, elbowing them out of the way without destroying them. If plants can survive with less access to sunlight, water, and nutrients, mugwort doesn't damage them. Likewise, mugwort has little toxicity when ingested.

Tiny seeds like those of mugwort can be intimidating to a new grower, but they shouldn't be. Just sprinkle the seeds over wet seed-starting medium and lightly press them in with your fingertip. Give indirect sun exposure or direct artificial light for germination in one to three weeks at a warmish room temperature—around 75°F

(24°C). If you want to be certain of the greatest amount of germination, cold stratify the seeds for a week (see chapter 2). As is true for most seeds of temperate herbs, don't make the mistake of trying to germinate them in too warm an environment.

After hardening off, transplant your seedlings to full sun and rich, moist soil (although they will grow in dry rocky soil once they get their sea legs). Space them one foot (30 cm) apart; believe me, they will fill in heavily. If you want to give plants to friends or put them in a different location, you can dig them up and divide them in the early spring, before they leaf out. Mugwort typically gets to be two to four feet (60–120 cm) tall, but mine easily grow to five feet (1.5 m) without any fussing over them. The plants are hardy down to −30°F (−34°C). Harvest at the beginning of blooming.

I can tell you from experience that cutting down a mass of mugwort to about the length of a forearm (which leaves plenty of stalk for the plant to form leaflets the following year) means that the plant will expand by underground roots (rhizomes) to a much greater extent than it would have done if you had just left it alone. Think of this as the plant reacting to threat, or perhaps as the plant realizing it is in a good environment for vegetative rather than seed reproduction. Remember, this is a plant that enjoys growing around people. It is not found deep in the woods, but rather along the edges of things, where it's sunny and we can spot them easily. Like many of the other witching herbs, it attracts our attention with its scent, the food of the spirit world.

Drying Mugwort

Because mugwort is a big plant and is pretty tough, it's a good candidate for drying by simply hanging. It's not only easy to dry this way (and keeps its goodies intact during the process), but it also looks nice while it's drying. If you can, choose a waxing moon and the beginning of a dry period to harvest mugwort. Just when the tiny whitish buds start to form at the tops of the plants, cut the stalks an arm's length or more from the ground, leaving something for the new leaves to get started on in the spring.

Make a bundle of the stalks as big as you can grasp in your hand and tie it toward the bottom. I like to use jute twine for this, because it holds the stalks securely and doesn't rot. Hold two sides of the bundle and open it like the blade of a scissor. Place the "crotch" of the bundle on a line strung in an area protected from the elements, or just make the tie of the bundle long enough to hang the whole thing from a nail in a rafter. I use my clothesline, which is under the patio roof. It helps if the herb bundle is outside, but it should be out of the sun and out of the elements.

Test the leaves every day for dryness; they should break instead of bend. It usually takes a couple days. If it's raining a great deal or is very humid, this kind of drying won't work and you're better off using a dehydrator. When the leaves are dry, take the bundle down and untie it. Strip the leaves off the stalks. Pick out all moldy or diseased bits and toss them. It's nice quiet work, although a little messy—a good time to get to know your herb in its final form. Breathe in that good mugwort scent. Store the dried leaves in jars. I like big bailed jars for this. Just make sure that all the leaves are thoroughly dry when you pack them away, or some will get moldy and ruin the whole batch. You can chop the stalks and dry them further, and then grind them for making incense and powders, especially for protection.

CHAPTER TEN

WORMWOOD

The Dead

C lose observation is the first step to spirit initiation in plant-based magic. One way to look closely is to study the medicinal uses of an herb. These often point to possible magical uses right away. Wormwood is a good example of how the way an herb works medicinally or how it relates to other plants is a reliable indicator of how the plant works in magic.

Although we can accept what the herbalist Nicholas Culpeper has to say about wormwood being heating (which is a Mars effect), wormwood looks nothing like a typical Mars herb. It doesn't have spines, nor is its sap caustic or burning. To me, however, it has always seemed as if it has some Moon in it, especially because of its odd, blue-white foliage. This bluish color is often characteristic of Moon plants, a particularly good example of this being poppy. And in fact, while wormwood almost always looks good, its pale, moth-dust foliage is especially attractive under a Full Moon when it's almost luminous. Its bitterness also seems to me to be much more cold Moon than hot Mars. And yet in so many ways, we can observe that wormwood is most definitely not Moon.

LORE

Agrippa connects wormwood with Hekate. I think this association arises from the fact that, like myrrh, it's bitter. Myrrh is associated not only with Hekate but also with death, not least because it was used to preserve bodies in Egyptian and other ancient cultures.

If wormwood is connected with Hekate, then it is good for celebrating Samhain—the Celtic festival and Wiccan Sabbat that coincides with Halloween, a time when the veil between the living and the dead is very thin. That's also when wormwood is ready to harvest. Wormwood is also one of the ingredients in the ink used to question the dead in the Greek Magical Papyri (IV:214): "red ochre, burnt myrrh, juice of fresh wormwood, evergreen, and flax. Write [on a leaf] and put it in the mouth [of the corpse]." A strong decoction can be used to purify mourners when hostile shades are around. Try this decoction as an asperger when you want to get rid of antagonistic ghosts. Conversely, it is also a good component in an incense for contacting the dead (combine

1 part wormwood with 2 parts myrrh and 1 part cypress) and is an ingredient in the bread for the dead.

....

☠ *Warning: Wormwood can be used externally—in inks and incense, for example—but should never be consumed in any form by humans or animals.*

....

Wormwood can be thought of as a sort of hinge between this world and the next, since it can be used to evoke the dead—to call them to us, the living. But it can also protect the living from the dead. Wormwood is not all about death and damnation, however. Like any plant, it has various facets to its personality and multiple possible uses. Culpeper considered wormwood an herb of Mars, hot in the third degree, as hot as blood. Because it is a Mars herb, he deemed it a remedy against injury from Moon critters like mice and rats.

Wormwood and the Warrior God Bes

According to the Greek Magical Papyri, wormwood is a component of an ink that was used to draw an image of Bes, or Besa, on the hand before retiring to request an answer from that spirit in dream. This demon protected sleep and childbirth and was popular for oracle requests. Bes is believed to be non-Egyptian, deriving perhaps from the Sudan.

The Fire connection here is that, apparently, the name "Bes" is related to the word for "flame" in ancient Egyptian. In terms of the Mars association of wormwood, the Fiery Bes is also often depicted wielding metal weapons like swords or knives. It follows, then, that in the Greco-Roman period that gave rise to the magical papyri, Bes was depicted most often as a warrior.

Wormwood is designated by the code phrase "Blood of Hephaistos" in the Greek Magical Papyri. "Hawk's heart" is revealed to be actually "heart of wormwood" in the same work. The hawk is usually considered a Sun (Fire) animal.

This makes sense because, as a Mars herb, wormwood is connected to Fire. Hephaestus (Hephaistos) is the Greek god of the forge and metalworking, and hawks are generally associated with Sun (the Fire element). Mars, of course, rules over war, which makes much use of metalwork. He also rules over blood and is of Elemental Fire.

Curiously, Culpeper maintains that wormwood is often found growing around forges and ironworks because it is a Mars herb, but also because of its possible use by metalworkers as an herbal quench. So we have a lot of unsuspected connections with Fiery Mars in an herb that may, on the face of it, seem Moon.

PRACTICE

In medicine, wormwood chases out parasites, tumors, and bacteria. It is so powerful—it contains one of the bitterest substances known, which can be a bit rough on the body—that only very tiny amounts are used. Its medicinal properties are lessened by heat, so for magical work, prefer cold macerations of oils, washes, or air-dried powders over incense. This is an herb that, like its sister mugwort, dries well just by being hung from the rafters.

A pinch of wormwood powder in a purifying oil or wash will help rid an area of spiritual varmints. I've used the fresh leaves as a rub on a staff I made from a piece of driftwood sumac I found at the lake. I alternated it with mugwort, because I wanted to use the staff especially for rituals at night that I hoped would continue or ripple over into dream. The wormwood acted physically to keep any gnawing critters off my staff (it still had bits of bark on it, which is a bug magnet); but it also worked spiritually to drive off scraps of negativity and spiritual nasties that might have latched on to the wood as it was tossed into the stormy lake. In my experience, storms can be grand times for gathering power, but you can also scrape up and carry along creepy entities much like a glacier drags along rocks.

If you are crafting your own yarn, cord, or fabric to be used ritually, wormwood can produce an olive green dye on wool with the addition of a copper sulphate mordant. (This is, interestingly, the same poisonous additive that once colored cheap absinthe, which depended on wormwood for its bitterness.) Moreover, the wormwood will keep moths from eating the wool.

Wormwood has long associations with alcohol, both as a preservative of malt liquors and as an ingredient in absinthe. Alcohol is fundamentally Fire, so wormwood's connection with it further indicates the herb's Fire. Culpeper says that wormwood was an ingredient in some beers that were drunk to cure "stinking breath."

Some consider wormwood, mugwort, and sagebrush (*Artemisia ludoviciana*) to be interchangeable for use in battles against demons. This makes sense, since they are all strongly aromatic, generally purifying, and pesticidal. Personally, given a choice, I choose wormwood over the other two for expelling a nasty spirit, because, on the physical plane, wormwood is extremely powerful. It can even get rid of the malaria parasite because it is so bitter and repelling.

I also like the idea of using Fire to fight fire—using a plant so connected with the Underworld to combat nefarious spirits. To work with the plant for this purpose, dry it and grind it into a powder, or just extract fresh wormwood leaves into alcohol and then mix the tincture with water to make a demon-ridding wash.

Magical Ink

Wormwood was a classic addition to ink, used to prevent insects from gnawing on manuscripts. In the Greek Magical Papyrus recipe mentioned above, the ink is applied to the operator's hand. The only other active ingredient in that ink is cinnabar, a form of mercury; but cinnabar would not have an immediate effect, even though it is orange red, a Fire/Mars color. Blood is another ingredient. In keeping with that history, try a modern-day version of the *PGM*'s Typhonian Ink that is good for writing messages to the dead or drawing sigils to keep them away.

Witch's Typhonian Ink

Myrrh, powdered or at least well crushed

Fresh chopped wormwood leaves or dried powdered wormwood

Red wine vinegar

Gum Arabic powder (optional)

Cast-iron skillet or pot/cauldron with cover

1. Char the myrrh and wormwood in a covered cast-iron vessel. You can do this quickly over a low gas flame or slowly over a tea candle if it's a small container. Add red wine vinegar and simmer with the cover off until it is reduced and slightly thickened.

2. Take it off the heat and add a little gum Arabic powder for further thickening if you've got it, but remember that magical ink has little in common with mundane ink; it's not made to be convenient.

3. You can strain the mixture through a steel sieve, but, in fact, the particles will just sink to the bottom anyway.

4. Pour into a red or black jar and store cool and dark until use with a steel nib pen.

Vermouth and Absinthe

Another great use for wormwood has been to make vermouth, the name of which is the French interpretation of the German word for wormwood, *wermut*. Vermouth is a fortified wine that has been infused with various herbs and was originally created for medicinal purposes. Wormwood was generally included in its formulation because of its ability to get rid of parasites. There are as many recipes for vermouth as there are makers. Here is a version for use in ritual work. A good time to make this vermouth is in the summer. The ratio of wine to brandy should be 5:2, the goal being to get an alcohol level of 20 percent.

Witch's Vermouth

750 ml bottle of red wine

Handful of mugwort

Handful of clary sage

Handful of vervain

Handful of yarrow

1.25 cups (300 ml) brandy

Sprig of wormwood to be used as a stirrer

Honey if you want it sweet (because bees are Martial insects and are said to communicate with the dead)

1. Steep the preferably fresh, chopped herbs in the wine overnight.

2. Strain and press out the goodies, then add the brandy.

3. Stir with the sprig of wormwood to get just a small amount of the herb's oils into the wine without making it too bitter. Then just throw the sprig on the compost with the strained-out herbs.

4. Taste; if you want it sweet, add honey a little at a time until it tastes right to you.

5. Seal well and store in a cool, dark place if you aren't going to use it right away. Once the bottle is open, use within 3 months and store in the refrigerator or other cold place. You can modify this recipe in a number of ways—for instance, by changing to white wine and more Sun-oriented or Moon herbs, or by switching to cane sugar for a more Sun product.

Of course, wormwood is most notoriously connected with absinthe. But we don't really know just how much wormwood was actually used in absinthe, and how much of it was wormwood (*Artemisia absinthium*) as opposed to Roman wormwood (*Artemisia pontica*), which is a very much smaller plant with a lot less bitterness and a more complex scent profile.

≋ The Green Fairy ≋

Absinthe, referred to in literature as the Green Fairy because of its color and potency, is totally different from a distilled product like vodka. The absinthe sold in England in the 19th century was made of alcohol; wormwood essential oil; other essential oils; sugar; chlorophyll from nettle, spinach, or parsley; and water. Another formulation called for dried wormwood, anise, and fennel steeped overnight in 85 percent alcohol, with water added the next day. The mixture was then boiled and the distillate collected and combined with an extract of dried Roman wormwood, hyssop, and lemon balm. Finally, this was filtered to give a liqueur that was 74 percent alcohol. Thus the damage that absinthe caused came from the high alcohol content (often over 70 percent, which is around the proof of 151 rum), from the addition of wormwood oil (which can cause seizures), and likely from the copper used to color the stuff green (heavy metals like copper being highly neurotoxic). No wonder they wanted to ban it![13]

Although some folks nowadays throw together an "absinthe" from essential oils (essential oils are not for drinking, period)—and some cheap absinthe tastes exactly as if that is what was done—in fact, true absinthe is a product of distillation and not made by combining essential oils. It does not, and did not *ever*, contain enough thujone to do anything to your brain, much less cause hallucinations.

That said, a lot of the "absinthe" sold in the days before laws concerning the purity of food and drugs were passed was, in fact, a kind of weird mishmash of herbs simply soaked in alcohol and colored with anything from nettle to spinach to parsley. This kind of thing is more like a bitters than a distilled liqueur. And remember that the heat of distillation changes the chemicals in an herb. The chemical profile of an herb that has been tinctured is different from that of an herb that has been distilled. That is one reason why I have described how to make a witch's vermouth instead of a witch's absinthe.

WORMWOOD IN THE GARDEN

Like those of mugwort, tobacco, and yarrow, wormwood seeds are tiny, and, like them, should be "surface sown"—simply sprinkled on the surface of whatever moist planting medium you are using and then gently firmed in with your fingertip. These tiny seeds don't have sufficient energy stores to push up through the soil.

Tiny seeds usually need light to germinate, but this means indirect sunlight (think of it lying beneath the leaves of its parents). When I start them indoors, I usually put them about one inch (2.5 cm) below a shop light (ordinary fluorescent light). If you start them inside a Moon cycle or two ahead of the last frost for your location, you will have a jump on them for the year. At normal room temperature, wormwood seeds will germinate in a week to ten days. Again, don't make it too warm—over 80°F (26°C)—because the seeds can die. Likewise, if it's too cold, they will just sit there; or if it's very moist and cold, they may rot. Just like people, seeds have a narrow window of environment that is good for them.

Water the seeds with a spray mist or put them in a tray and pour water into the tray. Let them soak up water for a half hour, then pour out the excess. Transplant the seedlings outside when they have one set of true leaves (the second set of leaves). This is a good plant to grow in the dry, rocky part of your garden that other plants don't like. Wormwood does like full sun, I have noticed, although it will grow in partial shade and lean always toward the sun. Space the plants two to three feet (60–90 cm) apart. In their second year, you can harvest the leaves and dry and store them for use throughout the year. I find it easiest just to cut them back to stalks two feet (60 cm) high once they hit their second year. If you cut them any shorter, or if you cut too many stalks, the plant will be set back and not produce as much the following year. Just hang the stalks upside down to dry. Once the leaves are crunchy, you can cut up the whole stalk with scissors or "garble" the leaves off the stalks and just save them—or preserve the stalks as bones.

These plants can grow quite tall once they're established—four to five feet (1.2–1.5 m). I had some that got to seven feet (2 m)! Wormwood is hardy throughout most of North America, but it can't tolerate a lot of humid heat, and it prefers the Eastern half of the continent.

Wormwood doesn't like other plants getting too close. It gives off chemicals in the soil that keep other plants from growing, so it should be in a place of its own. Even so, I have found that mugwort will overwhelm and kill wormwood, so give each one its own space. Some say that mugwort and wormwood are difficult to tell apart. This may be true when they are seedlings, because wormwood seedlings tend not to have the blue cast that is characteristic of the adult plants. They are as green as mugwort, and the leaf shapes at seedling stage are similar. The only noticeable difference in color is if wormwood babies are growing up from an overwintered root; then they do have the characteristic blue-white color.

Once they are grown, however, wormwood and mugwort are very easy to tell apart. Wormwood has distinctive silvery-white leaves and a peculiar bitter smell. Its leaves are also much more finely cut than mugwort's. Mugwort, by contrast, has silver only on the underside of the leaves, and you really have to crush the leaves (or least brush your hands through them) to get the mugwort smell, which is herby, not bitter. The two plants are not easily mistaken for each other once they are out of seedling stage.

CHAPTER ELEVEN

THORNAPPLE

Offering

Thornapple is a member of the datura family, which contains a number of species, including the *D. innoxia* of the Southwest with its fat cigar buds and lush flowers, the often double-flowered *D. metel* of India, and the scrappy, ragged *D. stramonium*, known worldwide as a "pest" of cultivated fields. Various peoples (and scientists) have not only conflated all the different datura species but have also put them together with other tropane-containing plants, like solandra or brugmansia, which are connected to magical or spiritual uses in their own environments. Our focus will here be on *D. stramonium*, also known as thornapple or jimsonweed, because this species has reached out to communicate with me and has turned up over and over in my work and life.

With the datura family, the waters of a witch's garden begin to get a bit deeper. Datura is not one of those forgiving herbs that can stand to be ignored or treated recklessly, and it can be dangerous. Some people just don't want to deal with any plants like this. That's okay. You can do a lifetime of magic with rose, for instance, and never fully exhaust the possibilities. But it's also okay to work with the more dangerous plants and their spirits. This does not mean that you should be condemned for practicing black magic. As for the danger, you need only be well informed about these plants and be patient. To that end, let's talk about alkaloids.

THE WEIRD SISTERS

Usually, plants create alkaloids when they are stressed (too much sun, not enough water) or when they are trying to protect themselves from predation (bugs, viruses, grazing). Alkaloids are chemicals that cause unexpected effects in those who ingest them—for instance, animals, including humans, can hallucinate, feel drunk, or even die as a result of consuming an alkaloid. Almost all alkaloids taste bitter to us. All sorts of them exist, and a number of them are well-loved by humans—morphine, nicotine, and caffeine come to mind.

Yet some alkaloids are significantly more problematic for us than others. The tropane alkaloids, which are found in what I call the Weird Sisters of the witch's garden—datura, henbane, belladonna, and mandrake—are among these. The Weird Sisters are more complicated to grow and more difficult to know than other plants. The alkaloids in them are primarily atropine, scopolamine, and hyoscyamine. Symptoms of tropane alkaloid consumption are dilated pupils—to the extent that some people can see fine at night, but daytime is just a blur—feeling very hot but not being able to sweat, reddened skin, extreme thirst, constipation and the inability to urinate, difficulty swallowing, and either very fast or very slow heartbeat. A number of these symptoms seem Saturnian—they're about being dried up. What's different and non-Saturnian about these effects are the heat and irregular heartbeat. This makes sense, however, when we consider that there are two groups of tropane alkaloids: the atropine group, as in the Weird Sisters, and the cocaine group, as in coca.

What's unique about the hallucinations caused by tropane alkaloids is that they often have a ferocious and sinister content, featuring threatening creatures and frightening vistas, as well as feelings of doom and paranoia. It's not unusual for people under their influence to believe they are being transformed into animals with claws and fur, which is interesting in the case of datura, because it is utilized by wolf shamans. Most important is that amnesia is a major part of the tropane experience. The first time Datura Spirit spoke to me, it was about forgetting.

⇒ Friday Night Fights ⇐

In Nigeria, the tendency of tropane alkaloids to precipitate or encourage violence is exploited by young men about to engage in fighting contests. Before the contest, they drink a tea made from seeds containing the alkaloid. This, they believe, makes them fiercer in battle and increases their chance of victory. It's almost as if the plant spirit deliberately torments those who consume it, urging them on to violence.

I will speak more about the forgetting aspect of this group of plants in chapter 13. Here, I want to discuss how the "magical forgetting" caused by the alkaloids of the Weird Sisters may be a material manifestation of the idea that magical knowledge is sometimes kept secret, even from the individual who holds it. Magical knowledge can rest in your brain or spirit like a seed germinating, sending out its roots and influencing everything around it. Yet you may know only that you have received knowledge and not be consciously aware of what that knowledge is. And you may not be able to remember it. I believe this is the actual truth regarding the keeping of magical secrets, which is not about going on social media forums and saying things like: "Well, I know, but I can't tell you because it's a secret." Magical "forgetting" is, I feel, fundamental to magical practice and secrets.

In the case of thornapple, the leaves contain higher levels of alkaloids (and more scopolamine) than the roots, even though the roots are where the alkaloids are produced. The highest concentration is found in the leaves of young plants. The Diegueño and Luiseño tribes of western North America, who utilized *Datura innoxia* for the initiation of boys, also used the dried or fresh root. In fact, in descriptions of exactly which part of the datura plant was used for religious purposes, it is often the root that is consumed.

That the roots contain so much less alkaloid than the leaves makes sense for an annual, because it does not depend on the roots to get it through the winter. So it throws the alkaloids upstairs to more vulnerable areas, those that are close to the seeds. Moreover, the seeds of these plants tend to have the highest concentration of scopolamine as well. Thornapple supposedly has lower levels of alkaloids than other daturas, and has more hyoscyamine than scopolamine—the reverse of other daturas. Hyoscyamine is a precursor to scopolamine; it turns into atropine in the dried plant material.

⇛ Leave It to Science ⇚

An awful lot of confusion and contradictory information exists regarding alkaloid content in the various parts of the Weird Sisters, even in terms of which alkaloid is where in the plant. I don't think this information is very dependable, despite being compiled by scientists and including all sorts of tables and molecular diagrams. I've noticed, for instance, that these scientific articles rarely note whether the plant material being examined is fresh or dried, or where or when it was gathered.

In fact, the slippery undependability of the information about datura alkaloids reminds me of this plant's approach to people: "Grow me—I want to grow around you very much!—But don't you dare eat me or touch me too much, or smell me too much, or, or, or . . ." And datura is serious in these threats. People have died from consuming datura. It is not quite as nasty as belladonna, but it is far from a benign and happy plant.

The alkaloids of the Weird Sisters are not psychedelics, like peyote or LSD. They're deliriants. This is one of the reasons why they trip people up—often literally! Deliriants are not especially favored in Western culture. Comedians may make jokes about a psychedelic high, but you don't hear much comedy about being delirious. If you've ever experienced a very high fever that included hallucinations, then you've experienced something close to what a tropane alkaloid can do to you.

Typically, with a deliriant, you don't know that you're hallucinating. You think it's real. There is a huge "body load" (unpleasant physical effects), and you experience blackouts. With an opiate, you may just lie there for a while, basically sleeping or dreaming. But with tropanes, you do things and wake up in the middle of them—things like strangling your friend's cat.

⇛Skill vs. Chemicals ⇚

Plant spirits are real and are no more dependent upon alkaloids for their manifestation than demons are dependent upon the presence of smoke for materialization. Nor does it appear that traditional societies necessarily used them. Using one of the Weird Sisters doesn't make you a powerful or "real" witch. Witches don't need chemicals to fly or to communicate with the plant spirits. To do those things (and many others), you only need patience, skill, and the grace of the spirits. A real witch can work with plant spirits through direct spiritual contact rather than through the rickety bridge of alkaloids.

Are we so jaded and so unsure of our magical abilities and those of the spirit world that we think we can only have magical experiences while high? We need to have more faith in our abilities as witches than that.

Patience is invaluable when working with plants and hoping to engage their spirits. Everyone who has gardened knows this. I grew datura for many years before I was approached by its spirit. It *might* have happened sooner if I had actually asked the plant spirit for contact, but I didn't even think of it. The point is that it took time for the spirit to manifest itself. But the patience and discipline that "time" implies seem to be in short supply for modern magic workers. Yet to me, they are the keys to acquiring any skill, including magical ones.

There's another important aspect of working with the Weird Sisters—your willingness to give. The Huichols, a tribe whose members work with datura, warn that, unless those who work with this plant spirit hold up their end of the bargain with an offering, datura can be brutal.

What offering did I make before Datura Spirit appeared to me? More than a decade of watering and feeding those plants, weeding their plots, and saving their seed and distributing it all over the world (through my shop) in a way that the plant could not have managed alone. I didn't "sacrifice" some animal or offer my own blood. Instead, I offered the real value of my time and my skill. To my mind, this was far more valuable to the plant than a bit of tobacco stuck in the ground. That may work well for wild plants, but even they can be cared for. Their immediate environments can be improved by weeding, or by adding nice organic fertilizer, or by grooming the plant itself, as Native people have done historically with wild plants. I can't see how any plant would not interpret such care as an honest and welcome offering, especially if it is done on a regular basis.

I can understand the point of offering tobacco to a plant spirit. The origin of the practice seems to be that the tobacco was precious to the individual, so the offering represented a sacrifice that embodied the time and skill of growing and processing it. But I think that today, when we can buy tobacco at any convenience store, a more valuable offering is our time and skill in another form—the time that goes into taking care of plants. This includes, not only time spent actually in the plant's presence, grooming and feeding it but also time spent learning about the plant, how best to care for it, how it grows, its history, and the skill that comes with practice and learning over time. So if you want to work with the Weird Sisters, consider if you are willing to make this offering. It is not as dramatic as slitting a goat's throat, but it is much more beneficial for the plant and for you as a witch. Skill grows from time and patience.

LORE

Some tribes of western North America used datura for fun, just as some cultures enjoy eating specially prepared poisonous fish or jumping off a bridge while tied to a rubber band. And datura has been incorporated into medicine. So considerable trouble has been taken, in different contexts, to know its levels of toxicity. It has been used in poultices, as belladonna has, and has also been smoked in many different places and times to stop asthma attacks. In the United States, dried thornapple leaves were combined with sage leaves and smoked in a pipe as a remedy for an asthma attack.

Ointments for topical relief of pain were made from fresh thornapple leaves processed at low heat. One part fresh leaves was tinctured for two weeks in ten parts 40 percent alcohol. In this case, a dose of five drops was used to treat frenzied, violent insanity (apparently on a sort of homeopathic basis) or epilepsy. In Ayurveda, a dose of dried *Datura stramonium* leaf is 50–100 mg, which is quite tiny. So you can see how potent this plant can be. Its alkaloids are soluble in water, alcohol, and fixed oils.

Kieri and the Huichol

Many Native peoples have worked with datura in one way or another, but here I'll focus on the Huichol of Mexico. They have traditionally resisted conversion to Christianity and have preserved their ancient religion, which includes much work with ancestor spirits and interaction with the spirits of plants, especially peyote. Huichol mythology tells of a war between a spiritual practice centered on datura and one involving peyote. The peyote won. And really, when you think about how these two plants interact with people, you can't blame the Huichol for switching plants. No one has ever died from consuming peyote, and it does not drive people mad. Compared to datura, peyote is easy.

The name the Huichols use for the primary opponent to peyote is Kieri. Solandra is the main Kieri plant and, in fact, the name for datura in Huichol means "like solandra." The Huichols put datura, solandra, and even brugmansia together in the Kieri category—which makes perfect sense, since they all contain the same kind of alkaloids, all have trumpet-shaped flowers, and all have five points, marks, or petal-like extensions to their flowers, like the five creases on peyote babies. For the Huichols, Kieri is the most quick-tempered and jealous of the spirit ancestors. They describe him as "a dangerous sorcerer who is to be propitiated lest he inflict harm." There are those among them who work primarily with Kieri instead of using peyote. But the Huichol do not consider them to be real shamans like peyoteros. They see them as sorcerers instead. From the perspective of Huichol peyote-centered spirituality, their attitudes toward datura and the spirit ancestor Kieri are reminiscent of how Christianity has viewed and demonized earlier pagan religious practices. However, we don't have to have this perspective about those who work with datura.

The Huichol believe that the negative effects that we attribute to alkaloids, especially insanity, can be experienced by someone who has had no physical contact with datura, but was simply related to or friendly with someone who had brought down the plant's anger by breaking their word about an offering. For them, winds, cyclones, whirlwinds, and tornadoes are associated with the dead or the gods—and in turn with Kieri—who designates and is associated with, not only a group of plant species but also individual plants that are recognized as persons.

The Huichol tell a lot of stories about people who had dealings with Kieri and paid for it with insanity or death. These were mainly people who asked Kieri for something mundane and promised an offering in return—for instance, abstaining from salt or sex for five months—and then broke their word. Kieri is unforgiving of such human lapses and is so interested in violence that he will help people magically kill others or hurt animals.

....

≋ The Jilted Plant Spirit

You may well wonder what made Kieri so angry and so violent. Is this just his nature, or did something happen? Author James Dekorne has an interesting theory about the Weird Sisters that relates to this. Because female sexuality and its representative spirits have been so brutally repressed in Western civilization for the past several millennia, he claims, the archetype of this energy has come to be seen as destructive and dangerous. He argues that it is our reception of these spirits that makes them seem dangerous and destructive. I would go further, however, and say that these spirits can be dangerous and destructive because of how humans have related to them. I think the Huichol overthrowing of the datura cult for the peyote cult is illustrative of this. Datura has been somewhat demonized by them. Perhaps it has adopted this dangerous and destructive behavior as payback for how it was jilted.

Wolf Shamans

The wolf shamans of the Huichol use Kieri in their vision quests, which are believed to be a vestige of a much older and more common religious practice whose traditions are echoed in the connection of canine animals, especially wolves and coyotes, with datura. Xolotl, an Aztec guide to the Underworld, is manifested as a black dog whose name is the Zapotec word for datura. In fact, in Zapotec stories about datura bewitchment, an individual may well become a black dog. Black animals in general are associated with witchcraft in that area of Mexico.

Huichols believe that wolves and coyotes are particularly affiliated with sorcery and with Kieri. Interestingly, some have described the symptoms of datura overdose as being similar to those of rabies, a disease associated with dogs. One of the symptoms of tropane alkaloids, the dilating of the pupils and subsequent ability to see better at night, is similar to the vision of wolves and coyotes. And of course, datura itself typically releases most of its perfume at night, when it is pollinated by large moths.

The walls of sacred caves near the Pecos River are covered with depictions of humanlike figures with datura-pod heads who are surrounded by canine figures. My own experience with Datura Spirit has likewise featured canine motifs. The Huichol perception of wolves is that, although they can be violent, they are wise and very community minded. They are believed to mate for life, and to be willing to give all for the pack.

This is quite a contrast to the Western stereotype of the wolf as a loner admired for its solitude and murderous nature. Just look at some of the popular images of wolves—even in occulture. Perhaps the present-day attitudes of Huichol wolf shamans about wolves derive in some way from what was once their culture's attitude toward datura. Was Datura Spirit once wise and, if a killer out of necessity, still dedicated to community, mating with its devotees for life in a postive rather than a jealous, violent way?

It's interesting how often canine imagery is connected with the witching herbs, whether in terms of the time of year when they are most powerful (at the rise of the Dog Star) or imagery of a black dog being somehow involved in an herb's harvest or use. This is certainly the case with datura or with mandrake, which, we are told, was traditionally harvested by a black dog. My dreams and visions related to Datura Spirit featured a black dog, a doglike child black as licorice, and a werewolf—which in turn was connected to *Amanita muscaria* images. (The Huichol wolf shamans who work with Kieri claim that wolves use *Amanita muscaria*.)

PRACTICE

Most cultures that have used datura for religious purposes do it once, as in a vision quest. For instance, Huichol wolf shamans use it only after a very long five- to six-year apprenticeship in shapeshifting to become a werewolf. Likewise, the Huichols, who make an offering to datura in order to get something like the ability to play the violin well for ceremonial occasions, don't ingest it. Most don't even know that it has hallucinogenic effects. They work with an individual plant approached as a person and make a deal with it, asking for some skill or luck in exchange for an offering of some type. To my mind, *this* is the best way to work with this plant.

However, my experience with datura is that, even if you do not petition the spirit, it may well come to you and, in doing so, scare the wits out of you. Why? Because it feels like doing so and because, in my opinion, it does not know its own strength relative to us. It's like a chimp playing with a person and causing injury because humans are nowhere near as strong or as sturdy as chimps. And chimps don't know that.

What's more, in my experience, datura gets a bang out of messing with people. Not as much or as badly as belladonna, but enough. And most people—including most witches—do not anticipate this. We act as if all herbs are innocuous cooking herbs. We've gotten so used to the War on Drugs baloney about marijuana leading to heroin addiction that we no longer believe *any* warnings about herb toxicity.

New Age approaches to the natural world have meant that many no longer expect plant spirits to have anything but calm and wise personalities. The New Age universe simply does not include prickly spirits who flaunt their power. However, in my experience, plant spirits are as different from each other and have as much personality as people. Some have an affinity for particular people; their plants will grow well for that person, whereas others will not. The way you come to know which plants want to work with you or which ones you have an affinity for is by actually giving it a try—especially if you feel a particular attraction to a plant.

I've always felt a strong attraction to the Weird Sisters and the nightshades in general. In turn, they grow well for me, whereas I have no luck growing some other plant families, like cucurbits. Years ago, a customer in Italy sent me some seeds for a variety of thornapple that has no spines on its fruit, only bumps (*D. stramonium* var. *inermis*). I grew it and liked it and offered it for sale in my shop. I then found out that it had once been native to where I lived in upstate New York and that the people indigenous to that area had used that particular subspecies of thornapple in initiations for boys. This rather odd coincidence occurs often in connection to this plant.

Binding Spells

In terms of ordinary magical uses, thornapple seems especially apt for binding spells. For instance, its flowers are often incorporated in binding love spells. Even though there is much that is Saturnian about this herb—its toxicity, its ability to thrive in "disturbed" or "waste" areas, its drying action—it has those lush flowers that are Venus in her darkest aspect. You can also use the emptied fruit (the usually spiked sphere that contains the seeds) as an imprisoning capsule for items related to the target of a spell—hair or bits of thread from clothing. Black wool yarn is also an appropriate binding aid.

I also recommend using various datura species as a bridge for approaching some of the darker goddesses, like Kali (*Datura metel*, in particular). I strongly suggest, however, that, if you are at all interested in working with this plant spirit, you prepare yourself to be frightened at some point. Most plant spirits will take care not to terrify their devotees, but thornapple seems unable to resist messing with people—even those who care for it and for whom, clearly, it also cares. We can't demand that a plant spirit show itself. It takes its time and comes on its own terms, if it comes at all. But I do believe that Datura Spirit has much to teach.

One of the main things we can learn from thornapple is that spirits can experience hurt, rejection, and resulting rage, and that pain can last for centuries. This doesn't mean we need to be sappy about it. It is capable of protecting itself. But it does mean we cannot approach plant spirits without a healthy wariness of their enormous power.

If simply tending your thornapple plants is insufficient, you can spend a summer evening sleeping next to them. Don't, however, bring the pots inside if you have other animals living with you. The scent of thornapple is psychoactive. Taking big whiffs of the flowers is not going to harm you—you can even try doing it deliberately before going to bed to see if it affects your dreams. Whether that happens depends on how sensitive you are to these alkaloids. In my experience, however, without even using the fragrance, dreams can be profoundly affected by Datura Spirit, especially if they occur during the day. Although the flowers don't release much scent during the day, try spending some time with the plant outside around lunchtime and then going indoors for a nap. This is how I have had my most profound experiences with this plant spirit.

Whatever you ask of thornapple, be prepared to give it an appropriate offering in return and to keep any promises you make. In my opinion, the greatest lesson that Datura Spirit has to teach us is the necessity for patience and discipline, and the importance of keeping our end of a bargain.

THORNAPPLE IN THE GARDEN

Thornapple seeds are large and easy to handle. Because this plant is an annual, it contains a lot of vitality and doesn't require much fuss. Thornapple seeds will germinate at warmish room temperatures in two to three weeks. Other daturas, such as *D. metal* or *D. innoxia*, like it warmer. I actually just poke seeds down into rich soil each year once the weather has warmed and settled. The plant is also easy to transplant, but needs full sun. It loves growing in containers with rich soil and seems to revel in displaying itself this way.

Do not place or site it near any member of the nightshade family that you will be consuming—tomatoes, peppers, or wonderberries—because their fruits will pick up unwanted alkaloids. Thornapple also acts as a reservoir for various plant viruses that don't affect it much, but that can make trouble for other nightshades. So give it its own area, where it can really shine. Space plants two to three feet (60–120 cm) apart. They can grow to four feet (1.2 m) tall.

Thornapple flowers produce a nectar that honeybees don't especially like, although it is not toxic to them (as wild tobacco is). It is usually pollinated by moths instead of bees, which makes sense, since the flowers exude most of their fragrance at night. These moths are huge and quite striking. The flowers have a pleasant citrus-sweet scent. But be warned: smelling them can give sensitive people extreme dreams or nightmares. The plant itself smells like peanut butter. Some people very much dislike the smell, so it's not a plant to position under a window.

If you want to harvest the leaves, pick off the pods as they begin to form so that more leaves and flowers are produced (and so that your entire garden is not overtaken by thornapple). Harvest leaves when the plants are blooming in the morning after the dew has dried. Dry the leaves and flowers at the low end of a dehydrator's temperature dial. Flowers typically last only one day on the plant and then fall off and turn brown. Seeds are easy to collect when the pods split and turn brown. Often, the plant will reseed, but it does not tend to spread all over the place this way, at least, not in my garden.

CHAPTER TWELVE

WILD TOBACCO

Smoke

T obacco is probably the most widely used magical, spiritual, or shamanic plant in the world. Certainly in the New World, it is used
more frequently than any other in all sorts of situations—for offerings
to plant spirits when harvesting a plant, for paying for some graveyard

dirt, for smoking as an aid in spiritual work, and for many other purposes as well. Even so, I hesitated to include wild tobacco in this book because not many European-style witches use it. It was its popularity in Hoodoo, aspects of which are rapidly being incorporated into all sorts of other magical paths, that made me decide it was appropriate.

The tobacco I talk about in this chapter is not the same species that is commonly smoked in the West. That's *Nicotiana tabacum*, which I will refer to as commercial tobacco. Instead, I want to talk about *Nicotiana rustica*, a species once known as yellow henbane, even though it doesn't look anything like a henbane. This is also called wild tobacco, although it has been cultivated by humans for at least 2,000 years. I chose this tobacco species because it has a history for us in North America—wild tobacco, not commercial tobacco, is what Native Americans shared with the Europeans at Jamestown. But also because it has a history that relates to me personally, since I live in the former homeland of the Seneca tribe, a people who, along with many others, made (and still make) use of this herb for both medicinal and spiritual purposes.

⇒ *Traditional, Wild, or Commercial?*

Native Americans often refer to N. rustica *as "traditional tobacco," "real tobacco," or "old tobacco," as opposed to* N. tabacum, *"commercial tobacco." And in fact,* N. rustica *was cultivated, not picked from the wild, by Native peoples. The truly wild tobaccos in North America are* N. attenuata *and* Nicotiana quadrivalvis, *and only two subspecies of this plant are actually wild—*Nicotiana wallacei *and* Nicotiana bigelovii. *The other subspecies were all cultivated only.*

Many witches consider tobacco to be a generally acceptable substitute for various baneful Saturnian herbs that are more difficult to obtain. And this makes sense if you think of Saturn as characterized by toxicity. Tobacco can indeed be quite toxic to many animals besides humans, and wild tobacco is especially toxic.

☠ *Warning: Nicotine can kill you—and I am not talking about lung cancer from smoking cigarettes. Do not ever drink a tea made of this plant or chew or eat the leaves, and always wear gloves when handling it. Some people are much more sensitive to nicotine than others, so don't use it as an insecticide, as some people do. Nicotine is a neurotoxin and is readily and quickly absorbed into human skin much more thoroughly on contact than when it is smoked. It is very easy to be poisoned by it. It kills fish and bees (and other animals), and it stinks.*

But for me, tobacco is not Saturnian. In the scheme of planetary correspondences, it's usually associated with Mars. However, it lacks thorns and is not hot in its taste. I think a better connection for tobacco is with Fire, especially because this herb has so often been smoked. Moreover, it is often dried by means of fire, it sharpens concentration (fires up thinking), and North American tribes historically offered it to Fire.

Wild tobacco is much less conspicuous than commercial tobacco, which is a big plant that enjoys heat and sucks all the nutrients out of the soil it grows in. Instead, wild tobacco is a much scrappier plant that grows better in a temperate clime. It has more resistance to cold than commercial tobacco does and is the tobacco Native Americans were growing in Manhattan when the Europeans arrived. This makes it a much better candidate for a witch's garden along with other temperate-climate plants.

LORE

Wild tobacco was the tobacco of choice for many of the tribes of North America before the introduction of commercial tobacco. It spread along with corn and was brought from South America up to the northeast by 160 CE. The Northeast woodland tribes, in turn, spread it to the Southwest, which means that, ultimately, it was grown by a good portion of the population of North America. What's more, wild tobacco had crossed the Atlantic and was being grown in European gardens by the 1550s, identified as "yellow henbane" or "English tabacco." So we know that European magic workers surely had an interest in it. Thus, wild tobacco has a history of magical practice far longer than any associated with commercial tobacco.

The Cherokee often used tobacco in rituals, although they also smoked it for pleasure. They only switched to commercial tobacco when they were forcibly relocated to a dry, hot area where commercial tobacco grew better than wild varieties. By that time, wild tobacco was already part of Cherokee charms used to ward off witchcraft. The Iroquois incorporated it into their ceremonies as well. The Hoodoo concept of putting tobacco into the ground as an offering in return for something taken—like a plant or graveyard dirt—derives from Native practices.

Various Native peoples considered wild tobacco to be a spirit, and it was strongly connected with Fire. It was often placed into a fire as an offering and was associated with thunderstorms. It was also used as a placating offering to evil spirits manifesting as snakes or sent by witches.

Henbane was often used in rain magic. In an interesting connection to that use, and in resonance with wild tobacco's old common name of yellow henbane, wild tobacco was smoked by Mesoamerican tribes known to others as "rain people." These tribes visited shrines to rain on four different peaks, where they smoked cigars made of this herb. With the help of wild tobacco smoke, they went into trances, during which they spoke in thundering voices. The combination of this "voice thunder" and cigar smoke was thought to bring on thunderstorms.

There are many magical uses of wild tobacco, including as the traditional payment for something taken from the earth. But you can also express thanks for particularly important dreams by offering some wild tobacco to a fire. Offer it to the Earth before planting. Or use its smoke as an aid to divination.

PRACTICE

Wild tobacco is different from many other herbs because specific methods have been developed for preparing it for use. We all know that tobacco is often ritually smoked. But this requires particular care in the case of wild tobacco. If you try to smoke wild tobacco on its own or before it is cured, or if you smoke leaves from a plant that has been deliberately stressed to increase nicotine content, you will get sick—and I mean *really* sick.

Even after curing, wild tobacco is typically incorporated in very small amounts compared to other ingredients in a smoking mixture. Sometimes the proportion of wild tobacco to other plant materials in ritual smoking mixtures is only 1:20; others use a proportion of 1:4. If the tobacco is cured, it can add a sweet richness to a blend. Today, most people who smoke wild tobacco combine it with commercial tobacco or with herbs that have no nicotine content—mullein or coltsfoot or even yauhtli (*Tagetes lucida*), which is said to have some hallucinogenic properties. There's some indication that wild tobacco contains beta-harmalines (like those in Syrian rue, *Peganum harmala*) that are especially concentrated in the smoke when the dried leaves are burned. These act together with nicotine in the plant to enhance memory and, according to some, to assist in communication between people, animals, and plants.

Wild tobacco contains more alkaloids than commercial tobacco, but it seems to me that the tribes of the Northeast woodlands, who smoked this herb mainly for spiritual purposes in pipes or cornhusk cigarettes, developed methods of growing it that reduced the nicotine levels greatly. This provided a smoking mixture that was not only less dangerous but also more pleasurable because it was not as harsh.

Drying vs. Fermentation

Wild tobacco can be dried like any other herb—in the sun, the shade, or over a fire. Native Americans certainly dried it using these straightforward methods. Today, a dehydrator works well for this, although, when you use a dehydrator the plant material remains green. And just to be on the safe side, don't use the dehydrator in your living space when doing this, because you don't want vaporized nicotine sprayed all over.

Green tobacco leaves have not been fermented and contain a ferocious amount of alkaloids. In fact, some folks don't harvest the leaves green, but wait until they begin to turn yellow. Various sources remark on how the tobacco that the Northeast woodland tribes used was in a green state and usually powdered. I believe they did not need to cure it, because they had taken care to grow it in a way that lowered its nicotine content greatly—by watering a good deal, by not fertilizing too much, and by not stressing the plants. If they used the flowers, they harvested them at the end of the season, when they reportedly have less nicotine. And they dried the plant material at a low temperature and used it with a mixture of a number of other plants, especially finely shredded barks.

You can reserve green wild tobacco leaves that have been dried for offerings, rather than using them for fumes, suffumigations, or smoking. Consider that the green dried leaves have a very high level of Elemental Fire to them.

To my mind, however, a more interesting choice for preparing wild tobacco leaves is to cure them. This entails fermenting the herb with moisture, rather than fermenting with liquid, as with wine. Curing is a means of modifying, not only the alkaloid content of an herb but also its scent and taste. Just like distillation's heat and steam, fermentation brings out certain chemicals in plant material, destroying some and creating others. Just think of the alcohol produced in liquid fermentation with yeast. The fermentation process changes the nature of plant material and affects how it interacts with us. To my mind, it is a way of asking for communication with the plant spirit on the material plane. Tobacco and black tea are the herbs most commonly fermented before use, but magic workers work with other fermented herbs, like patchouli and tonka beans.

Fermentation of tobacco lowers its alkaloid content and modifies its aromatics so that it is friendlier to the human palate and so that we can be affected by the alkaloids without them being as likely to injure us. Remember the importance of aromatics; scent is the closest to the spiritual of all the material "foods" our world provides.

The Secret Fire

There are numerous methods for curing tobacco, most of which involve the use of fire in some form, whether rays from the sun or actual smoke. I recommend curing wild tobacco using a method more aligned with magic—by using what alchemists call the Secret Fire: dew.

To use this method, harvest the whole plant a few weeks after the flowers are cut off. Hang the plants upside down outside during the night so they get wet from the morning dew. You will get the most dew where there are no overhanging trees. Allow the wild tobacco to dry in the air during the day, although not in the sun. You may have to move them morning and evening in order to catch the dew at night in the open and to dry them off in the shade during the day. Leave a bit of space between the plants so that the dew can reach them, but also so moisture won't cling to them and cause them to rot. The leaves should be able to breathe the dew in and out. You can string them through the stalks, knotting the string on each side of the stalk to keep space between the plants, then hang them in a row from this line.

Apply the Secret Fire repeatedly until the leaves are transformed, becoming brown and leathery and fragrant. The leaves should not be crispy; if they are, the smoke will be very harsh. You can try this same procedure with other herb leaves to change their alkaloid content or modify their taste or smell. Consider what the effects might be with other nightshades. I find it interesting that these Fiery plants can be transformed by water, not only while they grow but also after they are harvested. I think this demonstrates a fundamental quality of Fire: it hates Water, but loves it too.

Some tribes didn't use green leaf material, but didn't bother about curing much either. They just left the leaves on the stalks over the winter and picked them when they were dark brown, a kind of natural fermentation. To my mind, however, leaves cured in this way have a profile somewhat like Dead Bones (see chapter 6) and have possibilities for cursework. Yet tobacco was *never* traditionally used for cursing, only for blessing, protection, and divination. This makes it unique among the nightshades of the witch's garden, which I think says something about its fundamental nature.

Here is a recipe for a tobacco blend that can be smoked to shed Fire's light on dreams and aid communication between people, animals, and plants in dreams.

Witch's Smoke

3 parts mullein, dried, finely chopped

6 parts mugwort , dried, finely chopped

1 part sweetgrass (Hierochloe odorata) *or deerstongue* (Liatris odoratissima)

1 part traditional tobacco leaves, cured and shredded

Sufficient Witch's Vermouth (see chapter 10) or brandy (because of its Fire associations) to moisten the mixture

1. Blend the herbs and moisten with the liquid (don't drench). Pour out any liquid not absorbed.

2. Toss and jar the herbs.

3. Let sit for a couple of weeks. You can redo the moistening several times (and incorporate other alcoholic tinctures) or use as is.

Rather than incorporating sweetgrass or deerstongue, which can be diffi-cult to obtain, tincture a vanilla bean (or peru balsam or tonka beans) in brandy and use the tincture to moisten the herbs.

....

☠️ *Warning: If you smoke this blend, do not inhale. Native people traditionally smoke wild tobacco by allowing the smoke into the mouth and then rolling it out again without inhaling it, as one would with a cigar. If you don't want to take the smoke into your mouth, you can use this as a fume or suffumigation and simply fan the smoke toward yourself. Keep the smoke away from animals.*

....

WILD TOBACCO IN THE GARDEN

Wild tobacco has small leaves, so once the leaves are dried, you may end up with only about an ounce of dried plant material. Keep this in mind when deciding how many seedlings to plant.

Wild tobacco is among those plants that need increased warmth and light to germinate. I consider this combination of light and warmth to be a representation of its affinity to Fire.

Sprinkle the tiny seeds on wet planting medium and press them in with your fingertips. They need indirect light, not direct sun. A window is fine, although I use a shop light—the kind of cheap four-foot fluorescent light that is typically hung over a workbench. There are a number of options for maintaining warmth—a waterproof heating pad set on low, a bona fide propagation mat, or even the top of a hot water heater or a refrigerator in a warm kitchen. Keep in mind these plants want to be warm, but not hot. They will germinate in ten to twenty days at 70–75°F (20–25°C).

Regular watering from above will dislodge the tiny seeds, so either mist the surface of the soil to water them (don't let them dry out) or use bottom watering. Pour warm or tepid water in a tray holding the peat pellets or cell packs or small pots and dump out whatever has not been absorbed after a half hour. Once the seeds germinate, stop the bottom warmth or the seedlings will be damaged and perhaps even die. Once they come up, keep the seedlings at 65°F (18°C).

After the danger of frost is over and the weather is warmer, transplant the seedlings outside when they get their first set of true leaves (the second set of leaves that you see). Gradually get them used to being outside so that they won't be set back by cold or damaged by the sun. See page 24 for how to harden off.

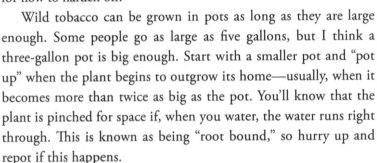

Wild tobacco can be grown in pots as long as they are large enough. Some people go as large as five gallons, but I think a three-gallon pot is big enough. Start with a smaller pot and "pot up" when the plant begins to outgrow its home—usually, when it becomes more than twice as big as the pot. You'll know that the plant is pinched for space if, when you water, the water runs right through. This is known as being "root bound," so hurry up and repot if this happens.

Don't be afraid to pot up. Just put your hand over the top of the dirt, letting the stalk come up between your fingers—be sure to wear gloves. Turn the pot upside down and, if all the dirt doesn't come out right away, tap the edge of the pot rim on something until it is loosened. Then put the whole root ball in a new larger pot, being sure to keep the top of the soil level with what was the top of the soil in the old pot—in other words, don't cover up the "crown" of the plant (the place where the roots and the stems meet) with mud or dirt. Some people break up the dirt at the bottom of the root ball if the plant is root bound, but I don't usually do this. Either the plant is strong enough to grow into new soil, or it isn't.

For all that it may sound a little persnickety, wild tobacco is actually pretty easy to grow. It likes rich soil. But remember: the more nitrogen in the soil, the higher the alkaloid level will be in this plant. Since wild tobacco already has far more alkaloids than is beneficial for us, make sure that, if you add any fertilizer, it is low in nitrogen. Good choices are composted manure or soybean meal.

One way to ensure fertility if you are growing these plants in the ground is to plant them in patches where legumes—beans, peas, or clover—were grown the previous year. It's optimal to till the legumes under before they flower, but I often don't do that. I just till them in at the end of the season and let the winter break down the material. This seems to give a sufficient boost to keep a patch healthy. We witches growing herbs for use in magic are not in competition with other farms looking for a bulk harvest, so we can be a bit more relaxed about how much production we get from our gardens. Quality, not quantity.

You can determine the alkaloid level of the leaves you harvest by where they grow on the plant. Nicotine concentration is greater when this plant is grown in hot, dry climates, but alkaloids also increase the higher the leaves are on the plant, because the plant focuses on conserving the newest growth. Native American tribesmen decreased the alkaloid level by giving the plants lots of water. In fact, tobacco is among the few crops that North American tribes irrigated by hand.

≋ No Women Allowed ≋

I say "tribesmen" here, because it was usually men who grew this particular plant. In fact, some tribes thought that exposure to outsiders or women (!) would make tobacco plants wilt. Men often put fences around their little plots and even made temporary shelters next to them where they slept to guard the plants. However, in tribes where folks smoked for pleasure, women certainly smoked as well.

For watering, I use soaker hoses made from recycled tires, but there are plenty of other ways to get water to these plants. You can, for instance, cut the bottom off soda bottles or milk bottles and turn them upside down into holes in the ground next to the plants. Just fill them up periodically. Don't use cat litter jugs for this, however; there seems to be something in the plastic of those things that kills plants.

The more these plants are stressed, the higher the level of alkaloids they will create to deter animals—especially bugs—from preying on them. When it comes to the nightshades, a happy plant that does not perceive threats will be easier to work with; wild tobacco is a good illustration.

Wild tobacco plants don't get anywhere near the size of commercial tobacco plants. They usually grow only two feet (60 cm) tall and not that wide—which is why, in my opinion, a five-gallon bucket is just too big. Like tomato plants, wild tobacco produces "suckers" that are basically whole new plants starting in the crotch between the main stalk and a branch. You can pinch these off (wear gloves) to get bigger leaves. You can even let the suckers get a little growth and then pinch them off to make new plants, or you can leave them to get more flowers and more seeds. If you cut off the tops before the flowers open, typically the leaves will be larger (and the honeybees will not be harmed by foraging for nectar from these plants).[14]

Some people like to harvest tobacco flowers. In fact, some tribes smoked the flowers separately. It even seems to me that some varieties of wild tobacco were developed to produce a lot of flowers. Wild tobacco has a number of named varieties, which shows that this is not really a wild plant at all, but a highly cultivated, human-friendly plant. Some of these varieties produce lots and lots of flowers. These varieties generally have small leaves, which makes me think that flowers were always an important aspect of this herb. But I suspect that the use of the flowers may generally be held secret. I haven't found any good information about how to prepare the flowers for smoking, even though a lot of information has been collected over the centuries about how wild tobacco has been used ritually all over the world.

⇛ Buffalo Bird Woman's Garden ⇚

Buffalo Bird Woman described her father harvesting tobacco flowers and mixing them with other ingredients as the first smoke that he would share with close friends. This plant, however, was not Nicotiana rustica, *but another tobacco,* Nicotiana quadrarivalvis, *which has white flowers. She actually helped him do this when he got older, so not all tribes, by any means, banned women from working with tobacco.*

Wild tobacco does not reproduce through underground runners. For one thing, it's an annual. These plants were often grown in patches and not sown again, because if you leave flowers on the plants, they become seed pods that guarantee natural reseeding. The pods are round and turn brown when the seeds are ready. You have to be careful when harvesting the seeds, however, because the ripe pods crack open and spill them. I usually use scissors to cut the seedpod stem so that the pod falls into a little bowl.

CHAPTER THIRTEEN

HENBANE
The Cauldron

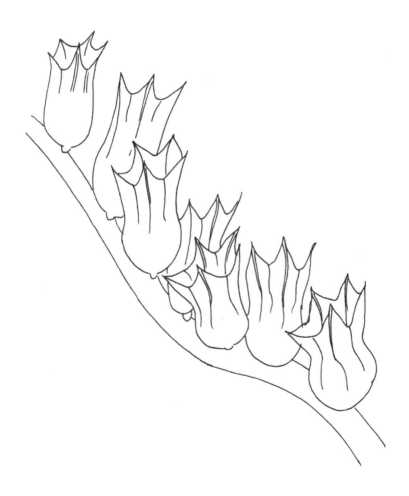

Saturn loves borders, ruins, and edges. So, as you might expect from a Saturnian plant, henbane occurs chiefly in waste places—near buildings, on roadsides, in graveyards, in old gardens, and in areas covered with rubbish from ruined structures. Yet I have never seen henbane growing in the wild. Perhaps it does so more commonly in the UK than here in North America.

What makes henbane a Saturn herb? For one thing, it is drying in its action on the human body, a characteristic of Saturn herbs. In the body, Saturn rules bones; thus the herbal use of henbane has often been connected to bones. For instance, it has been used to treat problems with teeth, the most commonly seen human bones. When henbane is applied to a diseased tooth, the tooth dries up and falls out. That tooth can then be put on a string and hung around the neck of a teething child, reputedly easing that painful process. Some think the calyx of the henbane flower resembles a tooth, especially if you look at it before the "skirt" begins to disintegrate. So there may be a bit of magic by association going on with relation to teeth.

LORE

Hercules is sometimes depicted wearing a crown of henbane. According to Pliny, Hercules discovered henbane while he was in Hades capturing Cerberus, the three-headed guard dog of the Underworld. Hercules had been initiated into the Eleusinian Mysteries to enable him to journey safely to the Underworld and return alive as part of his twelfth labor. Henbane's associations with Hercules's journey into the Underworld, as well as this herb's medicinal affinity for bone issues like toothache, are indicators of its connection to witchcraft, which has often had need of working with the Underworld and with bones.

Saturn, who rules henbane, is associated, not only with the Underworld but also with the underground—a place where bones often end up—and with all the wealth that it produces through agriculture or mining. From mining, it is not a huge leap to metalworking, a clearly Saturnian craft.

In some mythologies, humans were taught metalworking by angels from the heavens above. In Greek mythology, by contrast, knowledge of that skill came from Hercules—a half-human, half-divine being who traveled between this world and the Underworld, who had conversation with the inexorable and implacable Hades, and who lived to tell about it. Hercules's henbane crown is the symbol of his ability to travel to the Underworld and return in triumph. Instead of bringing knowledge from the heavens above, he brought it from below, from the place beyond death.

Hercules's henbane crown is a real contrast, however, to the henbane crowns of the dead who wandered the Underworld in Greek mythology. The function of their crowns was to cause them to forget their lives—perhaps so that they would not try to return and haunt or attack the living. Those who remained behind in the world of the living also decorated the tombs of the dead with henbane. This may have been partly as a protective measure—the dead cannot return if they cannot remember who they were—but it may also have served symbolically as a help for the living to forget their loss.

The important concepts for us here are forgetting and henbane's connection to the dead. We will see how these two threads are woven through the fabric of henbane's spirit. Keep in mind as well the difference between the effects of Hercules's henbane crown and the henbane crowns of the dead. Hercules did not forget who he was or his journey to the Underworld. His crown is one of action, determination, and triumph. By contrast, those of the dead who aimlessly wandered the shores of the Styx with no idea who they were certainly did not convey determination or action.

Perhaps one indication of what is different about Hercules is that, when he went to the Underworld, he asked Hades if he could take Cerberus, instead of just seizing the three-headed dog. Hades gave his permission with one condition—that Hercules could use no weapons, no iron, and none of the products of his own skill or craft.

Contrast what happens to Hercules to what happens to the two men he meets in the Underworld who approached Hades in an arrogant way. They didn't survive the trip.

These different results illuminate ways of behaving with henbane's plant spirit, although it is in no way as inexorable or implacable as Hades. If you approach henbane with an active goal in mind—sensibly and with humility—your experience will be far different from those who just want to wander around the shores of the Styx (i.e., get high) or who approach this plant spirit with arrogance. I think this is the case with any plant spirit, but henbane is a witching herb that can be physically and mentally dangerous—although certainly less so than datura or belladonna.

Forgetting

"Twilight sleep," an anesthetic once used during childbirth, was created by combining morphine with alkaloids like scopolamine or hyoscine. It became the boon of upper-class women in the Victorian period. The peculiarity of Twilight Sleep was that it not only dulled pain but also caused the person to forget having experienced it. Patients given Twilight Sleep were kept blindfolded in a dark room, with cotton balls in their ears. After an initial injection of both morphine and scopolamine or hyoscine, they were given repeated injections of scopolamine alone until they were unable to remember the answer to a specific question that they could answer properly at the beginning of the treatment.

This alkaloid, present in varying amounts in the plants we call the Weird Sisters—datura, mandrake, belladonna, and henbane—was also used as part of a flying ointment. When it was, memories of the experience (hallucination) may well have been obliterated, especially if the ointment were taking advantage of the interaction between morphine and tropane alkaloids—and it does seem that some flying ointments were designed to do precisely that. Perhaps henbane was incorporated into these ointments for its numbing properties, which minimized distraction when engaging in astral work.

Henbane fumes were inhaled by flagellants (Christian religious people who used the pain of self-flagellation for spiritual purposes) before a procession. This may have been to encourage hallucinations that could be interpreted as mystical experiences, or it could have been intended to help them bear the pain they inflicted upon themselves. If its purpose was to take advantage of numbness to the body's signals, then the forgetting of the material self could allow the nonmaterial self to extricate itself from the material and travel. This, however, contradicts claims that the flagellants achieved ecstasy through pain; if you don't feel the pain, you cannot attain ecstasy from it.

Henbane is not an ecstatic herb. So if the flagellants did experience ecstasy, it was not through their use of henbane. Rather than ecstasy, perhaps what they experienced was a vision of the Christian Hell, one where pain figures more as symbol than sensation. In other words, physical pain is transformed into spiritual pain—and again, there may well be a connection to the Underworld.

≋ The Third Degree ≋

The opposite of forgetting is remembering. In 1922, Dr. House (yes, really) developed scopolamine, one of the primary alkaloids in henbane, as a truth serum. He considered this a humane alternative to the Third Degree—better known as beating someone until they confess. House found that scopolamine could help an amnesiac remember what had been blocked. So henbane can provide a kind of gateway between remembering and forgetting—something like the portal between this world and the Underworld. This is interesting when we consider the difference between the henbane crown of Hercules and those of the dead on the shores of the Styx.

One problem with the incorporation of henbane into flying ointments is the possibility that people using the ointments will forget what they saw on a flight. Yet from all reports, European witches of the Early Modern period—who are the ones we think of today as the quintessential witches—*did* remember what they experienced during their night flights. Maybe they were not actually using alkaloids when they flew, but instead had learned the process of flying from these alkaloids. Henbane was, after all, being used medicinally at this time, so people would have been familiar with its effects.

To me, the descriptions of witch's flights that come down to us sound more like the effects of mugwort than those of henbane. Mugwort dreams are busy dreams, full of many actors and almost feverish detail. Crowd scenes seem to be frequent in them. Henbane may also have been involved in initiations. If so, then it is not what alkaloids show us that is important. What's important is that they show us how to "get there"—and that a "there" actually exists. Who among us, having been shown the way to some destination in the material world, has not eventually learned how to get there without directions, without aid?

The Cauldron

It is said that what is poured into the cauldron of the skull will be transformed. But forgetting transforms us as well. It is thus the equivalent of the witch's cauldron, beyond or within which the transformation from knowledge to action occurs. Knowledge is poured in and action on the material plane results, just as Hercules learned from the Eleusinian Mysteries and then was able to travel to the Underworld and complete his task.

The physical form of the henbane plant can be seen as an indicator of the nature of its spirit: As below, so above. Remember how the henbane calyces (plural for calyx) were thought to resemble teeth—their points representing the roots and the bottom of the rounded pod representing the crown. Now consider how a henbane seed pod has a lid that contains and protects the seeds until they are fully ripe and ready to be spilled out, sown by the wind. This pod closely resembles a cauldron. Here we find connections between death and rebirth—that is, the return from the Underworld—in the mythology of those parts of Europe where henbane plays an important role in witchcraft. Think of the lids on the seed cauldrons and how they hide the seeds, which are later revealed in their thousands. Similarly, the cauldron symbolizes the womb and regeneration. As such, it represents mystery.

The cauldron—a dry, nonfleshy womb—is usually associated with the elements of both Fire and Water, which may be beneath or within the vessel. The cauldron serves as a boundary between these two elements. What is poured into it is transformed and becomes unrecognizable. Pollen becomes seeds, which become plants, just as incense in the witch's cauldron becomes smoke—the food of angels and the clothing of spirits. The transformation of henbane's pollen into seeds resembles dream material that, although forgotten, is turned into actions.

The cauldron that serves as the location for incense fits nicely with henbane, not only because of the shape of the seed pods but also because of henbane's apparent historical use as a fume intended to stimulate prophecy. It is also appropriate because of how, in contemporary magical practices, the use of a smoke is often connected with the feeding, calling, or clothing of spirits.

Like henbane, cauldrons are connected to death and the Underworld in myth. In fact, cauldrons are often found in ceremonial burial sites in Europe. In Welsh myth, cauldrons were associated with death. These mythic cauldrons could regenerate the dead, but left them unable to speak. This is interesting, because memories are generally transmitted through speech, especially in those eras and regions lacking widespread literacy. Moreover, we've seen how memory of experiences with henbane can be erased, as with Twilight Sleep.

....

≡ Bloody Cauldrons ≡

One ancient Greek historian recorded how a northern European tribe used a cauldron to collect the blood of prisoners of war who had been slaughtered as part of a divination ritual.

....

In prehistoric Europe, cauldrons were often filled with things like metalwork and then placed in living waters—rivers, lakes, or swamps—apparently as a kind of offering. From prehistoric times through the Iron Age in Britain and Europe, cauldrons were put into burial sites in various areas. It is only after the beginning of the Middle Ages in these regions that cauldrons seem to lose their associations with death and regeneration. Perhaps the connection between henbane and cauldrons was preserved in folk magic or witchcraft. The cauldron-like shape of henbane pods is certainly striking to anyone who recognizes or recalls cauldrons as an important cultural symbol of death and regeneration.

Prophecy and Divination

Europeans and North Americans tend to treat alkaloid-containing plants as if they were drugs. This, in my opinion, is a mistake—and not only in terms of what I believe witches did historically. This misconception creates unnecessary issues regarding how to approach the spirits of these plants—spirits will not be commanded any more than Hades can be.

Similar issues have been raised around the nature of the fume used by the Oracle of Delphi. It has been suggested that the hallucinogenic vapors utilized by the oracle at Delphi were produced by henbane, jimsonweed, or mandrake. However, I think that the belief that the fumes at Delphi possessed verifiable psychoactive content betrays a fundamentally materialist prejudice that favors science and negates the actuality of the spiritual and of magic. This ideology—the assumption that the cause of prophecy must, of course, be material and discoverable through materialist, scientific methods—guarantees the belief that, from its earliest days, the Oracle of Delphi was not ecstatic but merely high. It suggests that prophecy is the result of alkaloidal fumes and brain fog, not of divine madness. The conclusion follows that neither divine madness nor magic exist; they are simply the product of a chemical reaction in the brain.

In other words, simply raising the question of what was in the smoke at Delphi is to conclude from the start that the divine was *not* in that smoke. But consider this: What if the smoke's function was purely decorative or intended to blur the image of the oracle herself, to erase her distracting humanity, allowing seekers to be more open to the divinity of her message?

Let's now turn this same approach to the use of henbane in witchcraft. What if henbane's involvement is not as a psychoactive substance at all but instead as a purely magical one? If we insist on the reality of henbane-containing flying ointments as an "explanation" for flying to the Sabbat, do we not from the outset deny the reality of magic? In my opinion, the assumption that alkaloids are responsible for visions of the Sabbat represents the pernicious encroachment of the ideology of science into every modern human endeavor.

So again I ask: Why bother with the heavy toll of unpleasant physical effects caused by some alkaloids when the spirit of the plant is right there for you to access with no unpleasant effects at all? Focusing on an alkaloid as a gateway to a plant spirit makes that chemical analogous to the priest in Catholicism who controls access to sacraments. Why not go directly to the spirit itself?

Because the presence of the plant spirit cannot be commanded, that's why. It will either come or not, and in its own time. It may take years before it turns up, no matter how you conjure it. As mortals, we're impatient and want contact *now*; when we call, someone had better pick up the phone. Moreover, many of us are not in a position to facilitate the process by growing our own plants.

Water Magic

The Oracle of Delphi had a strong connection to water. Plutarch said that the oracle was powered, more or less, by something that arose from the waters of the spring of Kerna. In fact, a number of the oracles in ancient Greece were associated with water, especially with springs. Apollo, among the reigning deities of Delphi, has his own connections with water. These links may shed some light on why henbane, a Saturnian plant associated with the fire festival of Beltane, also has associations with water.

The Saturnian stream of energy is associated with dryness. Henbane definitely likes dry conditions and is itself drying to the human body. However, henbane also has a peculiar relationship to water. For instance, this herb not only has hairs for water collection but also has played a part in Water magic, especially in the raising of storms by witches.

The *Libri Poenitentiales*, books that were used by local priests in England, Ireland, and Germany to describe various sins and outline their recommended penances, are a wonderful source of information about pagan practices that the Church was attempting either to stamp out or to incorporate. One of these books, *The Corrector and Physician of Burchard of Worms* (circa 1008–1012 CE), describes the following German folk ritual involving henbane intended to provoke a rain storm.

During drought, women chose a group of girls, one of whom acted as the leader. This girl was stripped and led out of the village. The women had her dig up a henbane plant with the little finger of her right hand—perhaps because this is a magical, not a mundane, way of digging something up. The plant was then tied to a string, which was in turn tied to the little toe of the girl's right foot. With the other girls helping and holding unidentified "twigs," the young leader dragged the henbane to a stream and threw it in. The girls then sprinkled her with water and walked her back to town in her own footsteps.

Those of us who have been involved with witchcraft for a while recognize the basic structure of this ritual as being similar to the harvesting of vervain and the digging up of a mandrake plant. Instead of the dog traditionally used to uproot the mandrake, the henbane ritual requires a girl—although, given that the dog in the mandrake ritual may well have originally been a sacrifice, one wonders about the girl! I wonder whether an older practice that is associated with working magically with plants lies behind these rituals, or whether they are all just the products of imaginative writers. Leaving aside the details of the ritual, however, the fact remains that henbane is still associated with raising storms and is literally connected to water in this ritual.

The German ritual for causing a storm is a bit involved and represents the action of a community. This may have been a community of witches, but it sounds more as if the people involved were simply ordinary citizens of a drought-stricken town. Yet even now, there are individual witches who use henbane to evoke storms, and storm raising was traditionally believed to be among the destructive talents of European witches. It is interesting that the covers of the cauldrons that contain the seeds on henbane are typically torn off by the wind during storms, a fact that the plant depends upon to spread its seed.

So why is a drying, Saturnian plant connected in this way to Water? I believe it's through its affiliation with Beltane.

Henbelle, Beltane, and Belenos

Some say that "henbelle," one of the old common names of henbane, derives from a reference to the bell-shaped calyces—what I call cauldrons. But there's another possible root for the "bell" of "henbelle." Another rather roundabout connection between henbane and Delphi is through henbane's association with the god Belenos, patron of the northern Italian town of Aquileia. When the town was attacked, Belenus floated above it and helped defend it in the same way that Apollo defended Delphi when it was attacked. Right away, we see a resemblance between the name of the god who is referenced in the word "henbelle" and Apollo, god of the sun and, by extension, fire.

Some connected the name Belenus with the names of henbane, which include *belenuntia* (Gaulish), *beleno* (Spanish), *belisa* (Gallo-Roman), and *Bilsenkraut* (German). A Latin name for henbane is Appolinaris, which, of course, refers to Apollo. This is made explicit in one of the common names for henbane, Apollo's herb.

Some say that the root "bel" that appears in "henbelle" and "Belenus" in fact means "white." But why would the color white be connected to henbane, which is generally called "black"? Linguist Edgar C. Polome, who was investigating the various appearances of the root word "bil"—such as in "bilsenkraut"—claims that nothing in the appearance of the henbane plant itself merits the word white. Its flowers are not white, and it doesn't have white sap. The only connection must therefore be from some other meaning of white, perhaps a ritual use associated with the solar god Belenus, and a healing deity like Apollo.

In his book, *The Encyclopedia of Psychoactive Plants*, German author Christian Ratsch claims that white henbane (*Hyoscyamus albus*), whose flowers do not have the purple veining of black henbane, was the plant used in ancient southern Europe for prophecy. If this is true, then perhaps the "bil" of "bilsenkraut" actually indicates white henbane as the proper ingredient, not black. This would explain using the word "white" in connection with henbane as a reference to *Hyoscyamus albus*, which in the past would not necessarily have been seen as a species separate from what we today call black henbane (*H. niger*). In the plant world, if a plant is defined as "black," it is safe to assume that there are other colors of that plant with which it contrasts—black spruce, blue spruce; black pine, white pine; black henbane, white henbane.

Although white henbane's flowers are not white, they are definitely pale yellow, which is a typical Beltane herb color. Most important of all, henbane begins blooming around Beltane. This seems to provide a lot of evidence that the real ritual version of henbane is not black henbane, but white. I do advise that witches try growing and working with white henbane as well as black, and allow their experience to determine which version of this plant is more helpful in magic. However, I will not argue with years of tradition working with black henbane. It is a powerful spiritual plant; no two ways about it.

Just as the fundamental symbol of henbane is the cauldron, the core concept of henbane is mystery. This fits, not only with henbane's historic use at Delphi but also with the mystery of the cauldron and its association with Water, which hides what is below. Perhaps the fact that henbane's foliage is often glaucous and has hairs is connected to the Water element as well, since hairs often appear on plants that are in environments where water is not common. Hairs act to concentrate the dew (the Secret Fire) that falls on the plant, allowing it to drip off onto the soil around it. This is different from plants with a more boat-shaped leaf where the dew collects and then evaporates. Such plants are more often found in watery environments. Henbane prefers dry, rocky places.

The concept of mystery also fits with henbane, because one easily forgets what is learned under the influence of this herb. However, "forgetting" may be an essential part of the acquisition of witchcraft skills. It may not be important that witches remember in their waking minds what they saw while under the influence of the Weird Sisters.

PRACTICE

Henbane has been part of the U. S. Pharmacopoeia since that listing began in 1820. It was more frequently used in medicine than belladonna or even mandrake, because it is more predictable than belladonna and not as strong as the other plants that contain this group of alkaloids. A typical 19th-century medicine employing henbane was used as a sedative (five drops of a mixture that was 1 part fresh leaves to 10 parts 70 percent alcohol, tinctured for ten to fourteen days).

Fresh henbane leaves have been used as a fomentation or bruised and applied to the body for nervous headache and various disorders like gout, nerve pain, and rheumatism.

....

☠ *Warning: Henbane is toxic. It contains lesser quantities of the same alkaloids contained in the other Weird Sisters. Unlike them, it has been used medicinally in many cultures all over the world, which seems to imply that it is more predictable in its action than, say, belladonna. But that does not imply that it's safe. It's a good idea to wear gloves when handling the plant. Just smelling the flowers can cause headaches, a common symptom of the action of this alkaloid group.*

Remember that every person is different, and every henbane plant is different. Alkaloid levels vary due to the growing environment of the plant. Some claim you can measure the alkaloid level of a plant using their seeds. But seed size varies greatly from plant to plant due to growing conditions, as well. Best to use caution when working with henbane.

....

Anesthetics made from herbs were used in southern Europe, especially before the advent of general anesthesia. Recipes for these anesthetics were often created by monks—for instance, one from a Benedictine monastery in southern Italy from circa 800 CE that combined opium, henbane, mulberry juice, lettuce, hemlock, mandrake, and ivy.

These natural anesthetics were apparently not used in the British Isles, but in medieval English manuscripts of household remedies and methods from the 12th to the 15th centuries, an anesthetic drink called "dwale" is described. Over fifty recipes for dwale have been identified, one of which is given below from Anthony Carter's "Dwale: An Anaesthetic from Old England." The "spoon" referred to here is probably a Troy spoon, equal to 11.6 ml.

Dwale

3 spoons of bile from a boar for a man or a sow for a woman

3 spoons hemlock juice

3 spoons bryony ("wild neep")

3 spoons lettuce

3 spoons "pape" (P. somniferum)

3 spoons henbane

3 spoon eysyl (vinegar). [15]

These ingredients were mixed, boiled a little, and kept in a well-stoppered glass bottle until needed. Three spoons of it were mixed into a "potel" of wine (2.276 l), which patients drank from while seated with their backs to a good fire until they fell asleep. Whatever surgery was necessary was then carried out without patients feeling pain. They eventually were awakened by washing their temples and cheekbones with vinegar and salt.

Housewives knew of this dwale remedy and used it on their own families. Bile was not usually used in pharmacy at the time, but it was used outside of it to emulsify fat. This recipe contains no fat, which makes me wonder whether this is actually a "translation" of an ointment version of this anesthetic. The name of this anesthetic is interesting, because dwale is also among the names for belladonna.

Bryony may well be included in this recipe as a substitute for mandrake, which would be another bit of evidence that this is a translated ointment recipe. Mandrake's hyoscine, which causes hallucinations as well as drowsiness, crosses the blood-brain barrier, but the atropine of henbane does not.

Flying Ointments

All this medicinal information puts a lot of focus on the physiological functions of the alkaloids present in henbane and in some other herbs used in witchcraft, like belladonna, datura, and mandrake. This begs the same important question that we have asked in other contexts: Are alkaloids necessary if a plant spirit is willing to work with you directly, without any chemical mediation? I question whether flying ointments—alkaloidal concoctions used specifically for gathering with other witches at a Sabbat—ever truly existed. And when I say "flying ointments," I mean an ointment specifically concocted for the purpose of flying to the Sabbat.

Did sensationalist witch hunters and historians simply invent these things? And did latter-day witches go along with them in their attempts to resurrect forgotten witchcraft knowledge? Or were "flying ointments" simply the same ointments that would have been compounded and used in any well-ordered European household as an aid to minor surgeries?

I tend to think this was the case and that no such things as flying ointments ever existed. The idea of a specially made ointment that allowed witches to fly to the Sabbat fits with other assertions by non-witches regarding the activities of witches—for example, that they kill babies for sport or make ointments from baby fat. These accusations may perhaps be a distortion of the identification of witches with midwives, who may actually have provided abortion services.

Poppets, Pods, and Incense

You can keep a particular individual away by stuffing a poppet with henbane leaves and putting it where the trespass most commonly occurs outside. This use is based on a 15th-century folk method for keeping rabbits out of the garden.

After the lids have come off the henbane pod cauldrons and you have harvested the seeds, the pods themselves can be used for magical purposes. They are wonderful as containers for incense, especially that of a Saturnian nature, or as magical tools. It is easier to remove the pods from the stalk with pruning shears than with scissors, although a craft knife can also work. The pods are strongly attached to the stalk and won't just snap off. Henbane pods also make good containers for binding spells. Write your binding spell on a small scrap of tissue paper, roll it up, and insert it into a pod. Then plug the pod with a little bit of black wool yarn, which has ancient associations with Saturnian deities like Hades.

A pod is also an excellent candidate for separating two lovers, since the interior of the pod is divided in two. Saturnian plants are often involved in binding, which can mean binding *away* as easily as binding together. For binding apart, add some iron filings or brick dust or anything red for Mars (anti-Venus) strength. Just as in ancient times, when love spells or curses were written on lead plates (lead being Saturn's metal) and thrown into wells—close to the Underworld, the abode of Hekate—henbane pods that contain spellwork can be tossed into holes in the ground. Remember that cauldrons were historically filled with ceremonial metalwork and then thrown into lakes. Add iron filings to the work you insert into henbane's small cauldron and then throw the pod into a bog or lake.

Dried henbane herb or its seeds are good for making incense to summon angels or demons, as well as for helping spirits to manifest themselves in its smoke. This is often mentioned in the grimoires. Keep a watch on popping seeds if you do this, because they tend to fly out of the incense container. And be sure to burn the herb outside, because you may be sensitive to the smoke, which was once used to dull tooth pain—so you know it does have some alkaloidal action.

HENBANE IN THE GARDEN

Some black henbane seeds produce an annual plant that flowers the first year and then dies; others produce a biennial that forms a rosette of leaves the first year and flowers the second. There's no way to tell which one a seed will produce. The biennial form is more common and hardier in cold environments; it can grow at elevations up to 11,000 feet.

I have had best success with germinating henbane using soaking. Put the seeds in a small jar and fill it with cold water. Keep it in the refrigerator for two weeks, changing the water each day. Then plant the seeds in your seed medium. They will germinate in two weeks at room temperature. They germinate best after the Winter Solstice.

Once they get their true leaves, you can transplant these seedlings outside to a sheltered location for hardening off. Henbane likes a dry soil on the alkaline side; a full-sun area next to a concrete wall is great. I have also grown it very successfully in pots. Henbane is extraordinarily prolific, however, which is what renders it a "weed" to monocultural farming. So be careful where you place it so as not to endanger your other plantings.

With henbane, belladonna, and mandrake, top-dressing plants in pots with some chick grit (finely crushed granite sold in farm supply stores) really helps to produce bigger, healthier plants. They do tend to flop over when they get larger, because the pods weigh more than the leaves. Henbane gets two to three feet (60–90 cm) tall and should be spaced three feet (90 cm) apart (or grow them in twelve-inch pots). The purple-veined flowers appear in summer and the plant keeps pumping out flowers and pods until it is killed by a hard freeze. If you want to try growing it, white henbane tends to be on the short side, about two feet tall.

Slugs enjoy eating the leaves of any kind of henbane. If you have this problem, I recommend using Slug-Go, which is approved for organic use and comes in small pellets you can sprinkle right around the plant. The biggest issue with henbane is the Colorado potato beetle, which attacks many members of the nightshade family, but absolutely loves henbane. If you see the colorful yellow-and-black striped beetles, smash them with your fingers. But it's their babies that decimate and can kill henbane with their ravenous appetites. They are small dark grubs that hang on to the underside of the leaves in a row and just eat the leaves down to nothing. The only thing I have found that works on them is spinosad. This is the weapon of mass destruction of the organic gardening world. A single application seems to be sufficient and has saved my henbane more than once.

The best time to harvest this herb is when it's flowering. You may want to collect it before the pods form, because they are quite difficult to dry well, being thick and crammed with seeds. If you want to save seed, harvest the pods before the capsules open and hang them upside down in a paper bag to collect the seed. I actually leave the pods on the plant until the whole branch is brown, but the cauldron tops are still on. Then I cut the branches and pop open the cauldrons to release the seeds.

CHAPTER FOURTEEN

BELLADONNA

The Evil Eye

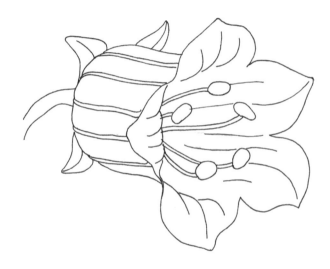

B elladonna is the most problematic herb on the Poison Path that is part of the witch's way. Even though datura (thornapple) can be quite brutal, that brutality is more or less expected—it does not arise out of meanness as much as out of the plant spirit's ignorance of its own strength and the flimsiness of mortals. The same cannot be said of belladonna.

Belladonna's brutality feels more like pure malice. For that reason, I associate this plant with the Evil Eye and with the malefic works of witchcraft that can indeed sometimes—without any help from a rede or karma or anything else—come back to bite witches just because they're there.

One way that poisonous plants warn us not to eat them is by producing substances that we interpret as very bitter. We have co-evolved with this indicator; if something tastes extremely bitter, we usually spit it out. Although some people—like me!—relish a certain amount of bitterness, like that of radicchio or endive, for instance, many others don't consider bitter things to be tasty or even edible.

In the past, Europeans often ate bitter herbs in the spring as a kind of tonic. I think that, as this practice has fallen away—in keeping with the fact that few of us now have kitchen gardens where those bitter herbs appear in early spring—we have gotten farther from our ability to tolerate alkaloids, which typically taste bitter. Perhaps one reason why we could consume or use very poisonous plants like monkshood or poison hemlock in the past is that we had a much greater tolerance for alkaloids. As we became more urbanized, we gradually lost that tolerance, much as a person who is constantly protected from allergens has a very intense allergic reaction when exposed to even small amounts of them. If our ancestors were regularly ingesting small amounts of alkaloids, they would have been able to tolerate larger amounts than we ever could today.

Belladonna is the exception, however. Even though this plant has played a role in pharmacy virtually wherever it occurs, it has never had the place of its sister, henbane. For one thing, belladonna has a lot higher alkaloid content than henbane does. But in my opinion, the more important reason is that belladonna is highly unpredictable in a way that the other Weird Sisters (henbane, datura, and mandrake) are not. Material harvested from the same belladonna plant and consumed in the same quantity by the same person cannot be depended upon to act in the same way. It is precisely this unpredictability that has kept belladonna from having a greater role in pharmacy.

LORE

But what about belladonna's role in witchcraft? Over and over, we see belladonna being prized in witchcraft. Perhaps it is precisely its unpredictability that has made it so attractive to witches. And yet, most practitioners probably aren't even aware of that aspect of this herb, especially today.

One possibility is that, as with so many other plants that are popularly associated with witches, this is just a manifestation of popular culture's historical idea of witches and witchcraft—a characterization that witches have in turn picked up and held close as some kind of fact, although perhaps a false one. We can find a parallel in how, having seen made-up depictions in movies of how the Mafia supposedly had some kind of blood rite to mark the acceptance of an individual into organized crime, the real Mafia actually began to perform this blood rite, and even claimed that they had always done so. They recognized it as having come down from ancient times, rather than from the imagination of a screenwriter. In the same way, if witches are paired with plants and animals considered obnoxious by the general populace, they may come to hold those obnoxious plants and animals dear and prize them as witchy when, in fact, they are not.

This is also seen in names that pair the devil with various nasty things. And, of course, European witches also came to be associated with the devil. Perhaps the connection between belladonna and witchcraft derives originally from outside the Craft and is not in any way indicative of any fundamental truths about it. Perhaps its spirit does not offer any insight to a witch that cannot be obtained in better ways and in greater quantity from another plant spirit.

I think, however, that the connection between belladonna and witchcraft is a valid one. What that means for us, however, is not obvious. In fact, I think a large part of the importance of belladonna in witchcraft is completely occult or hidden. Let's examine it closely, beginning with the basic structure of its stalk.

The Crooked Path

Each belladonna branch shoots to the opposite side of the stalk from the previous branch in a pattern that, in the plant world, is called "alternating." At the end of each branch, the plant produces buds that become flowers that will become fruits. Each branch is fruitful. The main stalk, however, is interesting because, unlike a lot of plants that just grow a straight stalk from which the branches emerge, belladonna's stalk bends back and forth. In other words, it is crooked, and very symmetrically crooked, so that neither side is favored. Both sides have the same number of flowers and fruits. In the context of witchcraft, this recalls the Crooked Path.

When viewed from above, the belladonna plant sends out branches in five equidistant directions. This shape is very striking, but we have to look at the plant from above to see it. The very same five-pointed star or pentagram shape is made by the calyx around the berry. Belladonna calyces start out with their five fingers cupping the flower. They gradually fatten, toughen, and pull back into a star shape holding the fruit, gaining a blood-colored speckling in the process. The ripe fruit detaches itself from the calyx and falls to the ground, but the starry calyces remain on the plant. The flower also has five scallops at the end. Five is a fairly common number for petals—the mandrake flower has five petals—but not that many plants send their branches out in five directions.

The Evil Eye

Another way to look at the strong connection between belladonna and witchcraft is to consider that belladonna represents malice or the Evil Eye. Belladonna berries are notable for how shiny they are. Lots of other black berries have a more satiny shine or dull gleam, but belladonna berries seem unique in their shiny blackness. It is precisely this shine that attracts children and even adults and entices them into eating the poisonous fruit.

There is another eye connection with belladonna. An old story without a scrap of evidence to support it tells how young ladies in Italy once used belladonna to dilate their eyes, which was perceived as making them more beautiful. This story, whether apocryphal or not, does connect with how seductive belladonna berries can be.

Perhaps it was not Italian ladies who dolled up their eyes in this way, but belladonna itself, tempting us with the shiny black eyes of its berries. In yet another example of how we cannot watch animals to determine whether a plant is safe to consume, these berries are heartily eaten by chipmunks without the slightest problem. People who have eaten them and lived to tell about it report that they actually taste somewhat sweet—in other words, they are not bitter, as one would expect from a poisonous, alkaloid-heavy fruit. It is as if belladonna tempts us with its berries, cajoling us to eat them, in order to then wreak havoc on our bodies. This plant just does not play fair. Its attractive berries aren't even bitter like the high-alkaloid products of other plants, which would make us spit them out.

Likewise, the eerily attractive flowers of belladonna actually have a slightly sweet smell, as opposed to those of henbane, which do not smell good at all. Yet a big whiff of the scent of belladonna's flowers can cause an instant headache. Talk about tricksy!

I think this tricksiness is a key quality of this plant and is fundamental to why belladonna is legitimately considered a part of witchcraft. Belladonna's unpredictability is like a curse that comes at you from out of nowhere. It falls out of the sky like a hex. Of course, in order to accept that idea, we first have to admit that cursing has always been a part of witchcraft.

The Ambiguity of Witches

Witches are frequently viewed by their neighbors as being scarily ambiguous. They can use their powers to help you find your lost cloak, but they can also dry up your cow's milk. This ambiguity is part of the Crooked Path that witches typically walk. The ambiguity

that folks feel about witches is reflected in how we feel about belladonna. It can be a painkiller, or it can kill you—and in a way that
makes an overdose of poppy look like a fun time. Belladonna, like
datura, is notorious for the horrific nature of the hallucinations it
causes when it is ingested in large amounts.

What do these physical characteristics tell us about the nature of
the spirit belladonna represents? That it does not respect the contract
that most plants make with us humans. Its sweet berries and sweet
flowers don't indicate a friend; they mask danger. Belladonna can be
depended on only to be unpredictable and to trick us into believing
that it is not harmful.

In some ways, this resembles how many people perceive witches.
We are often thought to be tricksy, because we can heal or hex, help
or curse. I think belladonna represents something extremely complex
about the nature of witches—something that many witches recognize, if only on a subconscious level. We find ourselves attracted to
belladonna without really knowing why.

Think about it. How many witchy formulae involve belladonna?
Not many. It's rare, even in flying ointments. Yet belladonna lingers
in the witch's world, enticing us with its gleaming berries, shining
with the blackness of the depths. It feels as if the plant is holding a
lot of knowledge in those depths, if only we could get to it.

Belladonna has several fundamental qualities for witchcraft:
unpredictability, ambiguity, trickiness, and as an indicator of the
Crooked Path. These qualities can be funneled into the concept
of malice, an essential characteristic of Belladonna Spirit. We can
respect something that is dangerous, like a tiger, and simultaneously
realize that tigers don't eat human beings out of any malice. They
may just happen to be hungry when a human is available. We know
there are dangers in our world, and we accept them. Generally, however, those dangers find ways to warn us off—with garish patterns,
spines, bad smells, or bitter tastes.

However, belladonna exempts itself from warning and steps into
the space of deliberately messing with us, betraying an intelligence

that materialists like to deny to the plant world. Like the witch in Hansel and Gretel who entices the children with her gingerbread house—because why else did she create it except as a trap?—and then shoves them into the oven, belladonna entices us with its luscious berries and then shoves us into the hell of its ferocious hallucinations. It can kill you, but even that's not dependable—today, three berries will kill you; tomorrow, it may take fifteen. That sounds like malice to me—which, in some societies, is the very definition of witchcraft.

I once created an image of the spirit Samael, the consort of Lilith, in the scheme of the *klippot* (husks or shells that contain a spark of the divine). Samael serves as an entryway to the Other Side; he is the *Malkuth* (Foundation, material manifestation) of the Klippotic Tree, the dark duplicate of the Kabbalistic Tree of Life. Samael appears as the snake in the Hebrew Bible's story of Adam and Eve; he is described as having many eyes. While drawing this image, I was struck, not only by how the berries of belladonna resemble the many eyes of Samael but also by how its crooked stalk is like the Crooked Path, like the shape of the Klippotic Tree. I also felt that the luscious but poisonous belladonna berry was a match for the eyes of Samael. Not only is Samael the snake in the garden; the tree from which he slithers is the Witch's Tree.

You could say that the tricksiness of belladonna is like the tricksiness of cursing. A curse may not have any effect on karma, or the Law of Three-fold Return, or any other accoutrements of the Just World Fallacy—the belief that, if you behave in an ethical way, you will never come to harm; that bad is eventually punished and good eventually rewarded. In fact, if this were true, we would not need magic. But it may also indicate that, when cursing, you should keep a sharp eye out for back-splatter.

When hexing, you must be exceedingly cautious. When someone approaches a witch in search of a curse, the witch hears only that person's side of the story, which may not always reflect the reality of the situation. The witch may read the story against the grain, so to speak, accounting for what may not have been said. But belladonna reminds us that a situation may be completely different in essence from what is being represented to us—that a story of being oppressed and harassed may actually mask a story of oppressing and harassing someone else. Moreover, belladonna teaches that the curse may deliver what we expect (the innocuous-tasting berry) or be far more deadly (the potentially lethal level of alkaloids). You may think you are shooting a bullet, only to discover that you have launched a missile.

Belladonna, tricksy and malefic as it is, has something very fundamental to teach us or remind us: that ambiguity is the essential nature of the witch. What may appear as tricksiness or malice to others is, to a witch, simply the Crooked Path. But as witches, we live in this world, not the Other, and so must deal with the consequences of being ambiguous in a culture that craves certainty and imposes limits and delineations on everything and everyone.

Ambiguity is always going to fall outside the lines of our cultures, because ambiguity undercuts the sanctity of meaning. Without order, meaning cannot exist. If someone is helping, but also hexing, we cannot "depend" on them to do one thing or the other, as we generally do expect of other folks. That can have very hazardous consequences for a witch, which may manifest in something as minor as being snubbed in the grocery store by a neighbor, to being harassed by threatening phone calls, or being fired from a job, or losing custody of children. In some societies, a witch can even be killed.

PRACTICE

The pull of witchcraft is strong—and rightly so. But the practice of witchcraft can be as dangerous as the gleam of a belladonna berry. It doesn't matter how many nice people appear on TV to talk about how witches just want to help people and worship friendly, happy nature gods. Many people don't believe that. And belladonna teaches us that they shouldn't—and that we should not forget that.

Here is a magical ink that can be crafted by infusing belladonna berries in vinegar.

Magick Ink

1. Put the berries in a clearly labeled jar and place it in the freezer overnight.

2. Take the berries out of the freezer and thaw, so that they break down and release their ink. Soak the thawed berries in 1 part white vinegar to 4 parts berries in a closed jar. (You can use the same jar you started with.) The vinegar should just cover the berries. You can put this in the sun to warm, but make sure to label it as poison if there is any chance that anyone will have access to it. And obviously keep it away from children, animals, and anyone unable to comprehend the warning label, especially teenagers or young men.

3. If the berries don't break down quickly enough, squash them with your hand. But make sure you wear a waterproof glove.

4. When the liquid looks good and dark, strain thoroughly in a baneful-dedicated strainer. (I advise storing equipment used for banefuls all together somewhere other than in the kitchen.) I like to start with a screen-type strainer, perhaps even using a piece of an old T-shirt or tea towel. First wet it with white vinegar, then wring the juice from the pulp. It's best to do this outside. Be careful not to get any on you; if you do, wash it off *immediately* with lots of soap. Strain one last time using a gold coffee strainer that is dedicated exclusively to baneful work. Store in a well-marked dark bottle in a dark place.

The ink will darken upon drying. It will be dark purple or purplish blue, but will gradually fade to brown. This ink is perfect for writing curse petitions, hexing sigils, and, of course, a sigil for Belladonna Spirit itself. Use a nib pen or paint brush, as it will clog a fountain pen. This ink still contains alkaloids, so it is crucial to label it well and never to allow it to come into contact with your skin.

Whole belladonna berries are hard to dry—they turn sticky—but you can dry a small amount of the pulp left over from ink-making on a piece of baking parchment in a dehydrator. Incorporate the dried pulp into a very potent incense dedicated to attack magic or war by combining it with Mars herbs like tobacco, peppers, myrrh, and perhaps a bit of well-boiled honey (bees are Martial insects). Grind the other ingredients with a mortar and pestle, then add the pulp and honey, if you're using it. Like all incense, it will improve with age, becoming less harsh. This incense should always and only be burned outside.

Belladonna leaves are wonderful additions to incense for hexing, binding, or attack. A little goes a long way, however. Burn all incenses that contain belladonna outside.

BELLADONNA IN THE GARDEN

Like the other Saturn plants mentioned in this book, belladonna's slow germination teaches us the worth of Saturnian slowness—that the reward that comes with delay can be much greater than that which comes immediately, as with an easily germinating annual. Belladonna seems to germinate more readily if the seeds are begun at the start of the waxing moon and after the Winter Solstice. Like some of its siblings, it seems to know that the days are getting longer. It is not that it will not germinate at all at other times of the year, but it does not germinate as readily.

Use the cold-water soaking method described for henbane seeds. Soak the seeds for two weeks in cold water in the fridge, changing the water daily. Then sow in typical planting medium, barely covering the seed. Like all the seeds discussed here, they don't like extreme heat—65°F (18°C) is a good temperature for them. Over half the seeds should germinate in two to four weeks once they are put in the soil. The rest of the seeds will eventually germinate, but it may take them a year or even two.

It is also possible to germinate belladonna seeds in a pot of soil that is left outside over the winter. Cover the pot loosely in plastic and keep it in full shade—no sun. Remember, this is a truly Saturnian plant that appreciates darkness.

Pot the seedlings once they have formed their true leaves. Then transplant them to a shaded area in the spring, once the danger of frost has passed. Belladonna likes soil that is "sweet"—that is, chalky or calcareous. You can add some gardening lime to your soil, grow the plants next to a concrete wall or cinder blocks, or top dress your pots with chick grit, as described for henbane. I've also found that belladonna very much appreciates a slow fertilizer like soymeal sprinkled over the bed right before or after the transplants are put in.

Since belladonna grows in open woodland in the wild, add plenty of organic matter to your soil. Composted leaves are great. The spot to which you transplant should not be dry, but it should not be sopping wet either. Belladonna dreams of the sun like an old vampire and will stretch toward its rays. But don't succumb to its begging to be moved to a sunny position. With anything more than just morning sun, belladonna will be injured and become pale and weak. Some think that the more sun belladonna is grown in, the more alkaloids it will make. That's true, but you will also have much less plant material. The plants will tend to be dried up, and I believe this fact accounts for the higher alkaloid content in specimens grown in sun. They are stressed.

Set your seedlings eighteen inches (45 cm) apart and make sure each plant has its own space. Be especially careful, as with other tropane-containing plants, not to grow it near nightshades that will be eaten or smoked, since its proximity will affect the alkaloid content of other plants. For instance, don't grow it near tomatoes, eggplant, or peppers. I have also found that it will sometimes kill plants grown near it, as it killed a rose bush I had growing in the same general area.

Belladonna can be grown in a good-sized pot and seems to really enjoy this, but don't try growing it inside. It won't be happy, and neither will you or your animals. This plant gives off chemicals that affect every living thing around it, either through allelopathy (destroying nearby plants through chemicals released into the soil) or through the volatilization of alkaloids from the leaves and flowers.

Belladonna is a perennial that spends the first year making leaves. If it's very happy, it may flower and fruit the first year. Generally speaking, however, the first year is reserved for establishing itself and absorbing energy rather than putting it out. The production of flowers and fruits requires a lot of energy. Young plants, however, often have larger leaves in general than plants that have gone through a winter. I've found that it's possible to get nice harvests of belladonna by growing it in pots and treating it like an annual. Top dressings of composted manure are very much appreciated.

The wonderful purplish-brown belladonna flowers that are beloved by witches have white stamens that look like little teeth. The flowers fall off when fertilized and berries form in their place. These begin as pale green and eventually become stained with purple. Then they plump and become a lustrous midnight purple.

....

☠ *Warning: It is when the berries are ripe that children are most attracted to this plant. Make sure to erect barriers around belladonna if children have free access to your yard. Impress upon them that the berries are not for eating, ever. Children have died from eating only a few, adults from eating a handful. All animals except a few rodents are susceptible to the toxins of the Weird Sisters and can be killed by them. Cats seem to ignore them because they smell bad. But dogs will eat anything, so always keep them away from any poisonous plants.*

....

If you let belladonna berries ripen, you will get a *lot* of seeds to propagate more plants, or you can just start more plants from cuttings of the tips of the stems. If you want to save the seeds, do the same as you would for a tomato plant, but be sure to wear gloves. Crush the fruits (not too brutally) and put them in some water. The seeds will fall to the bottom of the container and the fruit pieces will rise. You can skim off the fruit parts and end up with some pretty clean seeds by repeating this. Then spread the seeds on a plate (I like to use a paper plate) to dry. No need to put them in the sun.

Where winters are not too harsh, belladonna will winter over and become a much larger plant the second year, coming back from the roots. It can get up to three feet (.9 m) high in its first year, if it's started early enough and if it's happy. In the second year, however, it can grow to almost six feet (1.8 m). In my experience, it doesn't usually get quite that big, because it is competing with tree roots. Even so, it is not a small plant.

In terms of the alkaloidal strength of this plant, consider how it generally uses alkaloids as a defense against being eaten. It makes the most alkaloids in the parts of the plant that are most vulnerable at any given point. So in the fall, when the plant knows it will be depending on its root alone to get it through the winter, the root has the highest concentration of alkaloids. In the spring, the new leaves will have the most. When the berries are forming, the whole plant will have the highest amount of alkaloids because it requires a lot of energy—that of the entire plant, roots and leaves—to produce fruits and seeds.

The lowest alkaloid content for belladonna occurs when the plant is just beginning to flower. Leaves that have been subject to bug predation or mechanical damage can have double the amount of alkaloids, although it's not clear whether this doubling occurs in the whole plant or just in the predated leaves. Some people deliberately grow belladonna on a southwest slope to encourage a high alkaloid level. I think most witches prefer to create a place for belladonna where it will be happy and less stressed.

In wet years or climates, slugs can be a real problem. They seem to love eating the Weird Sisters and will strip the bark off the older stalks, which can kill the plant. I have often wondered if slugs do not get some kind of enjoyment from eating nightshades. I wonder the same thing about the Colorado potato beetle, whose babies love to chomp the leaves down to nothing. See chapters 2 and 13 for remedies to these issues.

Don't ever dry belladonna in the house. It may not kill you, but it will give you and your animals the worst headaches and constipation you have ever experienced. Wear gloves when harvesting the plant and dry it outside in a dedicated baneful herb dehydrator on the lowest setting. The stalks tend to be thick, so cut them up with a pruner before you dry them. You can even cut them in half lengthwise to help drying.

Belladonna roots can be very large if they come from plants that are more than a year old. This can make them very problematic for drying, because they tend to dry on the outside but rot on the inside since the moisture can't escape. If you dry them in a dehydrator, use the lowest heat. This can take weeks. Remember—keep the dehydrator outside when you are drying belladonna. I have also simply left the roots outside in a sheltered location (in my case, under the patio roof) to dry by weathering over the winter. The best thing to do if you want belladonna roots is to harvest first-year roots only. Of course, you can always preserve any root in 95 percent alcohol and then use the alcohol itself as a belladonna ingredient for incenses and inks. Just make sure it is labeled.

Despite belladonna's tricksiness, or maybe because of it, I have grown it every single year and have admired its deadly beauty. I hardly use it in spellwork, but there is just nothing else like those purple-brown flowers and those shiny black berries.

CHAPTER FIFTEEN

MANDRAKE

The Hanged Mannekin

In ancient times, mandrake root had many medicinal uses. Today it's primarily thought of as an aphrodisiac or as a treatment for infertility. This is based on the story told in Genesis 30:14–22, in which childless Rachel asks the very fertile Leah for the mandrakes— most probably the fruits, not the roots—that Leah's son has gath- ered. She promises that, in exchange, she will arrange for Jacob, their mutual husband, who prefers Rachel, to spend the night with Leah. Leah bears another son, and eventually Rachel gives birth to Joseph.

LORE

Many centuries later, we find British herbalist John Gerard (1545–1612) growing mandrakes in his garden for treating insomnia and infertility. He noted that, no matter how many he dug up, he never saw any that looked like the amulets sold for luck. Predictably, mandrakes were used to treat barrenness in Jewish traditional medicine. Sephardic women in Jerusalem either ate them or tied them around their bodies; Samaritan women of the 17th century put them under their beds. In his book *Theatrum Botanicum* (1640), herbalist John Parkinson says that women who want children should carry a mandrake fruit close to their person, which implies that it was not ingested but merely carried around. Mandrake fruits have been noted for their scent since ancient times. Carrying mandrake fruit in your pocket reminds me of the Tudor habit of carrying pocket melons for their scent. Perhaps that practice was originally based on carrying around mandrake fruits for fertility.

Mandrake and Aphrodite

Mandrake is also considered an aphrodisiac. The name in Hebrew, *dudaim,* is a combination of *daled-vav-daled* (which means "love," "carnal love," or "passion") and *ayim* (*aleph-yod-mem,* which means "terror"). According to the Song of Solomon 7:13(14), mandrake smells good, but once again, it's probably the fruits being described:

> *The mandrakes give forth fragrance;*
> *And at our doors are all manner of precious fruits,*
> *New and old,*
> *Which I have laid up for thee, O my beloved.*

The major chemical component in mandrake-fruit scent is esters, especially light ones, which also occur in apples and other fruits. The scent of mandrake fruit is often described as similar to an apple with a touch of clean sweat. Other mandrake scent constituents occur in guava, feijoa, papaya, mango, and passionfruit, but it also has sulphurous notes similar to onion, garlic, and cabbage just to add a little funk.

Renaissance Jewish physician Ovadia Sforno says that the mandrake fruit's apple-like scent excites men's passion, although this is not said of ordinary apples. So there has to be something more to the scent of mandrakes. Perhaps it excites the spirit rather than the body—the Talmud says that scent affects not the body but the soul (Berachot 43:2). And we now know that so much of sexual desire has to do with the mind.

If the scent of mandrake fruit is enticing, or at least exciting, the root of the plant has quite the opposite kind of scent. The freshly dug root is described in Saxon leechdom and sorcery as having a "powerful narcotic odor." I've smelled these roots quite often when digging them up, and they do have a very rootlike, earthy scent, with some pungency similar to horseradish.

In conjunction with mandrake's aphrodisiac aspect, some consider this plant to be the personification of Aphrodite. Alternatively, perhaps the connection between mandrake and Aphrodite exists precisely because of its use as an aphrodisiac. The word, in fact, derives from the name of this goddess.

Aphrodite, who is often depicted holding an apple, may actually be holding a mandrake fruit, especially in one image where she has a poppy in one hand and a small round mandrake-like fruit in the other. This makes sense, since, like poppy, mandrake can bring sleep. But it would make just as much sense if it were an apple, since then Aphrodite would be holding a Moon symbol in one hand and a Sun symbol in the other.

Mandrake is associated with deities and spirits in various cultures. For instance, although the present-day Arabic name for mandrake may be translated as "apples of djinn" or "testicles of djinn," an Ancient Arabic name for it is *abu'lruh*, which means "master of the breath of life" or "lord of the spirit." This name implies that mandrakes were connected to a pre-Islamic deity, although who that might have been is now unknown.

Mandrake and Hekate

It's common in contemporary occulture to ascribe the mandrake to Hekate, but no ancient sources seem to back this up. This association may have arisen from the black dog once sacrificed in the harvesting of mandrakes. According to medieval reports, the mandrake made a deathly scream when it was pulled out of the ground, so it was harvested by tying a dog (often described or painted as a black one) to the root and enticing the dog to run off, pulling the root out of the ground. This killed the dog instead of the root-hunter and the dog acted as a sacrifice to the root.

I have never been sure how someone could entice a dog to pull the rope without ending up hearing the deadly mandrake scream. Also, yanking a mandrake root out of the ground with a rope would cause the root to snap, because it's very brittle. In fact, that's the primary way it reproduces itself. It's true, however, that root-diggers of the ancient world may have used dogs to help them find roots, especially when the plants were dormant (i.e., seeming to be dead). And this may be how a dog was introduced into the stories about harvesting this plant. In that case, these dogs were not sacrifices, but work partners. In fact, at least one illustration shows a woman presenting Dioscorides with a mandrake root while she gives a treat to a dog she has on a leash.

Still, the black dog that dies as a kind of sacrifice to the mandrake is reminiscent of the black puppies that were the traditional sacrifice to Hekate in ancient Greece. Moreover, Hekate is often depicted in the company of dogs. So perhaps, in this story, we have a mangled version of an older story about sacrifice to Hekate.

The opposite may be true as well. It is possible that the mandrake was attributed to Hekate *because* it became associated with witchcraft. Hekate, of course, was the goddess of witchcraft and was associated with black dogs. Still, it is interesting, especially considering datura's association with black dogs. Curiously, the Romans called mandrake fruits *mala canina* (dog apples).

Mandrake didn't become strongly connected with witchcraft and flying ointments until between 1500 and 1700, the era when witches came to be identified as having made pacts with the devil. At this point, it pretty much lost most of its medicinal uses. This is also the time when the idea of witches' flight became a major part of the authorities' accusations of witchcraft. We have to wonder whether, prior to that time, mandrake was much used in witchcraft.

Mandrake and the Hanged Man

Some say that the root of a mandrake is no more like a human being than that of a parsnip, but I disagree. They are often curiously fascinating in shape. Around the same time that mandrake became associated with flying (the 1500s), little amulets called mandrakes or *alraunes* became popular. These were dressed and fed, and kept in a container. Even Joan of Arc was accused of having one. The image of a gibbet often appeared on the container's cover. And that brings us to the hanged man.

The belief that mandrakes grew from the urine and semen of a hanged man first became prevalent in the 16th century, coinciding with the era in which accusations of witches flying and making satanic pacts also rose to prominence. Jakob Grimm records a legend of mandrake growing from the urine or semen of a hanged man, especially a thief.

To me, the story of mandrake springing from the semen or urine of a hanged man seems very reminiscent of the story of the crucifixion of Jesus and the myths of his blood. However, the concept of the mandrake springing up beneath the gibbet may derive from Greek mythology. The ancient witch Medea dug up a plant, perhaps mandrake, which had been fed with the *ichor* (divine blood) of the wrongly chained and punished Prometheus, the thief who stole fire from the gods and gave it to humans. Here we have a sort of forerunner of the hanged man/mandrake connection. Even in the story of the dog harvesting the mandrake, a noose is involved.

The grimoire *Le Petit Albert* (1706) describes the making of the talismanic Hand of Glory (see chapter 8). In the traditional formula, the hand is taken from a hanged man. However, it seems very much more likely to have been crafted from a mandrake root. "Hand of Glory" in French is *main de gloire*, which so closely resembles the French word for mandrake (*mandragore*).

Mandrake is also associated with the biblical fruit of the Tree of Knowledge of Good and Evil. In Genesis, the fruit eaten by Adam and Eve gives them knowledge, but gets them kicked out of the Garden of Eden. They become mortal on the one hand and start having children on the other. The mandrake seems to partake of this very same binary split between life and death. It can increase life through fertility, or decrease it by causing death or being associated with death (the hanged man). In the same way, the hanged man of the mandrake origin legend produces life as he is executed. Often in mandrake folklore, the hanged man is someone wrongly executed, so his mandrake-producing semen is a kind of talking back to the authorities who execute him.

Urine is a fertilizer and semen, of course, is related to fertility. By the time the use of the mandrake fertility amulet became popular, women who wished to conceive were rubbing themselves with a hanged man's hand. This may have been because of the belief that, since a man ejaculates when hanged, he must be in an especially fertile state—and this state may be contagious.

Even when the mandrake/hanged man story comes down through the centuries and is moved to another continent, we can still see its outline and the mandrake's connection to both death and life. For instance, a Pennsylvania folk belief related to odd sounds heard in the woods described this noise as coming from an American mandrake being uprooted. These were said to grow from the skeletons of Indians or black panthers.

A possible key to the importance of mandrake to European witchcraft and magic is the fact that the root resembles a human being and can therefore be used as a substitute in a sacrifice. This may be connected to the black dog sacrificed for the mandrake harvest and may be an echo of earlier sacrifices of black dogs to Hekate. Apparently, in ancient Cyprus, sacrifices to the goddess Aphrodite included a person wrapped in the fleece of a sheep. If mandrake is Aphrodite's plant, then human sacrifice may be tied to it. Perhaps the roots evolved into a substitute for a human being. We see this in the way the roots are dressed, for instance—often in white, as a shroud or a fleece—and kept in a little coffin. This does connect the root up to the hanged man, but it also reflects what happened in a human sacrifice.

The word "mannekin" fits with the concept of a figure that stands for a real human being. So again we have a connection between mandrake and hanging, thieves, death, sex, fertility, dogs, and sacrifice. In addition to the dog story, various ways of ritually harvesting mandrakes have been described, as is the case with other herbs important in magic, like vervain. Theophrastus (371–287 BCE) instructs us to dig up mandrake root with a sword while saying "as many things as possible about the mysteries of love," which is a neat combination of life (sex) and death (sword).

Pliny (23–79 CE) advised us to keep windward of mandrake and use a sword to trace three circles around it while facing west. Hildegard of Bingen (1098–1179) was far more wary of this plant, and her attitude indicates that mandrake may already have had associations with witchcraft. She advised that the mandrake root be put into a spring for a day and a night as soon as it was harvested, because it has the devil in it and will be a good tool for dark magic if left unwashed for too long after harvesting.

The first mention of wrapping a harvested mandrake root is found in 1429 in Godefroy's *Journal d'un bourgeois de Paris*, which recommended swathing it in silk or linen. Jakob Grimm (1785–1863) described how mandrake roots were washed in red wine, dressed in red and white silk, and placed in a small chest if they were to be kept as amulets. This mannekin was then fed every Friday and given a new white shirt every New Moon. Both of these directions indicate that this folk practice came from the Jewish tradition, as they wear new clothes on the Sabbath, which starts on Friday night. And the New Moon is the beginning of the month in the Jewish calendar. In return, these mandrake amulets brought luck and money and answered questions.

Mandrake serves as a hinge, in the same manner as belladonna and henbane. Here, however, the hinge turns between life (fertility, aphrodisia) and death (the hanged man, the sacrificed dog or human). This coincides with the concept of the Crooked Path and with the ambiguity of witches, who now heal and now curse. This is part of why mandrake has become the witchcraft herb *par excellence*. It is the ultimate combination of two very different states.

I also think that there is some vestigial memory of human sacrifice associated with mandrake that peeks out through the folklore associated with it. It is the ultimate herbal code, in the manner of those masks mentioned as far back as the Greek Magical Papyri, in which an animal part in a spell formula is revealed to be a plant part instead. In this case, rather than a human being wrapped in a fleece, we have the mandrake root wrapped in silk. I believe that this substitution makes witchcraft all the more powerful—and all the more occult, hidden, and mysterious.

PRACTICE

If you want to harvest mandrake roots, do it in the fall, when it is at its fattest and most venomous. And be sure to wear gloves. For maximum strength, harvest the root on a Saturday and/or during a New Moon. Many people advise using song and flattery to approach this plant for harvest. I have not tried song, but I do speak to mandrake when I harvest it, complimenting its beauty and health and thanking it. If I dig a root, I promise the plant to sow its seeds and thus ensure its immortality. I usually do not use a knife or sword, but rather my own fingers and perhaps the tip of a shed antler. I anoint the roots with a few drops of red wine and cense them in myrrh, a resin associated with death that is therefore connected to Saturnian energies and to dark goddesses like Hekate.

The roots of this plant are exceedingly powerful. I find that handling them causes me to have a headache, even if I am wearing gloves and working outside. They must be washed gently, or bits will break off and the root's skin will come off in pieces. I usually dunk them in a bucket of water and sometimes, if there is a lot of dirt stuck in nooks and crannies, I leave them in the water overnight. Don't leave them too long, however, or they may rot.

Mandrake roots get big quickly, so even a first year plant can have a decent root that is sufficient for ritual work. Second- and third-year plants can have a root so big that it is difficult to dry without rotting. Roots dry down to just a tiny percentage of their fresh weight.

One nicely traditional alternative to drying these roots in a dehydrator (which involves spewing an alkaloidal miasma all over the place) is to use *Le Petit Albert's* method for drying the human hand that was to be used as a Hand of Glory. Because of the probability that the Hand of Glory was actually a root instead of a human hand, I decided to try this drying method with roots, and it worked well. You'll need a terra cotta (unglazed) flower pot with a terra cotta saucer to use as a lid. It should be big enough to hold the root with nothing sticking out. The pot has to be unglazed, because the moisture from the root has to be carried out of the pot. You'll also need a good amount of salt. You can usually get inexpensive salt in a five-pound sack at the grocery store, but if you want to be fancy (and expensive), you can use black salt. In *Le Petit Albert*, salt is mixed with long pepper (a hot spice similar to black pepper—not a chili pepper), but this isn't necessary. You can use any aromatic spice mixed with the salt, depending on the tasks you anticipate doing with the dried root.

Musk seeds as a Saturn herb or black pepper as a Mars herb (for attack magic) are especially good choices for this. Grind the herb and mix it with the salt. Put some paper in the bottom of the pot to keep the salt from running out the drainage hole, then pour in a layer of salt. Put the root in and fill the pot with salt (and spices, if you are using them). The root should be fully covered. Put the saucer on top. Then put the whole thing in a protected area in the sun during a warm time of year. The Dog Days of summer, when the star Sirius is rising, is traditionally the best time, because that's when it's warmest and because of the dog connections with mandrake. The terra cotta will conduct the moisture that is extracted by the salt out of the pot.

Leave the pot out in the sun for at least two weeks. Be careful that it doesn't get rained on, because that will let moisture back into the root and perhaps turn your salt into slop. Check the root for dryness after a couple weeks. Wear gloves and pour out the salt. You can even dedicate a pair of black gloves to working with this root, decorating them with appropriate symbols to honor the plant spirit. The root should be difficult to bend and should have shrunk a great deal. One problem with drying roots is that the exterior may be dried, but not the interior. This is why it's best always to dry roots with Saturnian slowness—at the lowest possible temperature. If the root isn't fully dry, put it back in the pot with the salt. When it is finally dry, throw away the salt or save it in a specially marked container. Make sure no one ever uses this salt for food. You can use the salt for drying the roots of another of the Weird Sisters, but don't use it to dry a root you may ingest at any point, since you can't tell how much alkaloid is present in the salt.

You can even then go a bit further, if you want, by censing the root in the traditional vervain smoke or using something Saturnian, like cypress, tobacco, Norway spruce, or cannabis. Holding the root in smoke will help to preserve it and is a way of charging any talisman.

This is a good time to infuse the root with energy as well. To store the root, you can wrap it in silk or paper and put it in a well-sealed cardboard box (something that will let what moisture is still present pass through). You can also store it in uncooked rice. This helps to absorb moisture, but be sure to mix the rice with bay leaves to repel pantry moths and keep it all in a tightly lidded jar. Again, make sure no one ever eats that rice. Whatever you do, don't try to dry a root in the microwave. It will explode. Once a root is dried and ready to be used in magical work, you can generally handle it without risking any alkaloid effects.

An even easier way to deal with mandrake root is to store it in 95 percent alcohol, rather than drying it. The alcohol itself can then serve as a substitute for mandrake, since it will be imbued with mandrake juice. As the alcohol is used, just top up with more. It's wonderful to have a jar of mandrake root in your witch's cabinet.

MANDRAKE IN THE GARDEN

Growing mandrake is not easy. This is why it is so rare to find it for sale commercially. Germinating the seeds requires a lot of patience, which most people lack. Moreover, the plant itself is notoriously given to dormancy if it's too cold, too hot, too wet, or too dry. I usually start seeds in December so that they hit the dirt right after the Winter Solstice. This is the time of year when seeds are waking up and considering germination as the sun ascends to power.

There are a couple of different ways to germinate mandrake seeds. One is to soak them in cold water for two weeks as I describe for henbane. Another is a method I've been using more recently, but it's riskier because the seeds can be damaged. This involves a mixture of 1 part ordinary hydrogen peroxide (3 percent solution) and 9 parts filtered water. Soak the seeds in this for twelve hours for a white mandrake and four hours for a black mandrake, which has much smaller seeds. Don't leave them in there too long, because they can be damaged by the acidity of the hydrogen peroxide. Then rinse them in cold water and plant them in planting medium.

I have been using peat pellets exclusively to germinate mandrake seeds (the outdoor method does not seem to work with them). Like henbane and belladonna, mandrake likes chalky soil, so a top dressing of chick grit is in order, even when they are in peat pellets. Something I've found works very well when germinating mandrake seeds is to fluctuate the temperature so that the daytime temperature is about 70°F and the nighttime temperature is about 55°F. This requires a cold room and a propagation mat. You can get the mat at horticulture supply sites online and sometimes at big-box stores in the spring.

Mandrake seeds can take several months (or even up to two years) to sprout. I usually quickly move them from peat pellets to four-inch pots filled with a mix of equal parts peat moss, perlite, and compost (I use organic composted cow manure). You can use sand instead of perlite, but that makes the pots heavy. And sand can create hairier roots, which is not desirable with mandrake. The composted manure provides some nutrients.

Because mandrake quickly develops a tap root, you have to keep an eye on the seedlings. This is where I usually don't keep a sharp enough eye on them and they end up twisting around in the pot. Instead of hurting them, however, this seems to make for more beautiful roots when they get larger. I gradually pot the plants up to a twelve-inch (30 cm) pot. I have not found that they need anything much larger, even after three years, although it's good to check them periodically.

I grow mandrakes in pots because there is nowhere in the United States where they will grow well outside. If temperatures get too low, the roots freeze and die. And they can't compete well with grass or tree roots. They can't handle too much sun or heat, or too much water, or too heavy a soil. Growing them in pots also allows me to take them inside in the winter, which very much increases the probability of their fruiting and just seems to make for happier plants. I take them inside before they get hit with frost.

Mandrake grows quite happily under lights inside in the winter. I have mine under the ordinary, cheap fluorescent lights that are used over a workbench (shop lights). Keeping the lights about an inch (2.5 cm) from the top of the leaves gives them enough light, but not too much. They are quite happy to grow in a cold room—my basement stays between 50 and 55°F (10–13°C) all winter—or something warmer. Look out for aphids when bringing your plants inside, because they attack a plant when it is stressed. If they turn up, use neem or azadirachtin, which is a fraction of neem (a component of neem).

CONCLUSION

P ractitioners of magic get all sorts of advice, some bordering on commands, about how to work with plants and their spirits. The one thing that I have learned is that any person—whether they have experience with magic or not; whether they belong to a group or not; whether they have been initiated into any practice or not—can learn to grow the witching herbs and can open themselves to direct interaction with the plant spirits with no mediation from anyone. This direct interaction with the plants and their spirits is exactly what our ancestors did, long before any magical orders or covens existed. And it is our right as humans to interact directly with the plants with whom we share the Earth.

Yes, we do have to learn how to grow these plants, and that knowledge comes as all knowledge does—from a combination of study and practice. The actual growing of a witching herb in a pot or in a garden plot, the study of that herb's lore, empirical knowledge of its behavior, and familiarity with its history as a medicinal plant can all combine to provide the perfect ground in which the seeds of spirit contact can flourish.

People make all sorts of claims in magic, most of which we cannot ever validate. But no one can gainsay healthy witching herbs that you grow yourself. They are there as proof of your hard-won expertise. I hope this book leads you to experience the satisfaction, confidence, and knowledge that are born from the serious practice of growing the witching herbs and devotion to their spirits.

May the spirits bless and guide you in your work.

NOTES

1 Charles G. Leland, *Aradia, Or the Gospel of the Witches*, p. 93. There is some argument about whether Leland's book was a fraud, but Carlo Ginzburg, a respected scholar of witchcraft, cites worship of Aradia in his book *Ecstasies: Deciphering the Witch's Sabbath*, which is highly recommended for those interested in shamanic approaches to witchcraft. Folkard, on the other hand, writes that "Conjugalis Herba" is the same thing as Concordia, which, he says, Gerard describes as *Potentilla asarina,* a kind of cinquefoil. I think Gerard is mistaken. It isn't the leaves that are described as having five fingers, but the roots. Folkard himself describes the plant as Palma Christi, better known to us as castor bean—*Ricinus communis* (*Plant Lore, Legends and Lyrics,* p. 109.

2 A gum harvested from *Ferula* species and once used medicinally. It's similar to asafetida, which is also from the *Ferula* genus. Sagapenum is described as smelling like onions. In the past, a mixture of galbanum and asafetida was sometimes sold as sagapenum, so that mixture would make a good substitute for this resin (see *Three Books of Occult Philosophy*, p. 129).

3 University of Illinois at Urbana-Champaign (October 27, 2006) "Honey Bee Chemoreceptors Found for Smell and Taste," *Science Daily.* Retried August 3, 2009, from *www.sciencedaily.com.*

4 "Herbaceous plants that have merely one blossom are rather rare. They belong predominantly to the group of monocotyledons in which the flowering process appears restrained because of the mercurial character affecting the blooms. . . . The summer, with its abundance of vegetation has few unifloral plants. The

poppy . . . [is an] exception." In Ernst Kranich's *Planetary Influences Upon Plants: A Cosmological Botany*, p. 38.

5 I would have thought that the number of pod sections would be related to the number of petals, but no. As I wrote this section, I had poppy pods with seven sections and some with up to thirteen sections. All of these pods were formed from poppies that had four petals, as is typical for a "single-petaled" poppy.

6 "Menstrua" is the plural of "menstruum," which is what an herb is macerated (soaked) in to produce a tincture. It's the same root as menstruation—month—because tinctures often went for a month and a day.

7 *Carmina Gadelica: Hymns and Incantations Ortha Nan Gaidheal, Volume II,* by Alexander Carmichael (1900), p. 95. Another version of this on the same page: "I will pluck the yarrow fair / The more brave shall be my arm, / That more warm shall be my lips, / That more swift shall be my feet; / May I an island be at sea, / May I a rock be on land, / That I can afflict any man, / No man can afflict me." This sounds much more Martial. Original Gaelic versions of both are given on p. 94.

8 See *www.ars-grin.gov/duke/*. As a side note, yarrow is often deemed "toxic" because it contains thujone, but ordinary sage contains far more, as you can see by comparing the two on Dr. Duke's site.

9 "The Evil Eye as Synthetic Image and Its Meanings on the Island of Pentelleria, Italy," *American Ethnologist*, Vol. 9, No. 4, p. 679; see also *Symbolism & Cognition II* (Nov 1982), pp. 664–681. Another version of *centelvo* is horehound in wine.

10 On the material level, the essential oils of biblical hyssop have been shown to kill thirteen different types of pestiferous microbes. See, for instance, Alma, et al., "Screening Chemical Composition and in Vitro Antioxidant and Antimicrobial Activities of the

Essential Oils from *Origanum syriacum L.* Growing in Turkey," *Biological and Pharmaceutical Bulletin*, Vol. 26 (2003), No. 12, pp. 1725–1729.

11 P. Burkhard, K. Burkhardt, C.A. Haenggeli, and T. Landis. "Plant-Induced Seizures: Reappearance of an Old Problem," *Journal of Neurology* 246 (1999), pp. 667–670.

12 From an unpublished manuscript dated 1752 (pp. 46–47): "This & vervain, flowring at midsummer time, they used with their great, & public midsummer sacrifice. The latter is called hierobotane the sacred plant for that reason; & columbaria pigeon herb, but the botanists are ignorant of the true reason. It was not that pigeons are fond of it, but that it was thus used in the midsummer festival, when pigeons were the accustomed sacrifice. So the Foxgloves has not its name from fox, but *folkes, popelli*, meaning in old language what we now call fairies: notions deriv'd from the Druids using it at that time; as they did the fam'd mistletoe at their midwinter sacrifice." Downloaded from *http://en.wikisource.org/* on 5/31/11.

13 See "Absinthe," *British Medical Journal*, Vol. 2, No. 1085 (Oct 15, 1881), p. 640; see also "Absinthe: What's Your Poison," *British Medical Journal*, Vol. 319, No. 7225 (Dec 18–25, 1999), pp. 1590–1592.

14 Flowers of *N. rustica* and *N. tabacum* provide nectar toxic to honeybees. See A. L. Kerchner, et al., "Protein and Alkaloid Patterns of the Floral Nectar in Some Solanaceous Species," *Acta Biol Hung*, 2015 Sept; 66(3):304–15. doi: 10.1556/018.66.2015.3.6.

15 The word "eysyl" seems to be related to the word for oxalis and perhaps referred originally to some kind of liquid made from sorrel. The combination here of *Papaver somniferum* and henbane is interesting because they potentiate each other. This is recognized as far back as Pliny, who, in his *Fourth Book of Natural*

History, cites Muesides as recommending that opium be mixed with henbane seeds to "preserve" it (*http://books.google.com/books/*, p. 277).

BIBLIOGRAPHY

Books and Primary Sources

Agrippa of Nettesheim, and Henry Cornelius. *Three Books of Occult Philosophy*. Woodbury, MN: Llewellyn, 2006.

Allen, D. E., and G. Hatfield. *Medicinal Plants in Folk Tradition: An Ethnobotany of Britain and Ireland*. Portland, OR: Timber Press, 2004.

Bartram, Thomas. *Bartram's Encyclopedia of Herbal Medicine*. London: Constable & Robinson Ltd., 1998.

Beasley, Henry. *The Pocket Formulary and Synopsis of the British and Foreign Pharmacopoeias*. Philadelphia: Lindsey & Blakeston, 1852.

Belchem, John. *A New History of the Isle of Man: The Modern Period 1830–1999*. Liverpool: Liverpool University, 2000.

Betz, Hans Dieter. *The Greek Magical Papyrus, Including the Demotic Spells*. Chicago: University of Chicago Press, 1996.

Bostock, John, EdMD, FRS, H. T. Riley, Esq., BA *Pliny the Elder. The Natural History*. London: Taylor and Francis, Red Lion Court, Fleet Street, 1855.

Boyd, Carolyn E. *Rock Art of the Lower Pecos*. College Station: Texas A&M University Press, 2003.

Britten, James, and Robert Holland. *A Dictionary of English Plant-names*. London: English Dialect Society, 1886.

Camporesi, Piero. *The Incorruptible Flesh: Bodily Mutation and Mortification in Religion and Folklore.* Cambridge, UK: Cambridge University Press, 1988.

Carmichael, Alexander. *Carmina Gadelica: Hymns and Incantations Ortha Nan Gaidheal, Volume II,* 1900.

Cole, William. *The Art of Simpling.* London: Printed for F.G. for Nath. Brook at the Angell in Cornhill, 1656.

Copland, James, MD. *Dictionary of Practical Medicine*, Vol. 5. New York: Harper & Bros. Publishers, 1847.

Cowan, Eliott. *Plant Spirit Medicine.* Louisville, CO: Sounds True, 2014.

Culpeper, Nicolas. *English Physician.* London: Champante & Whitrow, 1849.

Dasen, Veronique. *Dwarfs in Ancient Egypt and Greece.* Oxford: Oxford University Press, 2013.

Deane, Tony, and Tony Shaw. *The Folklore of Cornwall.* Totowa, NJ: Rowan & Littlefield, 1975.

DeKorne, Jim. *Psychedelic Shamanism: The Cultivation, Preparation, and Shamanic Use of Psychotropic Plants.* Berkeley, CA: North Atlantic Books, 2011.

Devillo, Stephen Paul. *The Bronx River in History and Folklore.* Charleston, SC: History Press, 2015.

Engstrom, A. G. "The Voices of Plants and Flowers and the Changing Cry of the Mandrake," in *Medieval Studies in Honor of Urban Tigner Holmes,* ed. John Mahoney and John Esten Keller. Chapel Hill: University of North Carolina Press, 1965.

Fairbanks, Arthur. *A Handbook of Greek Religion.* New York: American Book Co., 1910.

Faraone, Christopher. *Ancient Greek Love Magic.* Cambridge, MA: Harvard University Press, 1999.

Folkard, Richard. *Plant Lore, Legends and Lyrics.* London: Sampson Low, Marston, Searle, & Rivington, 1884.

Frazer, Sir James George. *The Golden Bough,* 3rd ed. Part VII. Vol. 2. London: MacMillan & Co., 1913

Freeman, Margaret. *Herbs for the Medieval Household for Cooking, Healing, and Diverse Uses.* New York: Metropolitan Museum of Art, 1943.

Furst, Peter T. "Introduction to Chapter 8," in Stacy B. Schaefer & Peter T. Furst, *People of the Peyote: Huichol Indian History, Religion & Survival.* Albuquerque, NM: University of New Mexico Press, 1996.

Ginzburg, Carlo. *Ecstasies: Deciphering the Witch's Sabbath.* Chicago: University of Chicago Press, 2004.

Goodrick-Clarke, Nicholas. *Paracelsus: Essential Readings.* Berkeley, CA: North Atlantic Books, 1999.

Green, Amanda J. "Back to the Future: Resonances of the Past in Myth and Material Culture," in Amy Gazin-Schwartz and Cornelius Holtorf, eds. *Archaeology and Folklore (Theoretical Archeology Group).* London: Routledge, 1999.

Green, James. *An Herbal Medicine-Maker's Handbook.* Berkeley, CA: Crossing Press, 2000.

Gutch, Mrs., and Mabel Peacock. "Country Folk-Lore," Vol. V., *Printed Extracts No. VII. Examples of Printed Folk-Lore Concerning Lincolnshire.* London: David Nutt, 1908.

Hamel, Paul B., and Mary U. Chiltoskey. *Cherokee Plants and Their Uses—A 400-Year History.* Sylva, NC: Herald Publishing Co., 1975.

Harris, J. Rendel. *The Origin of the Cult of Aphrodite*. Manchester, UK: The University Press, 1916.

Hazlitt, William Carew, and John Brand. *Faiths and Folklore*. New York: Charles Scribner's Sons, 1905.

Huson, Paul. *Mastering Witchcraft*. New York: G. P. Putnam's Sons, 1978.

Inderjit, K. M. M. Dakshini, and Chester L. Foy. *Principles and Practices in Plant Ecology: Allelochemical Interactions*. Boca Raton, FL: CRC Press, 1999.

Kellogg, Harriette S. "Native Dye-Plants and Tan-Plants of Iowa, with Notes on a Few Other Species," *Proceedings of the Iowa Academy of Science for 1912*, Vol. XIX: 113–128.

Kieckhefer, Richard. *Forbidden Rites: A Necromancer's Manual of the Fifteenth Century*. University Park, PA: University of Pennsylvania, 1998.

Koch, John T., ed. *Celtic Culture: A Historical Encyclopedia*. Oxford: ABC-CLIO, 2006.

Kranich, Ernst Michael. *Planetary Influences upon Plants: A Cosmological Botany*. Wyoming, RI: Bio-Dynamic Literature, 1984.

Lecouteux, Claude. *Witches, Werewolves, and Fairies: Shapeshifters and Astral Doubles in the Middle Ages*. Rochester, VT: Inner Traditions, 2003.

Lehner, Ernst, and Johanna Lehner. *Folklore and Symbolism of Flowers, Plants and Trees*. New York: Tudor Publishing, 1960.

Leland, Charles G. *Aradia, or the Gospel of the Witches*. London: David Nutt, 1899.

———. *Etruscan Roman Remains in Popular Tradition*. New York: C. Scribner's Sons, 1892.

Mackenzie, Donald A. *Myths of Crete and Pre-Hellenic Europe.* London: Gresham Publishing, 1917.

Osborn, Marijane. "Anglo-Saxon Ethnobotany: Women's Reproductive Medicine in Leechbook III," pp. 145–161 in Peter Dendle and Alain Touwaide, eds. *Health and Healing from the Medieval Garden.* Woodbridge, UK: Boydell Press, 2008,

Owen, Elias. *Welsh Folk-Lore: A Collection of the Folk-Tales and Legends of North Wales.* London: np, 1896.

Pendell, Dale. *Pharmako-Gnosis: Plant Teachers and the Poison Path.* Berkeley, CA: North Atlantic Books, 2010.

Petri, G., and Y. P. S. Bajaj. "Datura spp.: In Vitro Regeneration and the Production of Tropanes," pp. 135–157, in Y. P. S. Bajaj, ed. *Biotechnology in Agriculture and Forestry 7: Medicinal and Aromatic Plants II.* Berlin: Springer-Verlag, 1989.

Polome, Edgar C. "Germanic, Northwest Indo-European and Pre-Indo-European Substrates," pp. 47–56, in *Recent Developments in Germanic Linguistics,* Rosina Lippi-Green, ed. Amsterdam: John Benjamins Publishing Co., 1992.

Ramsey, Matthew. *Professional and Popular Medicine in France 1770–1830: The Social World of Medical Practice.* Cambridge, UK: Cambridge University Press, 1988.

Ratsch, Christian. *Ethnopharmacology and Its Applications.* Rochester, VT: Park Street Press, 1998.

Rendel, Harris, J. *The Origin of the Cult of Aphrodite.* Manchester, UK: The University Press, 1916.

Roberts, M. F., and Michael Wink. *Alkaloids: Biochemistry, Ecology, and Medicinal Applications.* New York: Plenum, 1998.

Robinson, William. *The English Flower Garden and Home Grounds.* London: John Murray, 1907.

Schulke, Daniel. *Viridarium Umbris.* London: Xoanon, 2005.

Schultes, Richard Evans, and Albert Hofmann. *Plants of the Gods: Origins of Hallucinogenic Use.* New York: McGraw-Hill, 1979.

Staller, John E., and Brian Stross. *Lightning in the Andes and Meso-america: Pre-Columbian, Colonial, and Contemporary Perspectives.* Oxford: Oxford University Press, 2013.

Tucker, Arthur O., and Thomas DeBaggio. *The Encyclopedia of Herbs: A Comprehensive Reference to Herbs of Flavor and Fragrance.* Portland: Timber Press, 2009.

Valadez, Susana Eger, "Wolf Power and Interspecies Communication," in Stacy B. Schaefer and Peter T. Furst, *People of the Peyote: Huichol Indian History, Religion & Survival.* Albuquerque, NM: University of New Mexico Press, 1996.

van Arsdall, Anne, Helmut W. Klug, Paul Blanz. "The Mandrake Plant and Its Legend," pp. 285–346, in *Old Names—New Growth: Proceedings of the 2nd ASPNS Conference, University of Graz, Austria, 6–10 June 2007, and Related Essays,* eds. Peter Bierbaumer and Helmut W. Klug. Frankfurt/Main: Lang, 2009.

van Wyk, Ben-Erik, Michael Wink. *Medicinal Plants of the World.* Portland, OR: Timber Press, 2004.

Watts, Donald. *Dictionary of Plant Lore.* Cambridge, MA: Academic Press, 2007.

Waugh, F. W. *Iroquois Foods and Food Preparation.* Ottawa: Canada Department of Mines, 1916.

Wilson, Roberta. *Aromatherapy: Essential Oils for Vibrant Health.* New York, NY: Avery, 2002.

Winter, Joseph C. *Tobacco Use by Native North Americans: Sacred Smoke and Silent Killer.* Tulsa, OK: University of Oklahoma Press, 2000.

Wood, Matthew. *The Book of Herbal Wisdom: Using Plants as Medicine.* Berkeley, CA: North Atlantic Books, 1997.

Woodhead, Eileen. *Early Canadian Gardening: An 1827 Nursery Catalogue.* Toronto: McGill-Queen's University Press, 1998.

Yasumoto, Masaya, "Psychotropic Kieri in Huichol Culture," in Stacy B. Schaefer and Peter T. Furst, *People of the Peyote: Huichol Indian History, Religion and Survival.* Albuquerque, NM: University of New Mexico Press, 1996.

Journals and Periodicals

"Absinthe," *British Medical Journal,* Vol. 2, No. 1085 (Oct 15, 1881), p. 640.

Albert-Puleo, Michael. "Mythobotany, Pharmacology, and Chemistry of Thujone-Containing Plants and Derivatives," *Economic Botany,* Vol. 32, No. 1 (Jan–Mar, 1978), pp. 65–74.

Alma, M. H., Ahmet Mavi, Ali Yildirim, Metin Digrak, and Toshifumi Hirata. "Screening Chemical Composition and in Vitro Antioxidant and Antimicrobial Activities of the Essential Oils from *Origanum syriacum* L. Growing in Turkey," *Biological and Pharmaceutical Bulletin,* Vol. 26 (2003) No. 12, pp. 1725–1729.

Andrews. Alfred C. "Hyssop in the Classical Era," *Classical Philology,* Vol. 56, No. 4 (Oct 1961), pp. 230–248.

Armstrong, Edward A. "Mugwort Lore," *Folklore,* Vol. 55, No. 1 (Mar 1944), pp. 22–27.

Berkov, Strahil, and Stefan Philipov. "Alkaloid Production in Diploid and Autotetraploid Plants of Datura stramonium," *Pharmaceutical Biology,* Vol. 40, No. 8 (2002), pp. 617–621.

Bonser, Wilfrid. "Magical Practices Against Elves," *Folklore,* Vol. 37, No. 4 (Dec 31, 1926), pp. 350–363.

Boumba, V. A., A. Mitselou, T. Vougiouklakis. "Fatal Poisoning from Ingestion of *Datura stramonium* Seeds," *Veterinary & Human Toxicology* 46(2), Apr 2004, pp. 81–82.

Briggs, K. M. "Some Seventeenth-Century Books of Magic," *Folklore*, Vol. 64, No. 4 (Dec 1953), pp. 445–462.

Brown, Theo. "The Black Dog," Folklore, Vol. 69, No. 3 (Sep 1958), pp. 175–192.

Bruch, Gerston, and Elmer H. Wirth, "Studies on Poplar Bud," *Journal of the American Pharmaceutical Association*, Vol. 25, Issue 8, Aug 1936, pp. 672–682.

Calvo, M. I. "Anti-inflammatory and Analgesic Activity of the Topical Preparation of *Verbena officinalis* L.," *Journal of Ethnopharmacology*, Oct 11, 2006, Vol. 107(3), pp. 380–382.

Carter, Anthony J. "Dwale: An Anaesthetic from Old England," *British Medical Journal*, Vol. 319, No. 7223 (Dec 18–25, 1999), pp. 1623–1626.

Chandler, R. F., S. N. Hooper, M. J. Harvey. "Ethnobotany and Phytochemistry of Yarrow, *Achillea millefolium*, Compositae," *Economic Botany*, Vol. 36, No. 2 (Apr–Jun 1982).

Clark, Raymond J. "A Note on Medea's Plant and the Mandrake," *Folklore*, Vol. 79, No. 3 (Autumn 1968), p. 227–231.

Drury, Susan. "Funeral Plants and Flowers in England: Some Examples," *Folklore*, Vol. 105 (1994), pp. 101–103.

———. "Plants and Pest Control in England circa 1400–1700: A Preliminary Study," *Folklore*, Vol. 103, No. 1 (1992), pp. 103–106.

Dubois, Constance Goddard. "Religious Ceremonies and Myths of the Mission Indians," *American Anthropologist*, New Series, Vol. 7, No. 4 (Oct–Dec. 1905), pp. 620–629.

Falconieri, D. L., A. Piras, S. Porcedda, B. Marongiu, et al. "Chemical Composition and Biological Activity of the Volatile Extracts of *Achillea millefolium*," *Natural Product Communications*, Oct 2011;6(10), pp. 1527–1530.

Fleisher, Alexander, and Zhenia Fleisher. "Identification of Biblical Hyssop and Origin of the Traditional Use of Oregano-Group Herbs in the Mediterranean Region," *Economic Botany*, Vol. 42, No. 2 (Apr–Jun 1988), pp. 232–241.

Fogg, Walter. "Wares of a Moroccan Folk-Doctor," *Folklore*, Vol. 52, No. 4 (Dec 1941), pp. 243–303.

Furst, Peter T., and Barbara G. Meyerhoff. "Myth as History: The Jimson Weed Cycle of the Huichols of Mexico," *Antropologica*, 17, pp. 3–39.

Galt, Anthony. "The Evil Eye as Synthetic Image and Its Meanings on the Island of Pentelleria, Italy," *American Ethnologist*, Vol. 9, No. 4, Symbolism & Cognition II (Nov 1982), pp. 664–681.

Geis, Gilbert. "In Scopolamine Veritas: The Early History of Drug-Induced Statements," *Journal of Criminal Law, Criminology, and Police Science*, Vol. 50, No. 4 (Nov–Dec, 1959), pp. 347–357.

Grendou, Felix. "The Anglo-Saxon Charms," *Journal of American Folklore*, Vol. 22, No. 84 (Apr–Jun, 1909), pp. 105–237.

Guarrera, P. M., G. Forti, S. Marignoli. "Ethnobotanical and Ethnomedicinal Uses of Plants in the District of Acquapendent (Latium, Central Italy)," *Journal of Ethnopharmacology*, Vol. 96(3), Jan 15, 2005, pp. 429–444.

Gunther, R. T. "The Cimaruta: Its Structure and Development," *Folklore*, Vol. 16, No. 1 (1905), p. 132–161.

Hocking, George M. "Henbane: Healing Herb of Hercules and of Apollo," *Economic Botany*, Vol. 1, No. 3 (Jul–Sept 1947), pp. 306–316.

Ingham, John M. "On Mexican Folk Medicine," *American Anthropologist*, New Series, Vol. 72, No. 1 (Feb 1970), pp. 76–87.

Kerchner, A. L, J. Darók, I. Bacskay, et al. "Protein and Alkaloid Patterns of the Floral Nectar in Some Solanaceous Species," *Acta Biologica Hungaricae*, 2015 Sep;66(3), pp. 304–315.

Krappe, Alexander H. "Artemis Mysia," *Classical Philology*, Vol. 39, No. 3 (Jul 1944), pp. 178–183.

Lachenmeier D. W. "Wormwood (*Artemisia absinthium* L.)—A Curious Plant with Both Neurotoxic and Neuroprotective Properties?" *Journal of Ethnopharmacology*, 2010 Aug 19;131(1), pp. 224–227.

Lai, S. W., M. S. Yu, W. H. Yuen, R. C. Chang. "Novel Neuroprotective Effects of the Aqueous Extracts from *Verbena officinalis* Linn.," *Neuropharmacology*, 2006 May;50(6), pp. 641–650.

Littleton, C. Scott. "The Penuma Enthusiastikon: On the Possibility of Hallucinogenic 'Vapors' at Delphi and Dodona," *Ethos*, Vol. 14, No. 1 (Spring 1986), pp. 76–91.

Lo, Vivienne. "Spirit of Stone: Technical Considerations in the Treatment of the Jade Body," *Bulletin of the School of Oriental and African Studies, University of London*, Vol. 65, No. 1 (2002), pp. 99–128.

Makino, Y., S. Kondo, Y. Nishimura, et al. "Hastatoside and Verbenalin are Sleep-Promoting Components in *Verbena officinalis*," *Sleep and Biological Rhythms*, Vol. 7, Issue 3 (Jul 2009), pp. 211–217.

Mason, James. "The Folklore of British Plants," *Dublin University Magazine*, Vol. 82, No. 491, (Nov 1873): pp. 179–195.

McNeill, John T. "Folk-Paganism of the Penitentials," *Journal of Religion*, Vol. 13, No. 4 (Oct 1933), pp. 450–466.

Miraldi, Elisabetta, Alessandra Masti, Sara Ferri, and Ida Barni Comparini. "Distribution of Hyoscyamine and Scopolamine in *Datura stramonium*," *Fitoterapia*, Vol. 72, Issue 6 (Aug 2001), pp. 644–648.

Mitich, Larry W. "Yarrow: The Herb of Achilles," *Weed Technology*, Vol. 4, No. 2 (Apr–Jun 1990), pp. 451–453.

Mooney, James. "Notes and Queries," *Journal of American Folklore*, Vol. II, No. IV (Jan–Mar 1889), pp. 65–73.

Moorhouse, A. C. "The Etymology of ΠΕΡΙΣΤΕΡΑ and Some Allied Words," *Classical Quarterly*, Vol. 44, No. 1/2 (Jan–Apr, 1950), pp. 73–75.

Newman, Leslie F. "Some Notes on the Pharmacology and Therapeutic Value of Folk-Medicines," *International Folklore*, Vol. 59, No. 3 (Sep 1948), pp. 118–135.

no author. "Panther's Cry a Plant," *Western Folklore*, Vol. 13, No. 4 (Oct 1954), p. 284.

Padosch, S. A., D. W. Lachenmeier, L. U. Kröner. "Absinthism: A Fictitious 19th-Century Syndrome with Present Impact," *Substance Abuse Treatment & Prevention Policy*, 2006 May 10;1, p. 14.

Patai, Raphael. "Jewish Folk-Cures for Barrenness," *Folklore*, Vol. 55, No. 3(Sep 1944), pp. 117–124.

Paton, C. I. "Manx Calendar Customs (Continued)," *Folklore*, Vol. 51, No. 4 (Dec 1940), pp. 277–294.

Pecetti, L. L., A. Tava, M. Romani, et al. "Variation in Terpene and Linear-Chain Hydrocarbon Content in Yarrow (*Achillea millefolium* L.) Germplasm from the Rhaetian Alps, Italy," *Chemistry & Biodiversity*, 2012 Oct;9(10), pp. 2282–2294.

Pettis, Jeffrey B. "Earth, Dream, and Healing: The Integration of Materia and Psyche in the Ancient Word," *Journal of Religious Health*, Vol. 45, No. 1, Spring 2006, pp. 113–129.

Rhode, Eleanour Sinclair. "The Folk-Lore of Herbals," *Folklore*, Vol. 33, No. 3 (Sep 30, 1922), pp. 243–264.

Robertson, H. M., and K. W. Wanner. "The Chemoreceptor Superfamily in the Honey Bee, *Apis mellifera*: Expansion of the Odorant, but not Gustatory, Receptor Family," *Genome Research*, 2006;16(11), pp. 1395–1403.

Robertson, Forbes W. "James Sutherland's 'Hortus Medicus Edinburgensis' (1683)," *Garden History*, Vol. 29, No. 2 (Winter 2001), pp. 121–151.

Siegel, Ronald, Peter Collins, J. Diaz. "On the Use of *Tagetes lucida* and *Nicotiana rustica* as a Huichol Smoking Mixture: The Aztec 'Yahuatil' with Suggestive Hallucinogenic Effects," *Economic Botany* 31 (1977), pp. 16–23.

Smith, William, ed., *Dictionary of Greek and Roman Antiquities (1870)*, Vol. 2, p. 726; *www.ancientlibrary.com*.

Soni, Priyanka, Anees Ahmad Siddiqui, Jaya Dwivedi, and Vishal Soni. "Pharmacological Properties of *Datura stramonium* L. as a Potential Medicinal Tree: An Overview," *Asian Pacific Journal of Tropical Biomedicine*, 2012 Dec; 2(12), pp. 1002–1008.

Steenkamp, P. A., N. M. Harding, F. R. van Heerden, B. E. van Wyk. "Fatal Datura Poisoning: Identification of Atropine and Scopolamine by High Performance Liquid Chromatography/Photodiode Array/Mass Spectrometry," *Forensic Science International* 145(1) (Oct 4 2004), pp. 31–39.

Strang, John, Wilfred N. Arnold, Timothy Peters. "Absinthe: What's Your Poison," *British Medical Journal,* Vol. 319, No. 7225 (Dec 18–25, 1999), pp. 1590.

Taussig, Michael. "The Language of Flowers," *Critical Inquiry,* Vol. 30, No. 1 (Autumn, 2003), pp. 98–131.

Urich, R. W., D. L. Bowerman, J. A, Levisky, J. L. Pflug. *"Datura stramonium*: A Fatal Poisoning," *Journal of Forensic Science* 27(4) Oct 1982, pp. 948–954.

Valbuena, Olga Lucia. "Sorceresses, Love Magic, and the Inquisition of Linguistic Sorcery in *Celestina," PMLA,* Vol. 109, No. 2 (Mar 1994), pp. 207–224.

Vickery, A. R. "Traditional Uses and Folklore of Hypericum in the British Isles," *Economic Botany,* Vol. 35, No. 3 (Jul–Sep, 1981), pp. 289–295.

Vlasopolos, Anca. "The Ritual of Midsummer: A Pattern for a Midsummer Night's Dream," *Renaissance Quarterly,* Vol. 31, No. 1 (Spring 1978), pp. 21–29.

Wilson, W. J. "An Alchemical Manuscript by Arnaldus de Bruxella," *Osiris,* Vol. 2 (1936), pp. 220–405.

Wright, A. R., and W. Aldis Wright. "Seventeenth Century Cures and Charms," *Folklore,* Vol. 23, No. 4 (Dec 1912), pp. 490–497.

Yamada, Keiji. *The Origins of Acupuncture, Moxibustion, and Decoction* (Kyoto: International Research Center for Japanese Studies, 1998), pp. 66–78.

ABOUT THE AUTHOR

Harold Roth is among the foremost authorities on plants within the modern occult community. For over fifteen years, he has owned and operated Alchemy Works (*www.alchemy-works.com*), an online store focused on herb magic, where he crafts and sells incense, potions, and magical oils, as well as seeds. He is also an artist and his images have an occult slant (*www.haroldroth.com*). *The Witching Herbs* is his first book.

TO OUR READERS

Weiser Books, an imprint of Red Wheel/Weiser, publishes books across the entire spectrum of occult, esoteric, speculative, and New Age subjects. Our mission is to publish quality books that will make a difference in people's lives without advocating any one particular path or field of study. We value the integrity, originality, and depth of knowledge of our authors.

Our readers are our most important resource, and we appreciate your input, suggestions, and ideas about what you would like to see published.

Visit our website at *www.redwheelweiser.com* to learn about our upcoming books and free downloads, and be sure to go to *www .redwheelweiser.com/newsletter* to sign up for newsletters and exclusive offers.

You can also contact us at *info@rwwbooks.com* or at

Red Wheel/Weiser, LLC
65 Parker Street, Suite 7
Newburyport, MA 01950